The Soul of Poetry Redefined

The Soul of Poetry Redefined

Vacillations of Mimesis from Aristotle to Romanticism

Mats Malm

MUSEUM TUSCULANUM PRESS
UNIVERSITY OF COPENHAGEN 2012

The Soul of Poetry Redefined: Vacillations of Mimesis from Aristotle to Romanticism

Consultants: Patrick Kragelund and John Pedersen
Layout and composition: Pernille Sys Hansen, Damp Design
Cover design: Erling Lynder
Printed by Narayana Press on Scandia 2000 Ivory
ISBN 978 87 635 3742 1

Cover: Mathias Lincopensis, *Poetria*. Codex Upsaliensis C521, fol. 169r. Uppsala University Library

This volume is published with financial support from
The Swedish Research Council

Museum Tusculanum Press
Njalsgade 126
DK-2300 Copenhagen S
Denmark
www.mtp.dk

MIX
Paper from responsible sources
FSC® C010651

Contents

Abstract

The essence – or soul – of poetry has been defined in many different ways throughout history. In the Aristotelian tradition, the key word *mimesis* has been characterized by a confusing, but also productive, ambiguity. This study sets out to shed new light on the notion of mimesis in the Aristotelian tradition by demonstrating how interpretations of Aristotle's *Poetics* have vacillated between two particularly dominating instances of mimesis, what is here labelled mimesis-composition and mimesis-representation. The vocabulary may be the same, but the definition of the soul of poetry may differ substantially depending on which instance dominates at any given time. Since Aristotle's poetological categories were inspired by those of rhetoric, the study begins with an analysis of Aristotle's *Poetics* from a rhetorical point of view. Subsequent chapters then study exemplary reinterpretations of the soul of poetry within the Aristotelian tradition from the 12th to the early 19th century: Averroës, Mathias Lincopensis, the Italian Renaissance, French classicism and the launch of the "fine arts" by Charles Batteux as well as responses from his German counterparts. Concluding chapters apply the perspective on issues concerning the aesthetics of the sublime, the symbol and the role of emotions in the system of genres.

Acknowledgements

The basic questions of this study have occupied me for quite some time. I have had the fortunate opportunity to discuss various parts of the book with friends and colleagues in different contexts. I would like to express my special gratitude to those who read the manuscript as a whole: Stina Hansson and Gunilla Hermansson, and to Susan Brantly, Scott Mellor, Anders Cullhed, Jon Haarberg, Otto Fischer, Ann Öhrberg and Håkan Möller for valuable discussions of separate chapters. Further acknowledgements regarding specific textual problems are made in the notes.

I would like to express my deepest gratitude to The Swedish Research Council for generously funding both the main work carried out on this book as well as its publication in the present form. I would also like to kindly acknowledge the Faculty of Arts at the University of Gothenburg for funding part of my research.

Portions of this book have appeared elsewhere. I am grateful for kind permission to publish revisions of the following material: "Mimesis: efterbildning *och* representation," *Samlaren. Tidskrift för svensk litteraturvetenskaplig forskning* (1993); "Uppenbarelse och poetik. Magister Mathias om effektiv framställning," *Tidskrift för litteraturvetenskap* no. 3–4 (1997); "On the Technique of the Sublime," *Comparative Literature: Journal of the American Comparative Literature Association* 52, no. 1 (2000); "Symbolen och den retoriska repertoarens gränser," *Tidskrift för litteraturvetenskap* no. 1/2 (2005); and "Nödvändighetens nytta. Förhandlingar om franskklassicismens *vraisemblance*," in *Kritikens dimensioner. Festskrift till Tomas Forser*, edited by Åsa Arping and Mats Jansson (2008).

Introduction

In the history of poetics, the essence of poetry – or its soul, as Aristotle influentially puts it – has been defined in numerous different ways. How this essence of poetry is defined at a specific moment in time depends on the cultural context, which in itself has many components which it brings to bear on the dicussion. The poetological tradition supplies the basic concepts for speaking about poetry, with every social situation contributing its own special demands. The developments not least of ethics, religion, philosophy and psychology clearly affect the notion of poetry, while the role played by language is less conclusive: although vernacular poetry has generally been produced under some kind of emulation of the classics, new and specific considerations have been added. Here, the issue of translation is crucial since the very concepts transmitted in the poetological tradition are apt to change their meanings when transferred to a new language. More could be added to the list of circumstances that affect the varying definitions of the soul of poetry, but the aspects of tradition, transmission and langauge are the ones that will dominate this study. In focus is the definition of the soul of poetry as made by Aristotle, and a series of illustrative reinterpretations of his view, ending at considerations on the 18th- and 19th-century aesthetics of the sublime and the symbol. Every new definition of the soul of poetry in the Aristotelian tradition is at the same time a definition of mimesis, this elusive and endlessly productive concept. Thus, the study will be an examination of the shifting notions concerning not only the soul of poetry, but also of mimesis until the early 19th century.

The soul of poetry – the definition of mimesis

Aristotle's *Poetics* has inspired discussion on a number of topics until the present day, not least the issue of the soul of poetry. Even though poetry is associated with mimesis or imitation, imitation broadly understood in itself does not constitute the soul of poetry, making the space for various interpretations considerable. The starting-point for discussions of the soul of poetry is Aristotle's formulation that "[p]lot [*muthos*], then, is the first principle and, as it were, soul [*psuche*] of tragedy."[1] Aristotle speaks of the soul of tragedy, not the soul of poetry, but as he consistently defines poetics from the viewpoint of tragedy, his words have commonly been taken as a description of poetry on the whole – even in later interpretations where the genre of lyric grew more and more prominent. In fact, Aristotle actually says that *muthos,* the "fable" or "plot," the construction of actions – and not mimesis in a general, wide sense – is the soul of tragedy/poetry. As it is clear that this is what Aristotle mainly understands by mimesis, the soul of poetry can be said to be mimesis, but it should rather be understood as one particular instance of mimesis. For mimesis is not always to be interpreted as *muthos,* not even within the *Poetics.*

The basic question concerning mimesis is simple enough: Aristotle's words that "the poet should be more a maker [*poiêtês*] of plots [*muthôn*] than of verses [*metrôn*], insofar as he is a poet by virtue of mimesis, and his mimesis is of actions [*praxeis*],"[2] seem straightforward, and have been repeated on innumerable occasions. It is evident that poetry is not defined by virtue of it being in verse; rather, it is obvious that the structure of action and event is the central issue to Aristotle. However, this formulation and all translations and paraphrases in the tradition of reinterpretations are constantly vague as regards the definition of mimesis. Does mimesis consist in composing actions and events into *muthos,* the plot or fiction, or does it consist in creating a verbal representation of the *muthos*? Or does it consist in both? Aristotle holds that *muthos* is the soul of poetry, but since mimesis is not always the same as *muthos* in the *Poetics,* this ambiguity has set its mark on the whole poetological tradition, with the vacillation between these two instances of mimesis structuring the definitions of the soul of poetry. When someone – be it Aristotle or any interpreter of his – says that poetry is mimesis or imitation of characters, actions, passions, etc., what is meant by "imitation"? Is it that actions and passions are *composed,* in the sense of construing a story, similar to how the historian arranges his account but with the freedom of invention, or that they are *represented* through words, just like the painter represents things and persons through colours? The relevance of this question lies not only in how we understand Aristotle today, but perhaps even more in how his interpreters throughout history have understood him. Aristotle held the composition of plot highest, but mimesis carried not only that sense but also the sense of representation, not least within the rhetorical discussion. This sense was – and would continue to be – a more self-evident one, but Aristotle did not make a clear distinction between the different instances of mimesis. His discussion in the *Poetics* lends itself to be understood now in one, now the other direction, an ambiguity that has subsequently become the hallmark of Aristotelian poetics. Aristotle developed his poetological categories from those of rhetoric, and to every interpreter until the 19th century it has been natural to consider the issue of language through rhetorical notions. Still, the rhetorical understanding of Aristotle has contributed immensely to the vacillation of the soul of poetry. The relation between these instances of mimesis, and their obscure demarcations, are vital to understanding the redefinitions of the soul of poetry.

The soul of poetry is continuously redefined as the interpretations and definitions of mimesis shift focus. Aristotle spoke of *muthos* not only as the soul (*psuche*), but also as the first principle (*arkhê*) and goal (*telos*) of tragedy.[3] Similarly, Aristotle's followers interchangeably speak of the soul, ends, goal or essence of poetry, using different terms depending on their respective language, with poetological problems regularly arising from the incompatibility between languages and the limitations of different terms.

Mimetic variations

The concept of mimesis has proven highly fruitful and highly problematic throughout history. The positive and the negative side of this are to a great extent two aspects of the same thing: the rich potential of meanings and thus ambiguity of the Greek word. The Latin translation *imitatio* is equally vague, but has come to represent a rather different set of meanings, which, in turn, have come to appear less attractive: whereas even today mimesis is used and developed as a tool within literary theory and dramatic areas, *imitatio* never really recovered after having been discarded by the romantic movement. While mimesis has been strongly associated with

Aristotle's *muthos*, the fable, and thus the dynamics of construction of epic and drama, the strongest associations of *imitatio* have been the more or less subservient imitation of previous great authors and the idea that poetry should imitate beautiful nature. It has thus been tightly connected to "classicism," or whatever term is used for that highly rhetorical way of regarding literature that dominated before aesthetics gradually developed during the 18th century, and before romanticism offered new ways of perceiving literature and the world by the turn of the century.

Precisely how great a change romanticism constituted is a controversial issue. The rhetorical tradition obviously lived on, but still the critique of the rhetorical system certainly made the theory of imitation more or less impossible. The classical distinctions of M. H. Abrams in *The Mirror and the Lamp,* defining the older view on poetry as mirroring the outside world and the new view as enlightening, inspiring and changing the world, have been nuanced but do elucidate the problem of the old theory of imitation and mimesis.[4] However, when the doctrine of imitation was questioned, it was imitation or mimesis in a very restricted sense. For several reasons, ranging from political considerations to linguistic problems of terms and translations, different thinkers have meant different things when speaking of imitation and mimesis. An even greater problem is that they have rarely meant the same thing even within their own work. This problem is very much at hand already in the major source, Aristotle's *Poetics.* Thus, any interpretation of the soul of poetry emanating from Aristotle's work is likely to hover between different meanings.[5]

Because of this elusiveness, the different interpretations, the diverse translations and adaptations of the concept are voluminous.[6] However, in Aristotle's *Poetics,* the most influential source of the concept, the definition has sometimes been considered to be quite simple, with Richard McKeon stating that it has one "single literal meaning," and Paul Ricoeur seems to agree: "Aristotle's *Poetics* contains just one all-encompassing concept, that of mimesis. This concept is only defined contextually and through one of its uses, the one that interests us here, imitation or representation of action".[7]

Still, it is obvious that mimesis in the *Poetics* is vaguely defined and that its meaning must be more or less extracted from Aristotle's use. This is apparent in the very structure of Aristotle's argument, since he discusses mimesis in relation to its media, its objects and its methods. Underscoring this, Gerald F. Else has pointed out the difficulties involved and described Aristotle's poet as "a maker of structures," with mimesis thus coming close to that of creation.[8] If the concept of mimesis was elusive in antiquity, it certainly did not become unequivocal as it was transformed into several new terms from the Renaissance and onwards. Renaissance authors often speak of "imitation" and "representation" and other terms as being more or less synonymous, and not least a concept such as "art imitates nature" is highly problematic, not only because of the vague definition of "nature," but also because "imitation" is equally vague.[9]

There is general consensus that what Aristotle considered to be the soul of poetry concerns structure, plot and fiction. As Stephen Halliwell has most efficiently pointed out, Aristotle's mimesis does not have one simple meaning, but he delimited the concept's meanings against the background of previous senses, primarily those employed by Plato. Halliwell has discerned ten different uses of the term in Plato's dialogues, ranging from the linguistic – words reflecting the essence of things – over the philosopher's "copy" of truth, the painter's copying things in paint, mimicry of different kinds, not least that of the actor, and dramatic impersonation within poetry, to music and dance.[10] Taking the tension between different notions of mimesis as his point of departure, Halliwell demonstrates how Aristotle in the *Poetics* sets metaphysical aspects aside and refines the technical aspects of mimesis in the arts. Basically, Halliwell discerns two necessary, not entirely separated but still identifiable, parts in Aristotle's use of mimesis: "The *Poetics* contains, side by side and sometimes overlapping, attempts to refine the understanding of two different aspects of poetic mimesis: in short, its true mode (enactment) and its true meaning (the portrayal of universals)."[11] In a later work, Halliwell ties the question of mimesis to that of aesthetics, positing that

> the importance of Aristotle's understanding of mimesis rests on its "dual-aspect" function as a way of holding together the "world-like" properties of artistic representation—its depiction ... of things which *could* be the case—with its production of objects that possess a distinctive, though not wholly autonomous, rationale of their own.[12]

This dual-aspect mimesis reveals itself in that "terms and standards of analysis throughout the *Poetics* are irreducible either to a reading of the poetic work as a surrogate for the audience's world ... or to aesthetic absolutisms of the contrary kind."[13] Thus, Aristotle liberates art from being judged by the same standards as life, and this is obviously of considerable importance to the development of aesthetics. Halliwell's distinction is thus to a high degree philosophical, resting on the relationship of discourse to "reality" versus autonomy. As he points out, the distinction was present in discussions of mimesis from a very early stage.[14]

To an extent, the distinction between these kinds of mimesis can be described as a result of the fact that the rhetorical tradition provided the most efficient tools for discussing the arts. We often view Plato and Aristotle from a rather purely philosophical point of view, but this study will be devoted to a rhetorical one. Instead of pursuing the philosophical scope or potentials of artistic autonomy in the *Poetics,* I will be following a more pragmatic line of thought in the *Poetics* and its reception. The concept of mimesis is very complex, forcing interpreters to simplify it – which, as is well known, has often been done in the rhetorical tradition. In many ways, this tradition would contort Aristotelian concepts, but it also rested on basic notions of language and representation, similar to those of Aristotle. Trying to clarify categories immanent in rhetorical tradition and in the *Poetics,* I will follow two instances of mimesis – what I will call mimesis-composition and mimesis-representation – which to a degree correspond to the abovementioned, but which are entirely the product of the categories of rhetoric. This is a means of understanding the reception of the *Poetics,* but it is also a means of understanding its conception, since Aristotle himself took as his point of departure the categories at disposal within rhetoric.

My starting-point is thus not modern aesthetics or notions of the role of the imagination and psychology. My questions concern how mimesis was developed in Aristotle's *Poetics* and how it was interpreted at different times up to the 18th century, starting with the basic conceptions of rhetoric, as they have been fundamental to the reception. Thus, when I approach 18th- and 19th-century aesthetics, this will also be from the viewpoint of rhetoric. The perspective is reductive and is intended to be so: it aims primarily at clarifying the reception of the concept of mimesis and reinterpretations of the soul of poetry through the centuries; secondarily – but not less important – it aims at using the rhetorical categories to illuminate issues concerning the aesthetic of the sublime, of the symbol and of the emotions. In order to do this, I will first present a reading of Aristotle's *Poetics* from a rhetorical point of view and attempt to clarify some of his points of departure in rhetorical tradition. My intention is thus to elaborate distinctions which will prove useful for interpreting various interpretations of the *Poetics* and definitions of the soul of poetry at different stages in history.

However widely different the contexts of the definitions of poetry have been, up until around 1800 they have had as one common denominator the rhetorical tradition and the ways it structures thought. I will be tracing different interpretations of Aristotle's *Poetics* in order to clarify how mimesis and the soul of poetry have been renegotiated over time and space. Seminal concepts such as "verisimilitude" and "probability" will also be treated as containers open to different definitions and emphases. While this study for obvious reasons cannot be exhaustive, the main focus of it will be on the two instances of mimesis mentioned above. To be sure, the rhetorical tradition within which Aristotle's *Poetics* was transmitted has been treated in several studies. This study, however, does not focus on audiences or on the ideas of the use of poetry more than marginally: instead the focus of attention is on what categories of language and thought are set in motion when the soul of poetry is discussed. In following the different attempts at categorizing mimesis and poetry, an important aspect will be the question of incompatibility between languages. The limits and possibilities of different words for "imitation," "verisimilitude," etc., will prove to be a dynamic force in the development of poetological theories. It will also be shown that, to an extent, the discarding of the doctrine of imitation was a discarding of terminology, not of the actual idea itself.[15]

Overview

In the first seven chapters of this study, interpretations and reinterpretations of mimesis from Aristotle to the late 18th century are treated. Three concluding chapters go beyond actual discussions of mimesis and

Aristotle, but examine issues closely related to the dynamic between the two central instances of mimesis to be discussed.

Chapter one consists in an analysis of mimesis in Aristotle's *Poetics*. The perspective is rhetorical in a double aspect. The leading question is what possibilities for understanding the soul of poetry are laid down in the text and especially how Aristotle's description of the soul of poetry would be understood from a perspective rooted in the Latin rhetorical tradition. This, obviously, is the prerequisite for the subsequent chapters. However, even though it is well known that later, rhetorically inspired interpretations of Aristotle's *Poetics* in fact moved very far from Aristotle's ideas, the rhetorical perspecive as such is congenial to the *Poetics* since it formed part of Aristotle's own background and offered him categories to think within – or outside – when developing his theory. The analysis will lead to the separation of two main categories, or instances of mimesis, one concerning what is said and the other concerning how it is said. I will label these instances "mimesis-composition" and "mimesis-representation" respectively.

Chapters two to six show how the history of Aristotle's *Poetics* up until the 18th century can be understood as the vacillation between these two instances of mimesis. Chapter two treats the Arabic interpretation which became so influential. The *Poetics* had soon disappeared in antiquity, reappearing through Averroës's commentary, which was translated into Latin in the 13th century and thus came to constitute that attitude towards poetry which was associated with Aristotle in Western learning. The differences between the Arabian Aristotle and the original are considerable, not least because of the instrumental attitude towards poetry. The reinterpretation, it turns out, can be described as a transference of the soul of poetry from mimesis-composition to mimesis-representation.

The third chapter treats a special case of Averroistic influence, the *Poetria* written by the Swedish monk Master Mathias in the 14th century. While Mathias, mostly known as the father confessor of Saint Bridget, follows Averroës, for various reasons his terminology and thus in the end his attitudes towards poetry is different. Mathias banishes that *muthos* which Aristotle extolled – the only place for fiction, according to him, is within metaphor – and his focus on the soul of poetry as persuasive, visualizing discourse is even greater than in Averroës.

Averroës's notion of poetry was that which was first associated with Aristotle's *Poetics,* but as the original text became available in editions and translations, the ground was laid for new interpretations – not seldom moving closer to Aristotle's original ideas.

Thus, the fourth chapter attempts to illuminate this development in 16th-century Italy, focusing on scholars such as Robortello, Castelvetro, Pallavicino and Scaliger, a context in which the issue of verisimilitude proved highly important, but was at the same time obfuscated simply by terminological problems. The Latin *verisimilitudo* was simply too wide to admit any precision in the analysis, which is clarified through the distinction between mimesis-composition and mimesis-representation. Emanuele Tesauro's famous mannerist poetics, *Il Cannocchiale Aristotelico* (1654), is also taken into consideration. The main feature of poetry according to Tesauro is metaphor and he leans heavily not on Aristotle's *Poetics* but his *Rhetoric.* Since Averroës converted the soul of poetry into imagery, particularly metaphor, the chapter examines Tesauro's poetics as a specimen of Averroistic elaboration.

Chapter five takes up the issue of verisimilitude which proved so problematic in the Italian Renaissance and examines its consequences in the French classicism of the 17th century. The discussion is based on the theories of Pierre Corneille and the "exemplary" drama of Jean Racine, *Phèdre* (1676), attempting to define the "necessary" as a central feature in the construction of drama.

The sixth chapter deals with the development of the "fine arts" and the oppositions – real or strategic – between a classicist and a more "pre-romantic" view of poetry. The curious debate around Charles Batteux's *Les beaux arts réduits à un même principe* (1746) is renowned not least due to the German translator Johann Adolph Schlegel's polemical comments, developed in several new, revised editions and translations. In addition to Schlegel, many later scholars have criticized Batteux's concept of imitation, derived from Aristotle's mimesis. Through the perspective of this investigation, it is shown how Batteux in his own manner developed Aristotle's system in a congenial way.

Chapter seven brings focus to the well-known fact that the doctrine of imitation was severely challenged by the proponents of pre-romanticism and was eventually discarded as an aesthetic concept. While it is true that very few would claim that imitation was the soul of poetry in the 19th century, the development of the concepts of poetry needs to be described with more precision. The terminology of aesthetics, as well as its underlying philosophy, certainly changed considerably. However, it is here shown that Batteux's much misinterpreted principle of poetry, diction proper, was in fact not discarded but on the contrary became even more important. The development is exemplified through August Wilhelm Schlegel, who made language as such the cornerstone of speculative philosophy. Thus, even though mimesis and imitation were no longer central terms, it can be said that mimesis-representation lived on as the soul of poetry, but under a new name and cast with new definitions.

Another side of the aesthetic development of the 18th century is the theory of the sublime. This concept has proved highly elusive, and it has been much discussed to what extent the sublime is rhetorical, psychological, or something else. Aristotle and mimesis are not included as part of the discussion here, but the aim of the chapter is to illuminate certain aspects of the sublime through the same governing distinctions as before. By defining what may be called the soul of poetry in the treatise *On the Sublime* by (Pseudo-)Longinus (first centuries AD), the reception of this seminal work can be clarified. Not least, the technique of the sublime is shown to coincide with one of the aspects of mimesis treated in the previous chapters.

While the sublime can be said to be central in the discussions leading to romanticism, the symbol seems to be equally central to romanticism itself. Chapter nine takes as its cue the fact that even though the symbol was not discussed as an aesthetic device until the late 18th century, symbolism and symbolic referentiality were in fact used long before. The discussion concerns how and why symbolic reference to such a great extent was kept out of rhetorical and stylistic discussions, thereby aiming at explaining the eventual aesthetics of the symbol. In contrast to today's juxtaposition of symbol and metaphor as stylistic devices, the symbol was commonly discussed as a category not of style, but of argument.

Finally, a tenth chapter is devoted to the role of emotions in the system of genres. It is well known that the main genres since Aristotle, drama and epic (sometimes completed with the didactic), were in the 18th century joined by a third major genre: lyric. Through a discussion of the definitions of emotion at various stages in history, an explanation of the development of the lyric genre is suggested. This development coincides with the changing categorizations of emotions from instruments into objects, and then, finally, into the soul of poetry.

Aristotle

Two instances of mimesis

In the discussions of poetry from antiquity to the present day, the key word has generally been mimesis, or, in Latin, *imitatio*. By the turn of the 18th century the concept certainly became considerably less popular, but it has nevertheless lived on. Discussion has mainly taken as its point of departure Aristotle's *Poetics* and the definitions there posited, however vague they may have been. It is more or less impossible to imagine a reader in this tradition who was not well versed in rhetoric. Thus, interpreting Aristotle's notion of poetry should be based on the categories provided by the rhetorical system. It is therefore important that the pedagogical distinction between what is said and how it is said – *res* and *verba* – must be taken into account in any historical interpretation of mimesis, including of course that of Aristotle himself. The significance of this emerges not least when the definitions of poetry are widened from Aristotle's focus on drama and epic to lyric. The common understanding in the Aristotelian tradition is that tragedy (representing poetry) is the mimesis of actions (*mimêsis praxeôs*). This focus on actions and events is what makes Aristotle's contribution so special, and it obviously makes the construction of plot and fiction central themes. However, the definition is ambiguous: mimesis is an imitating act, but in what way? Is mimesis the imitative construction of a series of events, i.e. the creation of content, or is mimesis the linguistic representation of those events? Both interpretations are not only possible, but even necessary. Yet, they are rarely distinguished from each other, giving rise to a fundamental vagueness in the tradition of poetics, since any interpretation will tend in the one or the other direction. Even though Aristotle's preferences are clear, this ambiguity is built into his *Poetics*.

In the very beginning of the *Poetics*, any reader will be persuaded that mimesis is the foundation not only of poetry but of the arts as a whole. Reading further, he or she will find in chapter six Aristotle's famous definition of the soul of tragedy, that which has come to comprise poetry on the whole:

> Thus, the events [*pragmata*] and the plot [*muthos*] are the goal [*telos*] of tragedy, and the goal is the most important thing of all.[1]

> Plot [*muthos*], then, is the first principle [*arkhê*] and, as it were, soul [*psuche*] of tragedy, while character [*êthê*] is secondary.[2]

The words concern tragedy, but apply also to the epic – both of them being, in Aristotle's view, the important parts of poetry. The words on the soul of poetry are a conclusion of the preceding argument, claiming that tragedy is mimesis of actions (*praxeôs*) (1449b23–24), and the idea is repeated in the statement "the poet should be more a maker of plots than of verses" (1451b27–28). Clearly, *muthos*, plot, close to "fiction" (but with no demand that the events be fictitious), is mimesis of events and actions, and with this sense of mimesis – the founding idea of Aristotle's *Poetics* – he departs from previous discussions.

However, this definition is not readily reconcilable with the definition of mimesis which the reader has met in the very first chapter of the *Poetics*:

> Now, epic and tragic poetry, as well as comedy, dithyramb, and most music for aulos and lyre, are all, taken as a whole, kinds of mimesis. ... Just as people ... use colours and shapes to render mimetic images of many things, while others again use the voice, so too all the poetic arts mentioned produce mimesis in rhythm, language, and melody, whether separately or in combinations.[3]

Here mimesis is produced through language, and poetry is defined as a mimetic art in accordance with, among others, painting. This comparison leaves little space for plot, structure of events.[4] Instead, it obviously refers to the conventional idea that words, like images, "copy" the object they refer to. Mimesis must here be understood as representation.

Greater still seems the distance between plot and mimesis when mimesis is paired with *diegesis*. Homer is said to be a mimetic artist in chapter three (*mimêtês*; 1448a26), and in chapter 24 he is praised because he, in contrast to other poets, knew

> the place of the poet's own voice. For the poet should say as little as possible in his own voice, as it is not this that makes him a mimetic artist. The others participate in their own voice throughout, and engage in mimesis only briefly and occasionally.[5]

This passage raises the question of how poetry, a mimetic art, can only briefly and occasionally be mimetic. The reader will realize that this is because Aristotle is here speaking of mimesis in the sense of direct speech as opposed to *diegesis*, reported speech. This means that mimesis in the sense of verbal representation, as presented in the first chapter, embodies mimesis, now in the sense of quotation. However, the question still remains whether this meaning of mimesis can possibly be identified as *muthos*, plot or fiction. The answer is, of course, that mimesis in Aristotle's *Poetics* is not unambiguous – even though the instance of mimesis that he proclaims to be the essence of poetry is in a sense unambiguous.

Systematically, Aristotle devotes the first three chapters of the *Poetics* to the media, objects and modes of mimesis, or rather: "the how, the what, and the through which" (*en ois te kai a kai ôs*; 1448a25) as it is formulated in chapter three. The first chapter is devoted to the media: this is where the comparison with painting and music is made. The second chapter treats the objects, "people in action" of various kinds, and the third chapter treats the modes, by which he here means the subdivision of mimesis into mimesis and *diegesis*. Still, the relation between different kinds of mimesis does not become very clear, a relation never made explicit, but which is evinced most clearly from the division of the parts of tragedy in chapter six:

> Since tragedy is mimesis of an action [*praxeôs esti mimêsis*], and the action is conducted by agents who should have certain qualities in both character and thought …, the plot is the mimesis of the action [*praxeôs o muthos ê mimêsis*]—for I use "plot" [*muthos*] to denote the construction of events [*sunthesin tôn pragmatôn*], "character" [*êthê*]

> to mean that in virtue of which we ascribe certain qualities to the agents, and "thought" [*dianoia*] to cover the parts in which, through speech, they demonstrate something or declare their views. Tragedy as a whole, therefore, must have six components, which give it its qualities—namely, plot [*muthos*], character [*êthê*], diction [*lexis*], thought, spectacle [*opsis*], and lyric poetry [*melopoiia*]. The media of the mimesis are two components, its mode one, and its objects three; there are no others.[6]

First, tragedy is said to be mimesis of action (*mimêsis praxeôs*), and as a consequence plot (*muthos*) is then said to be mimesis of action. Still, tragedy and plot are not identical since plot is described as one of tragedy's objects. Plot is merely the composition, *sunthesis or sustasis*, of action and events, which together with character and thought is presented through diction and/or lyric poetry.[7] (In the same chapter Aristotle dismisses spectacle, *opsis*, as pertaining to the art of acting but not to poetry; 1450b16–20.) Plot is mimetic in that it is the composition of actions – a composition which makes itself *like* that which has happened or could happen, a story expanding in time. This appears to be the vital part of tragedy, but tragedy on the whole is mimetic also in that it *represents* this composition through the means of diction (and lyric poetry): "through these mimesis is made."[8] This representation in itself is *another* mimetic act than the one resulting in plot, and it is effected through words, *lexis* (or song). It should be noted that *muthos* is primarily form, the composition of material, but it concerns the poem's matter and it becomes the object of *lexis*.

To make things more complicated, this verbal representation can be divided into mimesis and *diegesis*: direct and reported speech. The tragedy as a whole can then be the object of the actors' representation. Of these four instances of mimesis, only the first two will be discussed in this examination. That is, tragedy and thus poetry on the whole includes that instance of mimesis which is on the level of representation and words: *lexis*. It also includes that instance of mimesis which is on the level of content insofar as it concerns the composition of actions and events: *muthos*, and character and thought. It should be stressed that it is the aspect of *forming* that is central to the mimesis by which *muthos* is composed. Aristotle does speak of the matter of poetry, for example when he compares the poet to the historian and concludes that the events need not be fictional, but matter as such is not central in his definition of the parts of tragedy. It is form that is vital, and the act of mimesis is the act of forming. *Mimêsis praxeôs* is the composition, the forming of matter into *muthos*. In turn, composition, in the sense of putting together, is what Aristotle focuses on when using the words *sunthesis* and *sustasis*. The background and effects of Aristotle's establishing this new instance of mimesis will be touched upon in chapter 10.

In agreement with the traditional classification that *logos* is *what* is said and *lexis* is *how* it is said, Aristotle himself has chosen the term *lexis* for the "how." *Muthos* is not identical to *logos*, because it is not the only object of *lexis*, but it certainly corresponds to *logos*.[9] *Muthos* is the result of a mimetic act, composition, and it is the object of another mimetic act, representation. It is *muthos* which is appointed the soul of poetry by Aristotle, but the importance of *lexis* should not be underestimated in his thinking – in fact, his mimesis cannot be understood without it. Furthermore, the ambiguity between *logos* and *lexis* will prove to be fundamental in the reception of the *Poetics*. I will label the first instance "mimesis-composition" and the second instance "mimesis-representation."

THE ISSUE OF *LEXIS*

When Aristotle speaks of mimesis as opposed to *diegesis*, that is, direct speech as opposed to reported speech, this instance is very close to that mimesis in which the actor indulges when imitating characters on stage – since the poet or narrator here in a sense pretends to be the person portrayed (and this in turn is why Plato preferred *diegesis* to mimesis). When Aristotle treats this instance of mimesis, he is able to speak of poets who do not employ mimesis, although poetry in itself is mimetic: they do not employ that instance of mimesis which is opposed to *diegesis*. The actor's business, Aristotle has said in chapter 6, is not part of poetry itself (1450b16–20), but obviously mimesis as opposed to *diegesis* belongs to poetry and more specifically to the level of *lexis*.

However, *lexis*, "expression through choice of words" (1450b13–14), involves more. Aristotle starts treating different matters of *lexis* in chapter 20, and notably it is in this context, in chapter 21, that he discusses metaphor, one outstanding characteristic of the lexical level. The question of verse or prose, it appears in chapter 9 (1451a36–51b1; 1451b27–28), is also a matter of *lexis*: different kinds of linguistic representation.

Any comparison between the arts based on mimesis must focus on diction: the various arts have mimesis in common because they *represent*. In painting, the medium is colour; in poetry, the medium may be song, but first and foremost it is words: *lexis*. This instance is commonly recognized within the rhetorical and grammatical tradition, and Aristotle himself applies it in his *Rhetoric*: "words are imitations" (*onomata mimêmata estin*).[10]

Although Aristotle does not hold *lexis* to be the soul of poetry, it is an absolutely essential instance of mimesis. Clothing things in words is not necessarily an act of poetry, but construing poetic diction is. Not least, it is this instance of mimesis that makes possible the comparison with other arts and it is the obvious correspondence to colour in painting.[11] While Aristotle diminishes the attention on *lexis* and puts forth *muthos*, *lexis* is still vital, and besides being the starting-point of the *Poetics*, it is the topic of some chapters at the end of the treatise.

Admittedly, while Aristotle does not give diction a prominent position in the *Poetics*, the question is how to understand the chapters that are devoted it (20–22). Halliwell concludes that issues of style have been of little importance to Greek literary theory and states that

> indeed Aristotle himself says as much at one point in the *Poetics* (1456b13–19). Yet the fact remains that linguistic questions were not always properly separated from broader literary issues, and this too can be seen in the *Poetics*, for it has left its mark on Aristotle's own discussion on the style or language (*lexis*) of tragedy in chs. 20 to 22. Not only does this section of the treatise fail to focus at all clearly on the language of tragedy as such, despite its formal place as part of the analysis of this genre, but much of it is given over to a strictly technical treatment of linguistic points.[12]

When Aristotle in chapter 17 says that "one should construct plots, and work them out in diction [*tê lexei synapergazesthai*]" (1455a22), he firmly demonstrates that *muthos* is the kind of mimesis that comes first.[13] However, working it out in diction is an aspect which should never be neglected, being an instance of mimesis which although not constituting the soul of poetry is in reality equally necessary, it would seem. In chapter 19, Aristotle discusses "thought," *dianoia*, and "diction," *lexis*. He does so in order to rid himself of that which is not pertinent to his discussion in the *Poetics*, referring to his rhetorical writings for discussion of "thought." He then continues:

> As for matters of diction, one type of study concerns forms of utterance (knowledge of which belongs to the art of delivery and the person with this mastery) – namely, what is a command, prayer, narrative, threat, question, reply, and all the like. Knowledge or ignorance of these things can support no serious criticism of poetry. Why should anyone think it is a fault where Protagoras criticises Homer for purporting to pray but giving a command by saying "Sing, goddess, of the wrath..."? (To bid someone do or not do something, says Protagoras, is a command.) So, let this study be put aside as part of some other art, not poetry. (1456b6–18)

This may read as a dismissal of the whole issue of diction, but why then would Aristotle devote three chapters to it? In fact, he seems in chapter 19 to define what he will *not* take up. "Thought" is dismissed, as is "one type of study" pertaining, but not identical, to diction, that type of "diction" which concerns defining and putting statements into categories. Other aspects of diction are treated in the following three chapters: in chapter 20, syllables, auditive aspects, etc., are described, whereafter word classes are discussed. Chapter 21 takes up metaphor, neologisms, etc., while chapter 22 discusses ideals of diction: clarity versus that which makes diction special and grand – including different examples.

What connects these issues is the simple fact that diction is mimesis: words are the imitations of things, something which constitutes the basis for Aristotle's comparisons between the arts. This is not explicated, but diction can hardly have been conceived in any other way – even if it is not the primary instance of mimesis. Aristotle's words about metaphor here have always attracted the attention of readers. Even disregarding the considerable attention devoted to metaphor in the *Rhetoric*, it is evident that metaphor is the most important part of diction in the *Poetics*. As

Halliwell puts it, the "greatest attribute of all" is particularly suited for the central genres epic and tragedy, while not lending itself to a "technical understanding":

> It is only in the case of metaphor that we sense a complete harmony of meaning and style in Aristotle's view of language. The reason for this is that metaphor, although it *can* be regarded as a stylistic ornament alongside other types, is valued by the philosopher as a unique means of expressing certain perceptions.[14]

The treatment of metaphor is proof that diction is seminal in poetry. Moreover, the nature of metaphor, that which makes it an instrument not only of ornament but also of conceptualization, is described in terms which call for being understood in the light of mimesis: the "capacity for metaphor ... alone cannot be acquired from another, and is a sign of natural gifts: because to use metaphor well is to discern similarities" (1459a5–6). *Metapherein to to homoion theorein estin*: to discern similarities, find that which is alike, in this way is a functional development of simply letting a word imitate a thing. The common assumption is that a word represents a thing by imitating, copying it: if I say "lion," I imitate the lion verbally (as a painter would do with colours). In metaphor, a more philosophical imitation for the thing is chosen, an imitation or representation which catches the likeness not of one phenomenon, but of two. If I thus say "the lion," referring to Achilles, I create an imitation of the lion which in itself is an imitation, a verbal representation, of Achilles because of certain similarities. Mimesis in *lexis* is ordinarily to find the likeness of, the word for, one phenomenon. The verb *metapherein*, "transfer," thus appears to be a higher stage of *mimezein* on the level of *lexis*. While Plato considered words to be able to catch the essence of things,[15] Aristotle develops the wisdom of *lexis* one step further. Words are not only able to catch the essence of what they imitate/represent, they may even imitate in a higher degree when they are used in a metaphor. Poetry is a *techne* which can be analyzed and learned, metaphor is not. The mimesis of *lexis* is thus central, with metaphor providing a kind of double mimetic act.

The chapters on *lexis* are certainly abstruse and difficult. Still, second to *muthos* this is the most extensively discussed part of tragedy,[16] an indication that Aristotle considered *lexis* an important instance of mimesis. As we know from the *Rhetoric,* he (obviously) considers diction to be essential to any communication in words: his treatment of metaphor is a brilliant example. In the *Poetics,* the focus on drama – structure and enactment – relegates the importance of diction, consigning it to the late chapters. Quite naturally, *lexis,* while appearing to be a vital instance of mimesis – established at the very beginning in the comparison between poetry and the other arts – is not the foremost kind, though, and is thus placed late in the treatise.

Poetics – rhetoric

It is well known, and only natural, that Aristotle's *Poetics* has often been understood from a rhetorical perspective. It is also evident that he developed his poetics from an understanding of discourse based on the rhetorical tradition of his time. While it is equally evident that *lexis* in the *Poetics* corresponds to the rhetorical category of diction, mimesis-composition is connected with basic rhetorical thinking in a more complicated way. The common parts of the rhetorical working process are widely known in their Latin names *inventio, dispositio, elocutio, memoria* and *actio*. The latter two concern physical presentation and thus do not correspond to the central issue of Aristotle's *Poetics. Inventio, dispositio* and *elocutio,* the finding, ordering and dressing in words, usually translate the Greek *heuresis, taxis* and *lexis,* although Aristotle in his *Rhetoric* speaks of *dianoia* instead of *heuresis*. As in the *Poetics, dianoia* is one of the objects of arrangement and representation, but the difference is considerable: in the *Poetics dianoia* is one of the objects, in the *Rhetoric* it is *the* object, that which he will treat as a whole. Rhetoric's *heuresis* or *dianoia* (*inventio*) constitute the finding of material, and thus correspond to finding material for the *muthos*. *Taxis* (*dispositio*), ordering that material, corresponds to the structuring and composing of events and actions that make up *muthos*. Mimesis-composition thus corresponds to rhetoric's *heuresis/inventio* and *taxis/dispositio,* mostly to the latter, while rhetoric's *lexis/elocutio* corresponds to the medium of poetry, *lexis,* our mimesis-representation.

By rearranging the categories of rhetoric, Aristotle thus arrived at the productive categories of poetics.[17] The object to be presented was enlarged from the results of thought, *dianoia,* into *muthos, êthê* and *dianoia,* the objects of poetry. *Taxis* was included in the structuring of the *muthos,* while *lexis* stayed the same, perhaps why it is natural that readers through the millennia have interpolated the *Poetics* with the *Rhetoric.* This commonplace assumption must be stressed in order for the dynamics between mimesis-composition and mimesis-representation to become evident. Above all, it is important because in the reception of his poetics, Aristotle's focus on mimesis-composition would have seemed quite strange, while the notion of mimesis-representation would have been not only familiar but even self-evident to every reader up until the 19th century since the dichotomy *logos-lexis* lived on in Latin rhetoric in the formula *res-verba.* Plato had applied it without explicitly defining *logos* as mimesis, while Aristotle in the *Poetics* did not use *logos* as a bearing concept, understanding it as "that which is said" as opposed to "how it is said." He delimited it to "that which is said by the characters" and did not use it as a precise opposition to *lexis.* Even though *muthos,* mimesis-composition, is primarily form – the composition of material – it still has to do with matter and is itself turned into the object of *lexis,* mimesis-representation. Thus, the dichotomy mimesis-composition and mimesis-representation principally corresponds to the dichotomy *logos-lexis* or *res-verba.*

Plato's categories

Aristotle changed the meaning of mimesis in relation to Plato's usage, not least through launching *muthos.* The basic notion that words are mimesis is the starting-point for both of them.[18] Restricting discussion to matters concerning mimesis-composition and mimesis-representation, only a few differences and correspondences between them shall be mentioned. Something Plato and Aristotle do have in common is the dichotomy of mimesis and *diegesis* in the sense of direct and reported speech, which Plato makes in *Republic* III, 397. This division takes place within *lexis,* and it is mainly as representation that mimesis is discussed there.

Plato makes explicit the distinction between what is said in poetry, *logos,* and how it is said, *lexis*: "So this concludes the topic of tales [*logôn*].

That of diction [*lexeôs*], I take it, is to be considered next" (*Republic* III, 392C). Without at all discussing drama or analyzing literature, he makes the distinction that is common within the rhetorical system, and it becomes roughly equivalent to Aristotle's two instances – if one considers *muthos* as the object of representation and disregards the fact that *muthos* is also the product of mimesis. Plato too uses the word *muthos*, but in a negative sense of (detrimental) fable and does not really discuss it (391E; 392B). To both of them, *lexis* is, much like the painter's representation, mimesis, embracing the dichotomy of direct and reported speech. Thus Plato too can speak of mimetic and non-mimetic poetry.

When Plato discusses what poetry says, *logos*, he does not mention mimesis,[19] perhaps because he is more concerned with the content than with the composition of it. To Aristotle, *muthos* is an act of mimesis, but Plato rather discusses the results of that act. What concerns Plato is the actual truthfulness and the social advantages or disadvantages of the content. Artfulness, creativity and mimesis only become relevant when he turns to *lexis*. There, the basic conception is the same as in Aristotle: words represent things, not by imitating in the same way as music and painting does, but by representing them.

Probability – verisimilitude

The vacillation between mimesis-composition and mimesis-representation is confusing but important to our understanding of the *Poetics* and its reception. One of the major implications of it is a corresponding vacillation within the vital concept of probability. Poetry, as rhetoric, has to be convincing, and this is intrinsically connected to issues of credibility, plausibility and verisimilitude. These terms, as their Latin origins, are so all-encompassing that they blur important distinctions.

VERISIMILITUDE IN MIMESIS-COMPOSITION

When Aristotle discusses the structure and length of *muthos* in chapters 7–9, he stresses that the succession of elements should in no way be arbitrary but consistently progressing, and that they must convey truth albeit not necessarily a historical truth. This, of course, is where (chapter 9) the famous comparison between the poet and the historian is made, where the poet is said to capture the universal while the historian only describes the particular (1451a38–51b10). This is also where Aristotle speaks of the importance of beginning, middle and end, as well as the place of episodes within the whole.

The seminal terms here are "probability" (*eikos*) and "necessity" (*anankê, anankaion*), terms that Aristotle, as a rule, holds to be closely interrelated. This applies not only to the plot but also to character, as is declared in chapter 15:

> With character, precisely as in the structure of events, one should always seek necessity or probability—so that for such a person to say or do such things is necessary or probable, and the sequence of events is also necessary or probable.[20]

The importance of the formula "probability-necessity" is underlined by the fact that it occurs no less than three times in the lines quoted. Probability refers to what may be assumed as likely in one sense or the other, while necessity is more dependent on the sequence of events. Thus, necessity appears to be mainly text-internal, while probability concerns what one might surmise that anyone would do or say in a particular situation, i.e. more text-external. Halliwell thus concludes that the reason that probability and necessity are used together is due to Aristotle's emphasis on causality and unity in the structure of events, *muthos*. *Eikos*, being a rhetorical concept, to a certain degree concerns the expectations, while *anankê*, on the other hand, is a question of causality within the *muthos*.[21] Thus, one may say that probability is not as tightly connected to the literary work and its sequence of events as necessity. However, even if probability concerns what is needed to convince the audience of something, it is still tied to events. In his *Rhetoric*, Aristotle defines *eikos*: "that which is probable is that which generally happens."[22]

We may thus conclude that necessity, *anankê*, is entirely intrinsic to the sequence of events, that is, to mimesis-composition. Probability, *eikos*, is also firmly connected to the sequence of events, however not to the actual connection between events but rather to a more general credibility of things happening. This is one aspect of verisimilitude which belongs to the temporal structure of *muthos*: a different aspect of verisimilitude is connected to the atemporal mimesis-representation.

VERISIMILITUDE IN MIMESIS-REPRESENTATION

Probability evidently is important to mimesis-representation as well, but not in relation to the actions, events and their structure. Instead, the choice of words is vital for producing a convincing scenery and setting for what happens. Introducing the issue of *lexis* in chapter 19, Aristotle states that thought (*dianoia*) and speech (*logos*) largely follow the same principles as those that we have seen apply to *muthos*,

> when one needs to create impressions of what is pitiable, terrible, important, or probable [*eikota*] – with this difference, that the latter effects must be evident without direct statement, while the former must be conveyed by the speaker in and through speech.[23]

Probability, *eikos*, is thus used as a transition to the discussion of *lexis*, but Aristotle does not use the term when discussing how to achieve credibility through *lexis*.

The chapters devoted to *lexis*, 20–22, start out dryly with discussions of syllables and word classes, but they also treat metaphor in ways which have received much more attention. As Aristotle emphasizes in chapter 22: "Excellence of diction means clarity [*saphês*] and avoidance of banality" (1458a18). Anyone familiar with Aristotle's *Rhetoric* would know that especially in his discussion of metaphor, but also on other issues, a vital idea is that things represented should be put "before the eyes" (*pro ommatôn*), as it were, of the receiver.[24] This aspect is part of the abovementioned clarity, but it is not given much weight in the *Poetics*. Curiously, Aristotle there uses the concept *pro ommatôn* once, treating mainly *muthos* in chapter 17:

> One should construct plots, and work them out in diction, with the material as much as possible in the mind's eye [*pro ommatôn*]. In this way, by seeing things most vividly, as if present at the actual events, one will discover what is apposite and not miss contradictions.[25]

Visualizing the scenery is thus very important for the poet, and tightly connected to clothing the events in diction. From this, we may conclude that it must be vital for the receiver of a text that its discourse is clear and visualizing, in the way that Aristotle describes it in his *Rhetoric*. While this aspect has frequently been expanded in later tradition, it should be repeated that Aristotle is not particularly preoccupied with it in the chapters on *lexis*. One reason for this is obviously that it is mimesis-composition which is the most important instance of mimesis, while another reason may be that in drama, with its visual enactment, visualizing a scenery in words is less important than in epic or in speech. Aristotle could not possibly have accentuated visualization more than he does – in a treatment of drama. In turn, when he does discuss epic, in chapters 24–25, he stresses the need for credible representation.

The analogy between the arts must be based in the level of representation. The painter represents an object in colours; the poet represents it in words, on the level of *lexis*. This results in one specific way of achieving credibility, which is elaborated in the discussion of epic in chapter 25:

> Since the poet, like a painter or any other image-maker, is a mimetic artist, he must represent, in any instance, one of three objects: the kind of things which were or are the case; the kind of things that people say and think; the kind of things that ought to be the case.[26]

The poet is a *mimêtês* in much the same manner as any *eikonopoios*: image-maker. The objects described are not necessarily physical objects that are to be represented through a medium of language or paint, but the demands for credibility are made more definite in the same chapter. Aristotle distinguishes between two kinds of fault in poetry: one intrinsic and one incidental. The incidental kind is when, for example, a horse is portrayed moving its legs in an unnatural way (1460b13–19). In the same way, "it is less serious not to know that a female deer has no horns, than to depict one unconvincingly [*amimetôs egrapsen*]" (1460b30–31). In these examples poetry is similar to painting, with the discussion taking place on the level of mimesis-representation. Faults within representation, i.e. in poetry *lexis*, are intrinsic to poetry.

* * *

Verisimilitude is of paramount importance in Aristotle's *Poetics*. The main way of achieving verisimilitude in mimesis-representation is, still in accordance with the painter, by describing the things portrayed as convincingly as possible – *pro ommatôn*, as Aristotle says in the *Rhetoric*. This does not necessarily have to be done in a "realistic" fashion – it can also be done in the form of an overwhelming, "unnatural" representation. But as far as the question of verisimilitude is concerned, it is the convincing representation of things – similarity to the actual things – that constitutes credibility in mimesis-representation.

In mimesis-composition, on the other hand, verismilitude is achieved through necessity in the structure of events and probability in the sense of general plausibility. Terminology is not precise in the Greek,[27] but the difference between these instances of verisimilitude becomes practically wiped out as discussion is transferred into concepts such as 'verisimilitude', 'credibility' and 'plausibility' in various languages. Thus, as we shall see, the inherent imprecision of vocabulary makes ample space for renegotiating not only the soul of poetry but also the question of verisimilitude in poetry.

Points of departure

Aristotle's dictum that "the poet should be more a maker of plots than of verses, in so far as he is a poet by virtue of mimesis, and his mimesis is of actions" expressed a forceful doctrine. At the same time it conveys an ambiguity, that between mimesis-composition and mimesis-representation, which dominates the poetological discussion as a whole. Is mimesis to be understood as the creation of *muthos*, or as the verbal representation of it?

The relation between these two instances is the subject of this study, but additionally the *Poetics* also includes the mimetic business of acting – which is not regarded as part of poetry – and that form of mimesis which is opposed to *diegesis*, not identical to mimesis-representation, but rather a subdivision of the lexical level meaning "direct speech." In addition, mimesis and *imitatio* occur in even more meanings, from the child's imitation of adult behaviour to the well-known meaning of imitation of *auctores*, as Pseudo-Longinus among others describes it. Many of these senses of mimesis will be actualized in the following chapters, but it is the two instances of composition and representation that will be the main focus of attention.

In the Roman tradition, imitation of *auctores* is what is foremost connected with the term *imitatio*. As we have seen, one seminal instance of mimesis concerns the level of *lexis*, and it is this instance which is accentuated in any rhetorical approach. Thus, Aristotle's demand for probability is replaced by a focus on verisimilitude on the lexical level. This focus on mimesis-representation was of course even more strengthened through the influence of Horace, whose formula "ut pictura poesis" exerted a tremendous impact throughout the Middle Ages and beyond.[28] Evidently, by stressing the analogy between painting and poetry, Horace practically extinguished Aristotelian mimesis. But any rhetorical approach to Aristotle's *Poetics* seems naturally to tend in that direction.

Among followers of Aristotelian poetics up until, say, the 19th century, *muthos* is rather seldom discussed. Instead, the important objects of poetry are usually seen to be character, thought, persons, things.[29] Aristotle held that character and thought should enhance the probability of the story, but later they are more connected with mimesis-representation than mimesis-composition. When questions of truth in poetry are raised, they mostly concern whether this or that really did happen, or whether a thing is really such as it is described. In other words, the probability of *muthos* is replaced by the verisimilitude of *lexis*.

In the reception of Aristotle's *Poetics*, interpretations and reinterpretations stress either of the two instances. In rhetorical tradition, mimesis-representation is the instance which dominates, but it does so with widely varying results and with the tension between the two proving highly productive. The consequences of these distinctions will be traced in the following chapters, which certainly do not aim at telling the whole story: rather, they bring forth a series of illustrative examples.

While it is well known that Aristotle works out his own adaptation of mimesis, what needs to be stressed here is that his definition in *Poetics* is so far from common understandings of mimesis, and in particular rhetorical conceptions, that it has been doomed to be constantly reinterpreted in a rhetorical direction. At the same time, the text of Aristotle's *Poetics* clarifies its own application of mimesis to which the receiver is led. It is the dynamics between the two directions of mimesis – towards content and towards form – that is our topic. The directions, or instances of mimesis, that will be followed are thus mimesis-composition, selection and arrangement aiming at probability, and mimesis-representation, rhetorical, lexical representation, description of objects, aiming at verisimilitude of a kind corresponding to the painter's representation.

In following the redefinitions of the soul of poetry, it is important to note how Aristotle's categories are changed and adapted. An essential aspect in this respect is the diffusion and relocation of categories, and thus it will not always be possible to define exactly what different theoreticians have meant. To a certain extent, therefore, I will have to speak of the direction towards this or that category rather than precise categorization. For the sake of clarity, I will be referring to the following scheme, which will represent Aristotle's originally designated parts of poetry with English translation:

object	plot	*muthos*
object	character	*êthê*
object	thought	*dianoia*
medium	diction	*lexis*
medium	lyric poetry	*melopoiia*
mode	spectacle	*opsis*

Adaptations

CHAPTER TWO

Averroës's adaptation
(12th–13th century)

The *Poetics* practically vanished from literary discussion in the West after the time of Aristotle. It seems that key concepts influenced Horace's *Ars Poetica* by way of a certain Neoptolemus, but the original text was not to be available to a European audience until the Latin translation of Giorgio Valla in 1498.[1] In turn, Aristotle's *Poetics* came to exert its impact on the European Middle Ages in an Arabic adaptation.

Aristotle's *Poetics* was translated from Greek into Syriac, and in the 10th century into Arabic and commented upon by Averroës in 1176. Averroës's commentary was translated into Latin by Hermannus Alemannus in 1256, and in this guise Aristotle's *Poetics* was first presented to the medieval European audience. Similarly, also Aristotle's *Rhetoric* was transmitted through Averroës and Hermannus Alemannus. A translation of the *Poetics* was made directly from the Greek original in 1278 by William of Moerbeke, but this never came into use,[2] while his translation of Aristotle's *Rhetoric* directly from the Greek enjoyed wider influence. Averroës's commentary in Latin translation was printed in 1482, but before that it had already exerted great influence through manuscripts. This was the version of Aristotle's *Poetics* that was first known to learned Europe, and the Averroistic poetics enjoyed great influence during the 15th and 16th centuries. A Latin translation of the Greek original was published in 1498, the original itself not until 1508. The first important work that decidedly broke with the Averroistic interpretation of Aristotle was Lodovico Castelvetro's *Poetica d'Aristotele vulgarizzata et sposta*, published in 1570.[3]

As is well known, Averroës's deviations from Aristotle's *Poetics* are largely due to his rhetorical apprehension of poetry. He refers poetry to the rhetorical categories *ars laudandi* and *ars vituperandi*: poetry should thus be used either to praise or to vituperate, according to the *genus demonstrativum* of rhetoric. This idea may be considered an extreme interpretation of Aristotle's mention of the oldest poetic forms as vituperating (satire) or praising (hymns, encomia), and his point that tragedy presents humans more virtuous than ourselves, while comedy presents ones less so (ch. 2, 4). The consequences of this pragmatic view of poetry can hardly be overemphasized.[4] In the Arabic tradition, Aristotle's *Poetics* and *Rhetoric* were categorized as parts of logic and considered to be instrumental: their function was to convey philosophical and moral education, a function which spread to Latin scholasticism through the translation-adaptation of Hermannus Alemannus.[5] As poetics was linked with rhetoric, it was also ordained the purpose of rhetoric: persuasion.[6]

In this tradition, the task of poetry and rhetoric was thus to effectively and persuasively convey truths. Since their object is philosophical truth, fiction as a category is undermined: poetry should present what is true, not inventions. Imaginative presentation, similes and rhetorical devices are meant to persuade by addressing the emotions of the hearer/reader, while rhetoric seeks the same effect mainly by focusing on the intellect.[7] The consequences for the *Poetics* being treated as an instrumental art were considerable, as described by Alex Preminger, O. B. Hardison Jr. and Kevin Kerrane:

> To include the *Poetics* in the *Organon* is to assert that it is an essay on method, and that the method itself is a "faculty" without "content." Furthermore, since each of the logical faculties was supposed to be distinguished from the others by its use of a unique logical device, the inclusion of *Poetics* in the *Organon* shifted emphasis from "imitation," the key term in the Greek *Poetics*, to the "device" which differentiates poetry from its sister faculties.
>
> This interpretation ignores imitation, plot, characterization, catharsis, and most of the other subjects stressed by Aristotle in favor of an element – the imaginative syllogism – for which the reader of the Greek text will search in vain.[8]

The "device" or "element" of "the imaginative syllogism" is certainly central to the Arabic tradition, but as we shall see the key concept of imitation was not entirely ruled out. On the contrary, the imaginative syllogism should be seen as a development of mimesis, a reorganization of the instances of mimesis inherent in Aristotle's *Poetics*. Averroës was obviously not acquainted with the Greek literature Aristotle discusses, which accounts for some of the differences. But far from consisting of chaotic misunderstandings and in spite of confusing terminology, Averroës's commentary is to a great extent consistent. As poetics and rhetoric are defined as instrumental parts of logic, they are considered to be different ways of conveying philosophical truths, and not least morals; rhetoric through intellect and argument, poetry through imagination and visuality. In this tradition, poetry becomes exclusively epideictic poetry, intended to praise or vituperate,[9] a notion of great importance to the understanding of the immensity of occasional poetry during the 16th and 17th centuries.

Averroës's *imaginatio* and *assimilatio* serve as translations of mimesis. To Bernard Weinberg, this meant that "the notion of 'imitation' is essentially lacking" and that "the notion of imitation has been reduced to that of figurative expression." Hardison comes close to Weinberg's figurativeness when stating that "Averroës defined poetic imitation as the use of metaphor."[10] On the other hand, Minnis and Scott describe the consequences of Averroës's interpretation:

> The crucial point to grasp is that the concept of imitation (*mimesis*) has largely been replaced with that of imagination (*imaginatio*) or imagistic "likening" (*assimilatio*), representation of a kind which arouses the emotions of the audience in a way which encourages them to follow virtue and flee from vice.[11]

Averroës himself did not employ a clear terminology, and there are a number of obscurities as to how his adaptation relates to Aristotle. It seems clear that he redefined the essence of poetry, but does that mean that *imitatio* disappeared or was redefined? If the latter, then how? How should "imagination" or "imagistic 'likening'" be understood in relation to mimesis, and do they include metaphor, or are they metaphor exclusively? How can this have replaced mimesis? Averroës changed the *Poetics* significantly, but he did so within a system. While consenting to the main course of events, I will try to re-examine the assertion that emphasis shifted away from "imitation" in this tradition. The question, then, is more precisely how the soul of poetry was redefined by Averroës.

The poetics of visuality

It seems almost impossible to get a firm grasp on Averroës's terminology. His use of *representatio, assimilatio, imitatio* and *imaginatio* sometimes seems to be a way of distinguishing aspects of representation from each other, sometimes they appear to be synonymous. The word *assimilatio* calls for being understood in terms of figuration or simile while *representatio* and *imitatio* seem more like plain representation, but then *assimilatio* is suddenly qualified as *metaphorica*.[12] On the other hand, when Averroës uses the words *assimilationes et imitativas representationes*,[13] he seems to mean that "representations" are plain while "assimilations" are figurative. The relation between these and *imaginatio* is also diffuse, even though *imaginativus* must be understood more as relating to the effect of an utterance than the qualifier *representativus*.

Averroës's stress on metaphor is considerable. Early on he states:

> Poetic forms of speech are based on images. There are three modes of imagination and of "likening" [*modi imaginationis et assimilationis*]. There are two simple modes, and the third is a compound of those two. One of the two simple modes is the "likening" of one object to another and its exemplification in terms of that object. This is achieved in all languages by words peculiar to that language, for instance *quasi* or *sicut*, or similar words which are called particles of comparison, or else by adopting that which is "like," together with the thing to which it is compared, or in place of it. And in this art this process is called a "trope" [*concambium*].[14]

This trope embodies both simile and metaphor, the difference being, as usual, that the word "like" or "as" is spelled out in the similitude,[15] resulting in no word being used in a figurative, improper sense in the simile, while tropes consist of (at least) one word which is used in a figurative, improper sense:

> You must understand that the forms [*species*] which our modern writers call substitution [*transumptio*] and figurative usage [*translatio*] fall within this category, as for instance we read: "the meadow is smiling," "the shore is ploughed."[16]

Translatio is traditionally the most common synonym of *metaphora,* and the examples show that Averroës chooses metaphors as his examples of trope, *concambium*. The second kind of *assimilatio* is when a simile or metaphor is reverted, as when saying "the sun is like this woman" instead of "this woman is like the sun," and the third kind, then, is a mixture between the two.

To be sure, Averroës later on devotes much space to metaphor. He treats it for instance when he speaks of the representation of abstract things through concrete ones (*representatio intellectualium rerum per res sensibiles*; 59), with the technique of presenting one thing through the image of another being explicitly called *representatio*. He discusses six categories: the third kind is when memories are aroused and the fourth is that kind of metaphor which consists in calling Socrates "the second Plato" (60/367). The fourth kind of representation or imitation is "metaphoric assimilation" (*Species autem quarta representationis seu imitationis, id est metaphorica assimilation*), Averroës says, which further confuses the distinction between figurative and non-figurative. The fifth kind is hyperbole and the sixth is prosopopeia (61/368).

Metaphor is quite clearly discerned as an eminent technique of poetry because of its ability to spur the imagination. However, Averroës's terminology does not clearly distinguish between figurative and non-figurative ways of expression. Metaphor, together with simile, is treated separately from other forms of representation, but it is overall clear that all presentation that enhances imagination is good – including vivid representation.

Thus, while it is obvious that metaphor is very important to Averroës, it cannot be defined as the substitute for mimesis. The major argument of Averroës implies that metaphor is only a subdivision of the essence of poetry.

From the first moment, Averroës underlines the analogy with the sister arts – which imitate poetry (*artibus representativis, que imitatrices sunt poetrie*; 41). Following this, he describes poetry as *sermones imaginativi* and discusses simile and trope, before returning to Aristotelian reason again to discuss the media of poetry:

> In poetic discourse imagination and representation is produced by three things: the harmonious sound, the measure, and the assimilation itself. ... Representation or imitation occurs in speech, that is, in discourses which represent or imagine, without metre or rhythm.[17]

This passage is vital, since it not only identifies *imaginatio* with *representatio* – notwithstanding the inconsistency of terminology – but also because it is a redaction of Aristotle's definition of the two media of poetry: *melopoiia* and *lexis*. *Melopoiia*, song, has turned into harmony and metre, while *lexis* is rendered "imitation in speech" (*imitatio in dictione*). Even though metaphor and simile are accentuated, they are only part of visualizing representation. This is also clear when Averroës elaborates further on Aristotle's comparison between poet and painter:

> Assimilation and representation relate to praise of things which are at the summit of virtue and goodness. Just as the skilled artist depicts an object as it is in reality, so that he can represent a furious, a laughing and a slothful person in his paintings ... in the same way in his representation the poet should depict and form the object as it is in itself and as he is able to do it, so that he imitates and expresses the character and habits of the soul.[18]

The poet, as the painter, depicts the visible in order to convey the invisible, such as emotions – by portraying for example a laughing person. In a sense, this can be compared with figurative language: metaphor, too, has the ability to convey the invisible through a visible, concrete image. However, this passage – in which clearly no kind of figurative representation can be at stake – deals with non-figurative representation and description.

We will return to the categories of Aristotle later, but for now it must be concluded that Averroës's different terms *imaginatio, assimilatio, representatio* and *imitatio* can all indicate figurative language, foremost metaphor, although this is not the proper meaning of the terms.[19] What they indicate is primarily re-presentation, evocation of images through words that "imitate" things. Secondarily, as this mimesis-representation is tied to a considerable urge for strong visualization, they indicate imagery in its widest sense of description, visualization, and the figurative language of tropes.

The place of metaphor

To be sure, Averroës's great focus on figurative language, including both visualizing techniques and tropes, is an addition to the *Poetics*. The focus on visualization is largely imported from Aristotle's *Rhetoric*, where it is not least connected to metaphor: metaphor and visualization proper, setting "before the eyes," *pro ommatôn*, render "smart sayings," *asteia*.[20] The blending of *Poetics* and *Rhetoric* account for the great focus on metaphor in Averroës, but his focus on imagination is yet another supplement. It has been recognized that the role Averroës attributes to *imaginatio* does not come from the *Poetics* but rather from Aristotle's *On the Soul*.[21]

The Arabic exegesis of Aristotle – by Alfarabi, Avicenna and Averroës – attempted to define the logic of poetic language, and in so doing they focused on imitation as distinguished from the "real" and the impact of imitation on the imagination. The syllogistic argument was not much at hand in Aristotle's *Poetics*, more so in his *Rhetoric*, but the Arabic interpreters supplemented it not least by using the *Prior* and *Posterior Analytics*. Aristotle had connected both metaphor and the enthymem to issues of resemblance and recognition, and his interpreters thus developed the *poetic syllogism*. The imaginative is that part of poetry which concerns logic and truth, and that is what attracts the Arabic philosophers' attention. In their view, the imitation of an object creates a distance to it, and the imagination resulting from such an imitation creates an equivalent distance. As Alfarabi states, "The syllogistic nature of poetic discourse depends on the power of imagination to retain and manipulate representations." The essence of the idea of the poetic syllogism is metaphor, as appears from an example provided by Avicenna: "the evening of life" consists of two terms which can both be used literally, but in order to understand the metaphorical statement one must find the similarity between life and evening. The meaning of the metaphor then is the conclusion of the syllogism.[22]

Following Aristotle, the Arabic philosophers conclude that metaphor gives an immediate kind of learning, perspicuity and pleasure. Salim Kemal demonstrates how Averroës develops the idea:

> He points out that learning and wonder are pleasurable and that the use of imagination and representation are likewise pleasurable because they are similar to learning. Thus, drawing, sculpture, poetry and other imaginative representational arts are pleasurable not because the forms they present are beautiful or ugly but because there is a kind of syllogising (or comparing) in them, a matter of making known the absent or concealed thing by presenting an imaginative image. This allows our understanding of representations and imaginings in the art form to be a species of learning through syllogising: the imaginative image presented to us serves as a premise and the thing we want to make known serves as a conclusion. Averroës maintains also that because of the similarities between such use of imagination and learning, the evocation of imagination is pleasant.[23]

In the Arabic tradition, imagination is much more stressed than in Aristotle's *Poetics*, and this becomes essential to the concept of the poetic syllogism. It should be noted that metaphor may be the starting-point for the argument; however, the definitions are not always restricted to metaphors but rather cover any imaginative representation: any conclusion deriving from the imaginative act could then be described as syllogistic.[24] It should also be noted that Averroës's reasoning on the poetic syllogism and the nature of imagination mostly takes place in connection with Aristotle's *Rhetoric*. Even if metaphor is emphasized in the idea of the poetic syllogism, in Averroës's commentary – in the terms of the Latin translation – the essence of poetry is not metaphor, but imaginative representation. Metaphor, and tropes on the whole, are one instance of the latter, the other instance being visualization. In this tradition, imitation and representation is a sincerely creative act, producing insight, knowledge, new perspectives and pleasure deriving from logic.[25]

As Kathy Eden has demonstrated, Aristotle's theory of drama was closely connected to his theory of juridical practice. The question of insight is central both to poetry's *anagnôrisis* and rhetoric's proof, the mutual judgement of probability, actions and intentions, the ways of using *pathos* as a means of reaching a conclusion or verdict, and, essentially, those stylistic devices which are most useful in this context. Eden points to metaphor and visualization, and she does so by showing that Aristotle's *Poetics* and *Rhetoric* need to be understood in the light of *On the Soul*. The central issue is his conception of how imagination works: the "capacity for judging ... is intimately linked in the human soul to the act of imagining, so crucial to both rhetoric and poetry."[26]

In the Arabic tradition, the *Poetics* was consistently interpreted in the light of the *Rhetoric* and *On the Soul*. The rhetoricizing of the *Poetics* is obvious, the psychologization of it somewhat less so. In principle, images are always useful for purposes of convincing the receivers, be they literal or figurative. The distinction between literal visualization and figurative imagery such as metaphor was clear in Aristotle, but he did connect the two in the *Rhetoric*. While praising metaphor, he lavishly explained that setting things "before the eyes" (*pro ommatôn*) was the best way of achieving effect, both in metaphors and in other cases. "We ought ... to aim at three things – metaphor, antithesis, actuality/visuality" (*metaphoras antitheseôs energeias*), he states in III.x.6, and then goes on to demonstrate how metaphor and actuality/visuality support one another.

In *On the Soul*, the basic idea is that we think through images – and thus literary images must be considered the most efficient means of instruction and persuasion.[27] In both the *Poetics* and *Rhetoric* Aristotle maintains that metaphor has an instructing capacity,[28] and while he does not stress visuality in the *Poetics* (for reasons discussed above), he certainly does so in his *Rhetoric*. Averroës, on the other hand, not only elaborates on metaphor and visualization, but also stresses their effect through imagination. Through the *Rhetoric* and *On the Soul*, his view on *Poetics* is dominated by the persuasive power of imagination. Still, metaphor may be the most interesting feature, but it is only one aspect of imagery and visualization.

Averroës and the soul

Averroës does not speak expressly about the soul of poetry, even though he often uses the word *anima*. Significantly, it mostly occurs as a synonym for the receiver, discussing how to move and lead the soul/receiver. He repeatedly describes how the soul's ability to receive and learn depends on the imaginative qualities of assimilation and representation.[29] As the impact on the receivers is what interests Averroës, one might possibly say that the soul of poetry is now placed in the soul of the receivers. However, by turning to the very beginning of Averoës's commentary, the transformation of the soul of poetry becomes clearer.

Averroës is so intent on exploiting poetry's means of manipulating passions in order to move the receivers in the right direction that Aristotle's *pathos* could be seen to have become the central issue. While the passions obviously are a great means for affecting the imagination, this aspect remains one of poetry's functions, not its essence. Averroës defines the essence, or end and substance, of poetry as follows:

> And the end in respect of substance [*terminus substantialis*], or what makes intelligible the substance, of the art of praise is that it should be the likening [*assimilatio*] and representation [*representatio*] of a full [*complete*], voluntary and virtuous action which has universal efficacy [*potestas*] in relation to virtuous actions, and not just a particular efficacy in relation to any specific virtuous actions whatever. A representation, I add, which arouses in souls certain passions which moderate themselves [*or* which moderate the souls] to feel pity or be fearful or to other similar passions which the representation induces and stimulates by what it images [*ymaginari facit*] in the form of virtuous men.[30]

From this description it might appear that Aristotle's *muthos* is what is thought to induce morals, but structure and content, in spite of Averroës's words about action, are in effect dispelled from the essence of poetry. He stresses that *sermo fabularis representativus* is the fundamental principle and foundation of poetry:

> The principal and fundamental part of these [six] parts is fictional language [*sermo fabularis representativus*]. The second most important part is 'typical characteristics' [*consuetudines*]: originally that was the part upon which representation was employed; in other words, that

> was the part which was represented. Indeed, representation or imitation is the foundation or sustenance in this art, because no pleasure is derived from mentioning a thing which we want to, without it being represented. But when it has been thus represented, the result is pleasure and it becomes acceptable.[31]

As we shall see, this principal part, which derives from Aristotle's *muthos*, is now taken to mean "linguistic representation." Later on, he elaborates on visualization:

> The excellence of poetic narration and what brings it to the fulfilling of its goal is when the poet in his stories and narratives writes so vividly that the audience considers what is narrated almost before its mind and eyes, so that it both understands what is narrated, and also does not fail simultaneously to understand things which are not narrated.[32]

Thus, we may conclude that although metaphor is fundamental in the theory of Averroës, it does not constitute a redefinition of the soul of poetry, mimesis. The essence of poetry, rather, is visualization, an important part of which is metaphor. Averroës's various synonyms should not be too enthusiastically interpreted as metaphor or trope: the origin of the idea of imagination is image, evoking a picture or a scene in the mind.

The word *imaginatio* easily associates to psychological faculty and phantasy, but it displays the quality of representation if we consider it a translation of mimesis. A painting of a vase is mimesis of the vase, with the word "vase" being mimesis of the same thing. The painting represents by virtue of establishing an image, *imago*, and from the frequent comparison of word and image follows that the word is also an *imago* of that which it represents – not metaphorically or figuratively, but by presenting a sign. In the same way, *assimilatio* may associate to the word *simile* and imply figurativeness, but it can essentially be understood as a sign which looks like, represents, the thing. A psychological understanding of Averroës's concepts would simply necessitate that the image or the word creates a mental image of the thing which they represent. By extension, any vivid description will be even more efficient.

While its merits are pronounced in Aristotle's *Poetics*, metaphor does not occupy a prominent place there – and although it is addressed in an influential way in the discussion of *lexis*, mimesis-representation, it is clearly subordinated to mimesis-composition. Visualization, the importance of which is also clear in the *Rhetoric*, is not accentuated in the *Poetics*. Nevertheless, as we have seen, Aristotle in chapter 23 does express the potential of metaphor in passing: "[Metaphor] alone cannot be acquired from another, and is a sign of natural gifts: because to use metaphor well is to discern similarities" (1459a5–6). Metaphor – a gift with the potential of creating knowledge – is also the highest instance of imitation and imagery, since it aims not merely at finding a proper representation for the thing intended, but an imitation or representation which captures the likeness of two phenomena at the same time. Although metaphor thus turns out to be the best way of finding and presenting similarities, *to homoion theorein* – which also seems to be Averroës's conclusion – it does not become the soul of poetry here. Furthermore, it is not that "imitation" has disappeared out of sight, but rather that mimesis-composition is replaced by mimesis-representation.

The soul of poetry: muthos *replaced by* lexis

In order to find out what happened to *muthos*, we need to see how Averroës deals with the different parts of poetry. Introducing his topic, he states that poetry always amounts to blame or praise. Since it consists mainly of actions, ruled by will, which are deemed as praiseworthy or reprehensible, action is obviously important to the poetics of Averroës. However, action is not really discussed, only the ways of representing it. Initially, Averroës takes up Aristotle's comparison with the other "representative arts," and this is the aspect of poetry he then follows. The consequence is a seminal displacement of the soul of poetry.[33]

What constitutes poetry, then, is vivid description, be it of events resembling the elements of Aristotelian *muthos* or the exploiting of metaphor, but it is in itself diction, Aristotle's *lexis* – with a strict demand for vividness. This redistribution of the soul of poetry is specifically delineated when Averroës presents his version of the six parts of tragedy:

> [N]amely fictional language [*sermo fabularis representativus*], typical characteristics [*consuetudo*], metre or measure [*metrum seu pondus*], belief [*credulitas*], consideration [*consideratio*], and musical intonation [*tonus*]. An indication of this is that all poetic discourse is divided into "likening" [*assimilatio*] and the means whereby "likening" is achieved. These [means] are three in number: representation [*representatio*], metre and music. And there are three things which are "likened" in the poetry of praise: typical characteristics [*consuetudines*], belief [*credulitates*], and consideration [*consideratio*], which is the process of proving a belief to be true.[34]

Averroës seems to be substituting terms continuously, but it is fairly clear how his categories compare to those of Aristotle.[35] Aristotle's *muthos* has often been understood as the Horatian *fabula*,[36] and Averroës's first category indeed should be understood along these lines. Importantly, when Averroës at the same time names the first of the three means, he does not say *sermo fabularis representativus* but *representatio*. This implies that story, plot and content are no longer really part of poetry. Instead, what is essential to poetry is pure representation, mimesis-representation. The importance of visualization is underscored effectively, but not entirely consistently, as Averroës subsequently says that there are three means which effect *representatio*: *sermo ymaginativus, metrum* and *tonus*.[37]

However, when Averroës speaks of the three objects of poetry, they are *consuetudines, credulitates* and *consideratio*. That is, Aristotle's *opsis* has turned from mode to object – a kind of proof, not the "persuasive" kind but the "representative" kind.[38] To Averroës, rhetoric is persuasive speech (*sermo persuasivus*), while poetry is representational speech (*sermo representativus*). That is, *consideratio* in fact concerns the essence of poetry as opposed to rhetoric, its visualization. Aristotle's *opsis* has been transformed not only from mode to object, but also into something which parallels the other definitions of poetry's essence, the representational force of language.

Averroës thus defines three objects by speaking of "that which" is represented. "That which" is close to Aristotle's own words about the objects, but it is apparent that Averroës redefines the meaning of this kind of object. *Consideratio* in fact concerns visualizing diction, and it must be noted that his definition of the Aristotelian notion of thought, *credulitates*, is made very much in the same way:

> The third part of tragedy is "belief" [*credulitas*], that is, the ability to represent a thing in terms of what it is and what it is not. This is similar to what rhetoric tries to achieve in its attempt to prove that a thing is or is not, except that rhetoric attempts to achieve this end through persuasive speech, and poetry through representational speech.[39]

In effect, of the three "that which is represented," only *consuetudo* is really an object. It is those features, those typical characteristics, in an object that the representation of the object can focus on. All the other parts concern visualizing representation. So, even though Averroës formally speaks of three objects within the six parts of poetry, he really defines only one as an object. His argument thus results in the following scheme:

	Aristotle		Averroës	
object	plot	*muthos*	*sermo fabularis representativus/representatio*	medium
object	character	*êthê*	*consuetudines*	object
object	thought	*dianoia*	*credulitates*	"object"/technique
medium	diction	*lexis*	*imitatio in dictione*	medium
medium	lyric poetry	*melopoiia*	*tonus/metrum seu pondus*	medium
mode	spectacle	*opsis*	*consideratio*	"object"/technique

The changes in terminology mostly mirror substantial changes in the meaning of the concepts. It is not possible to reconstruct an entirely consistent system here, but the effect of the argument is clear – as linguistic representation has become the soul of poetry. Aristotle's *muthos* is described as something which in fact looks more like his *lexis*: *sermo fabularis representativus* or *representatio*. This means that it *can* concern structure of events but that it *must* concern diction: *lexis*. While Aristotle separated object (*muthos*) from medium (*lexis*), Averroës introduces medium – *sermo, representatio* – as the base word in Aristotle's object category. This is all the more evident, as Averroës, before introducing the six parts, does speak of something which is close to Aristotle's *muthos* but is *not* one of the six parts:

> Fables [*fabulae*] refer through *assimilatio* and *representatio* or *imitatio*. By "fable" I mean a composition of things which are intended to be represented either according to how it is in itelf, or according to how it is conventionally feigned in poetry, even though it is mendacious fiction. And this is why poetic speeches are "fables." Reciters and enunciators, in sum, are men who have the ability to represent character and belief.[40]

Averroës's *fabula* has connotations of the animal fable, but his definition is very much that of Aristotle's *muthos*: "the composition of things which are to be represented."[41] He even goes on to state that *sermones poetici* are *fabulae*, but, importantly, in his list of the six parts of poetry he has replaced *muthos* with something much closer to *lexis* since *sermo fabularis representativus* cannot be understood as *fabula*, only as diction associated somehow with *fabula*. Even if *sermo fabularis representativus* has been removed from action and described more as diction, this does not mean that action has disappeared entirely. *Praxis*, the action which *muthos* structured according to Aristotle, is transferred to *consuetudines*, which are expressly said to "embrace actions and morals."[42] Transferring action to Aristotle's *character, êthê*, is quite logical within Averroës's system, since the deeds of people clarify their ethics. As Averroës states in the very beginning, poetry portrays voluntary actions which are either praiseworthy or deprecable (41).

While Aristotle obviously regarded *lexis* as an instance of mimesis, it was the instance of mimesis that is inherent in the construction of *muthos* that he held to be important. In Averroës's view, *muthos* or fable is part of poetry, but it is not central to it. The poet should avoid inventing fabulous creatures, such as Aesop does in his fables; he should instead represent that which is or that which is possible (51). The poet uses stories, mimesis-composition, but the whole discussion of how to achieve imaginative commotion, *ymaginativa commotio*, focuses on mimesis-representation.

As Aristotelian *muthos* is put back in rank, it becomes even more dependent on the lexical level of poetry. The poet must avoid the suspicion of lying, and when he construes or delivers his poem there is one really efficient way of doing so. By employing mimesis-representation to such an extent that the receiver is effectively persuaded or even overwhelmed by it, the poet can make the fiction seem more plausible than it in fact is:

> Fictional invention intended to inspire grief or fear must be invention that is "set before our eyes," so that it may convince us, as if we had actually seen the event happen. For when a fictional account is untrustworthy and is clearly made up on the basis of doubtful material, it will not produce the effect [*actio*] which it was intended to produce. For a statement which someone has not really believed will not move him to fear or pity.[43]

If the story is not credible enough, it can be lent credence by means of persuasive description. This has been a commonplace maneouver through the ages, not least within the "realistic" movement, but the effect of it can always be noted: the probability of mimesis-composition is aided through verisimilitude in mimesis-representation.

Averroës does not deny that poems must portray actions. He even speaks of completing the action of a poem, and, as we have seen, he speaks of *fabula* in a manner reminiscent of *muthos*.[44] But he does not count *fabula* as a part of poetry, noting that "representations arrived at by means of false and invented fictions are not part of the work of a poet."[45] These *figmenta* are not plot but rather inventions of things which cannot be found in nature, such as the speaking animals of Aesop, etc.:

> [I]t is clear that a poet is not a poet unless he uses fictions and metres and measures in such a way that he is successful in producing "likenings" and imitative representations. He does not employ "likenings" except for matters relating to the will which exists in nature. It is part of his task to imitate and represent [*imitetur seu representet*], not just things which exist, but also those things which it is thought can exist. ... Nothing prevents him from taking and using those [possible] things as he uses things which exist here and now. So, made-up

> stories are not lacking in poetry which is intended to stimulate the imagination.[46]

Still, Averroës certainly downplays the role of action as he transfers the soul of poetry to representation. Actions to him are as a rule either effects in the receivers, or exemplary patterns intended to produce such effects. As a consequence of his focus on verbal representation, metre becomes a prerequisite for poetry. In the end, he formulates an idea which seems eternal, but which for him derives directly from the notion that poetic discourse is persuasive and that *lexis* is more powerful than *logos*. Whatever is described will gain credibility if it is said in a visualizing way, placing things before the eyes of the receivers.

It is not correct to say that the notion of imitation is lacking in Averroës: it has been redefined from mimesis-composition to mimesis-representation. Neither has the soul of poetry been defined as metaphor. Tropes, especially metaphor, are certainly dominant, but they are only one instance of that representation. Nor has the soul of poetry been defined as *imaginatio*: while the term occurs more or less synonymously with *representatio, assimilatio* and *imitatio*, it is an aspect of the psychological effect of *representatio*. The terms mentioned sometimes seem to be used in a more restricted sense, sometimes without discrimination. According to Averroës, the essence of poetry – *terminus, finis, substantia, principium, fundamentum* – equals *lexis*, but not in the pure sense of *lexis*: it is supposed to be metric, and above all it is required to be of a highly visualizing standard, including figurative language. To be sure, *lexis* in Aristotle and elsewhere is always presupposed to be artistic, but in Averroës the visualizing aspects which Aristotle propounded in the *Rhetoric*, and the effects on the imagination which he discussed in *On the Soul*, have been fused into the essence of poetry. The soul of poetry thus becomes equivalent to the rhetorical devices of visualization: *enargeia/evidentia*, or with the concept Aristotle applies focusing on both "actuality" and "visuality," *energeia*. In the tradition of rhetoric, *repraesentatio* is known to be a synonym of *evidentia/enargeia*, for example in Quintilian's *Institutio oratoria* (8.3.61).[47]

Aristotle appeared to define metaphor as perfect mimesis – but within *lexis*. When Averroës makes *lexis* the soul of poetry instead of *muthos*, the place of metaphor becomes much more central.

CHAPTER THREE

Mathias Lincopensis

Representation and revelation (14th century)

Saint Bridget of Sweden came to play an important role in both national and international politics as a result of those revelations for which she became renowned. Immediately after her death in 1373 preparations were made for her canonization, and a redaction of her revelations was delivered to pope Gregory XI in 1377. The former bishop of Jaén, Alfonso, was responsible for the redaction, but it was introduced by an authoritative prologue written by master Mathias, the confessor of Bridget and the original promotor of her great career.[1] The ambition of the prologue is evident from the start: "Stupor et mirabilia audita sunt in terra nostra." "The astounding and miraculous" that has made itself heard is of course Bridget's revelations, and the importance of these, according to Mathias, is greater than the human mind and heart can grasp. In fact, Christ's apparition to Bridget is even greater than when Christ appeared as a human being on earth:

> Indeed, this apparition is more amazing than that by which [Christ] appeared in the flesh. That apparition demonstrated a carnal surface to corporeal eyes, this one demonstrates God and Man to spiritual eyes.[2]

This sensational claim should perhaps be understood as relating to the apocalyptic theories of Joachim de Fiore, where the new age was considered to be highly important.[3] In any case, it raises certain questions as to how the revelations were presented.

Mathias's task was to convince the Christian community that the revelations of an unknown woman in a remote country were not only authentic but also of utmost importance. How should documents of this kind be written in order to convince Christianity of something so incredible that Mathias himself, he had to admit, could hardly understand? Of course, Mathias does not discuss this issue in his prologue. In order to find an answer, we will have to examine his ideas of divine truth and literary representation.

Mathias's distinction between "corporeal eyes" and "spiritual eyes" derives from Augustine, primarily the fifteenth book of *De trinitate*. This is where he discusses the words of Paul, 1 Corinthians 13:12: "Now we see only puzzling reflections in a mirror, but then we shall see face to face" (*Videmus nunc per speculum in ænigmate: tunc autem facie ad faciem*).[4] According to Augustine, what we see *per speculum in aenigmate* (literally: through a mirror in an enigma) is ourselves and creation. He discusses the *aenigma* of rhetoric and describes it as an obscure allegory: something is represented by way of something else. His conclusion is that *per speculum in aenigmate* should be understood as an obscure image.[5] The issue is that of human interpretation and the search for God: until we finally meet him, we can only discern the traces of him in creation. Belief and intellect are thus both engaged: this is where Augustine expresses his influential doctrine that who does not believe cannot understand.[6]

The spiritual eyes of man are employed to interpret this tempting and vague image. With corporeal eyes one can see material things, the obscure image of truth, but with spiritual eyes one can see other dimensions:

> For who does not see his own thought? And who does see his own thought, not I say with the eyes of flesh, but with the interior gaze itself? Who does not see it, and who does see it? For in thought we look, so to say, into our own mind, whether those things are present which we also see with our bodily eyes or perceive through the other senses, or whether they are not present, and their likenesses are seen in thought; or whether it is neither of these, but we think of those things that are neither corporeal nor the likenesses of bodies, such as the virtues and the vices, as, in a word, thought itself is thought.[7]

Here, the faculty of imagination is positioned in Augustine's view on interpretation. Obviously, focusing on the interpretational strength of the spiritual gaze, Mathias in his prologue discreetly turns to Augustine: what is seen with spiritual eyes must be of higher authority than what is seen with corporeal eyes, since wisdom is the light of the spiritual eyes (*De trinitate* xv.viii.1–3).[8] This idea is also emphasized in Bridget's revelations, in which spiritual and corporeal eyes are often discussed, and frequent mention is made of the visions as images expressing higher truths – the reader is even at times supplied with thorough explications of how the visions are to be interpreted. Christ himself tells Bridget that her visions of devils, hell and so forth are images of higher truths that she could not otherwise grasp.[9] It has been demonstrated that theories of revelation, not least those of Thomas Aquinas, are at work in Bridget and then particularly through the influence of Mathias. Man is unable to understand without images; the visionary is furnished with a certain consciousness by God, and it is the visionary's responsibility to formulate the message, to find the right images to convey insight and learning.[10]

Bridget received visions where the images were adapted so that she could understand them, but she herself was responsible for the way in which they would be presented to the world – and in this she received aid from her confessors. We may thus ask which is the most efficient way of representing revelations so that they strengthen belief and understanding, while also instigating the receivers to continue their search for divine truth. Bridget's tutor Mathias does not discuss this question in a religious context, but he develops his idea of literary presentation elsewhere.

Master Mathias on literary presentation

Around 1300, Mathias studied in Paris and he brought a considerable amount of learning back to Sweden. Manuscripts of his concordance on the Bible, *Alphabetum distinccionum,* have been preserved in several libraries throughout Europe. Among other things, he wrote a work on rhetoric, *Testa nucis,* and one on poetics, *Poetria. Testa nucis,* which has only been partly preserved, is based on the translation of Aristotle's *Rhetoric* that William of Moerbeke made in the 13th century. *Poetria* is based on Averroës's commentary of Aristotle's *Poetics,* as translated by Hermannus

Alemannus in 1256, discussed in the previous chapter. Here, some illustrative aspects of Mathias's redaction will be discussed.[11]

Mathias's view on poetry is close to that of Averroës, but he elaborates and sharpens the distinctions considerably, arriving at a definition of the essence of poetry which corresponds to that of Averroës, but is even more remote from Aristotle. Initially (§ 5–6), Mathias discusses poetry in a manner quite similar to the premises presented by Aristotle:

> Whereas in our opinion all the resources of language are normally used for rational statements, we maintain that poetry alone deals with statements that are imaginative [*sermones imaginatiuos*]. This is why the poet is rightly compared to the painter. For the skilful painter, by the harmonious arrangement of the different parts and colours of the picture, turns out to give an agreeable representation of something that would not in itself be agreeable to look at, and in the same way the perfect poet gives pleasure by making us imagine a thing in accordance with its characteristics.[12]

The poet uses "statements that are imaginative," *sermones imaginatiuos,* to establish something corresponding to the painting, the seat of the images being the imagination of the human mind. *Imaginatio* is in the following paragraph described as the result of literary technique:

> This imagination, however, is accomplished by three means, viz. *representacio, intonation* and *metre,* but representacio alone is an essential part of poetry.[13]

Although he continues to discuss the means for achieving it, the concept *imaginatio* is no longer a central topic of discussion. Mathias states that what belongs to the essence of poetry is *representatio,* the echo of Aristotelian mimesis.[14] The *tonus* and *metrum* in the quotation correspond to Aristotle's *melopoiia,* while *representatio* corresponds to *lexis.* As opposed to Averroës, Mathias does not use *imaginatio* synonymously with *representatio,* and thus after stating its importance he does not discuss *imaginatio* further. Another difference from Averroës is that Mathias strictly defines *representatio* as the equivalent of *lexis,* where Averroës's *sermo fabularis representativus fabularis* or *representatio* was intended to be the equivalent of *muthos*. As in Averroës, linguistic representation has taken over the role of the essence of poetry, but to an even greater extent: Mathias offers no equivalent to *muthos* at all but discards fictional narrative more consistently.

Discussing *representatio*, Mathias stresses that what is presented should be conjured before the eyes of the hearer/reader.[15] The emotions, which Mathias in his rhetoric (*Testa nucis*, § 12–14) describes as a fundamental means of persuasion, can thus be evoked through poetical image, and this is precisely the aim of poetry.

Mathias distinguishes between two ways of accomplishing *representatio*: "a thing can be visualized by its characteristics, which enable the intellect to grasp it. ... This form of visualization may be called *descriptio*."[16] *Descriptio*, we are told, should place that which is presented before our eyes (*ante oculos*), and preferably consist of actions that express presence (*acciones presenciales*) (§ 10–12). Mathias here refers to the methods of visualization which he has treated in *Testa nucis*, that is, where he has rendered Aristotle's discussion of *energeia* and *pro ommatôn* in his *Rhetoric* (unfortunately, this part of *Testa nucis* has not been preserved).

The other way to achieve *representatio* is *conformatio*, which can be divided into *assimilatio* (simile), *concambium* (trope), illustrated by a metaphor, and a kind of blend of these (§ 13–14). Mathias's categories are thus more precise than those of Averroës, and different. *Representatio* is used consistently as the overarching level of – visualizing – representation. Below this level is, on the one hand, *descriptio*, visualization of the kind of *energeia* or *enargeia-evidentia*, and on the other hand *conformatio*, a new term which substitutes Averroës's *concambium*. In turn, *concambium* is defined as trope as separate from simile, while *assimilatio*, which Averroës could use synonymously with *imaginatio*, *representatio* and *imitatio*, is defined as simile. The effect – changing the soul of poetry from mimesis-composition to mimesis-representation – is the same as in Averroës, the execution more distinct. As Averroës, Mathias devotes lavish space to metaphor (§ 16–25), which again proves its central position. But Mathias manages to elaborate metaphor further, at the same time downplaying fiction.

From mimesis to representatio*: Fiction boiled down to metaphor*

To Aristotle, the soul of poetry was *muthos*, the structure and content of fiction. As we have already seen, Mathias, as Averroës, displaces the essence of poetry from mimesis-composition to mimesis-representation, and *representatio*, the equivalent of *lexis*, thus moves to the centre. Also Aristotle's *melopoiia* is discernible in Mathias's *tonus* and *metrum* already in § 7, but other pieces of Aristotle's six parts of poetry are not discussed until § 63, where Mathias takes up that which "poetic representation deals with" (*hiis, circa que est representacio poetica*): *consuetudines, credulitates* and *consideratio*. *Consuetudines* are briefly described as that which men "get used to through frequent actions," while *credulitates* are notions which are stabilized not by habit but by legislation (§ 64–65). Aristotle saw character as something which emerges through actions, but Mathias, like Averroës, sees actions more purely as a means of displaying character (and as a way of gaining visuality). However, these actions are not given much attention, especially not as composition: Mathias simply does not mention the six parts of poetry as such, and nowhere does he suggest an equivalent to Aristotle's *muthos*. Focus is always on *lexis*, not only when *representatio* is said to be the essence of poetry, but also in discussing the other parts:

> *Consideratio*, however, is nothing but the presentation of uncertain things – not, however, through rational arguments or persuasions (since that is not the poet's business) but through representations so certain and plausible that the matter does not seem to have been made up.[17]

Mathias thus follows Averroës's development of *consideratio*, Aristotle's *opsis*, into visualizing suggestion. Here, it becomes even clearer how poetic persuasion and argument is supposed to consist in visualization: had Mathias used the term *evidentia*, he would have provided a good example of the term's development into "evidence." Even this category thus turns into linguistic representation, and of the kind that explicitly supports or dominates the content of poetry. Positing *consuetudines, credulitates* and *consideratio* as that which "poetic representation deals with" suggests that they are the objects of poetry, but they are not really objects, rather technical conditions of poetic representation and thus to a high degree concern mimesis-representation. Mathias lessens the status of *consuetudines* as object even more than Averroës, so that five of Aristotle's six parts of poetry are turned into representation or suggestion. Aristotle's soul of poetry, *muthos,* is not even treated in this context. Actions are mentioned as aids to visualization (§ 12), as means of representing persons (§ 31), or as the cause of customs, *consuetudines* (§ 64). Aristotle's six parts of tragedy in relation to Mathias can thus be schematized as follows:

	Aristotle		Mathias	
object	plot	*muthos*	–	–
object	character	*êthê*	*consuetudines*	"object"/technique
object	thought	*dianoia*	*credulitates*	"object"/technique
medium	diction	*lexis*	*representatio*	medium
medium	lyric poetry	*melopoiia*	*tonus, metrum*	medium
mode	spectacle	*opsis*	*consideratio*	"object"/technique

Mathias does give clues as to the nature of *muthos.* Regarding the three species of simile and metaphor, he states that they are employed either in order to demonstrate the honourable or to vituperate the shameful, or they may be used for both purposes (§ 29–30). This leads to the declaration: "All poetic representations thus express either praise or censure" (§ 31).[18] This, in turn, leads to the conclusion that the poet should not create fictions, but on the contrary refrain from them:

> In consequence, it is not the poet's affair to make up fables [*fabulas*] and insert them in his verses, since such inventions do not create the kind of credibility required in eulogy.[19]

While Averroës prohibited fictions, in the sense of supernatural creatures, etc., but allowed for *fabulae,* stories of diverse kinds, Mathias is even closer bound to the verisimilar. What then, one may ask, happens to the Aristotelian *muthos*? Mathias immediately addresses the issue:

> Nevertheless, if they [inventions] are made up with care and convey probability, they are now and then admitted of, primarily in order to give pleasure, sometimes also to conceal some truth which is understood by the very fables. In such cases the result may perhaps be not fables but either metaphors or allegories of the kind just dealt with.[20]

The element of fiction should consequently be limited to metaphors and other tropes: an exchange of words or phrases. Evidently, Mathias holds that metaphor, such as the old one of calling a man a lion (§ 20), is necessarily false, since the word "lion" is used in a transferred sense. The metaphor is thus a lie, but as the lie is limited to a metaphor it is acceptable and even recommendable, since it promotes an imaginative impact. The lies, inventions and fables which are to be avoided by the poet are thus longer invented stories. To be sure, Mathias suggests that *acciones presenciales* are good for visualizing, but this is far from the Aristotelian *mimêsis praxeôs*; rather, it designates movements or events that create presence.[21]

Although the aspect should not be exaggerated, poetry in the Arabic tradition had increasingly become defined as a *means* to present truths.[22] In the end, content appears to be seen as a given – what concerns poetics is rather the way of representation. Principally, there is no room for a story of the kind Aristotle discusses as *muthos,* since it, as shown above, has been hidden away in metaphor. In this respect, Mathias is stricter than Averroës, perhaps because Mathias was more familiar with Western literature than Averroës, who did not know the genres about which Aristotle was speaking. At the very least, poetics according to Mathias is a subject redefined and associated with the level of representation. This, of course, is congenial to the "Horatian" tradition of poetics, whose focus was held on versification, grammar, rhetoric and not least the idea of *ut pictura poesis*. To illustrate this point, Mathias ends his *Poetria* with a poem in honour of the town Uppsala, exemplifying the devices discussed. As Mathias says that "visualization alone is an essential part of poetry," the soul of poetry distinctly resides in mimesis-representation.

Revelation and poetics

Would Mathias then have thought his prescriptions in *Poetria* valid only for profane, metric poetry? This is most unlikely, since Mathias himself gives a reference to (a now lost passage of) his own work on rhetoric for further discussion of placing *ante oculos.*[23] It was also in his *Rhetoric* that Aristotle originally discussed the ability of metaphor and other devices to conjure things before the eyes (*pro ommatôn*), and the formula *ante oculos* is frequent in the translation by Moerbeke.[24] Since Aristotle's mimesis turned into this kind of visualization in *Poetria,* one could say that rhetoric and poetics have fused. Mathias's poetics expresses a general attitude towards literary representation, which is congruent not only with the homiletic tradition and the theological ideas derived from Augustine and formulated in the 12th century by Anselm of Canterbury, *credo ut intelligam,* but also with Thomas Aquinas:

> Just as human reason fails to grasp the import of poetical utterance on account of its deficiency in truth, neither can it grasp divine things perfectly on account of their superabundance of truth; and therefore in both cases there is need of representation by sensible figures.[25]

Aristotelian mimesis is thus converted into rhetorical visualizing and figurative language, in accordance with common theological notions as well as homiletic practice: the preachers' use of *exempla* and other devices to move the listeners should probably be directly related to the theories of Mathias, who also displayed a great interest in image in his *Copia exemplorum,* a collection of "abstracts" of *exempla,* edifying images to be used by preachers.[26]

The issue might also be directly relevant to the revelations of Saint Bridget. Their enormous impact on Christianity, of course, cannot entirely be explained by their literary technique, but it is apparent that part of their reputation and influence is due to those techniques proposed by Mathias: commentators rarely omit to speak of the stunning "realism" or "naturalism" of the revelations, and it has been shown how in the revelations biblical scenes or Christian works of art have been used as models.[27] Also, within the revelations great weight is placed on the interpretation of the forceful images, that is, in the terms of *Poetria*, on both *descriptio* and *conformatio*, resulting in *representatio*.

This is too general to prove that the vivid description of the revelations has anything to do with the literary theories of Mathias, and it would hardly be possible to find actual evidence within the revelations. The revelations have often been described as the product of genial inspiration or at least intuitive originality.[28] It has been noted that Bridget defines eloquence as verbosity, and that she, thanks to a "good psychological intuition," recognized the use of some rhetorical devices, primarily imagery.[29] The question is, however, whether it is at all possible to suppose that her confessors did not convey any notion of literary technique: the revelations constantly reveal a thorough consciousness of their own imagery and capacity as persuasive objects for interpretation. What the records do evidence is that the confessors of St Bridget took an active part in redacting and finishing the written versions of her revelations.[30] And among the confessors, Mathias was clearly the most influential one.[31] It was he who launched and modelled her career as visionary; and, as we have seen, in doing so he spoke in terms of spiritual eyes in a manner most reminiscent of the wording in *Poetria*.

In revelation VI:18, Christ himself tells Bridget that her way to knowledge must be through figurative representations of spiritual truths.[32] A revelation such as VI:52 is a good example of this, offering an overwhelmingly vivid description:

> The aforementioned dead mother seemed to creep out of a dark and dirty puddle. Her heart was pulled out and her lips cut off, her cheek was trembling and her long, shining white teeth were rattling. Her nose was corroded and her eyes torn out, hanging down on her cheeks on two strings. Her forehead seemed pushed in, and in its place was a great dark gorge. There was no cranium in her head, her brain flowed forth like melted lead and poured out like tar. Her neck was spinning like a piece of wood in a turning lathe with the sharpest iron against it, mercilessly grinding it down. Her chest was open and filled with long, thin worms, wriggling all over one another. ... A long, great snake stretched from the lower part of her stomach to the upper part, joining its head and tail like a bow, coiling constantly in her

> intestines. Her shins and legs looked like thorny rods, filled with the sharpest thorns, her feet were like those of toads.[33]

The passage is filled with similes, but the most prominent feature is what has often been called Bridget's "realism" or "naturalism": detailed descriptions where the elements are chosen and elaborated in an overwhelming way. It has been demonstrated with precisely this revelation how Bridget used art and sculptures from churches she visited as inspiration for her descriptions.[34] This "ecphrastic" method clearly shows how carefully Bridget nourished the potentials of imagery.

Apart from visualization and similes, Bridget has become well known for her use of effective metaphors. One example of her way of clarifying abstract theological concepts through everyday images is when she says that "penitence is a good laundress, who removes spots ... but remorse is a good bleecher."[35]

Another aspect of imagery, namely allegorical interpretation, is highly relevant in the revelations and not least in the one quoted above. Following her description, Bridget has the woman dictate how the import of her own spiritual meaning should be interpreted. She says to Bridget,

> You who see me, you only see me through bodily similes. For if you saw me in the form I really have, you would die of terror, because all my limbs are demons. Therefore the Bible is right, saying that as the righteous are God's members, so the sinners are the Devil's members. Thus I now experience that demons are attached to my soul, since my heart's will has destined me to such deformity.[36]

This, then, is the starting-point and motivation for the images: just as Christ told Bridget elsewhere, visualization is the only way to knowledge and truth. The dead woman very carefully explains the horrid details of her own appearance:

> It seems to you that my feet are like those of a toad. This is because I stood firm in sin, and therefore the demons now stand firm in me, biting me without ever being satisfied. My legs and shins are like thorny rods, because I had my will directed towards my carnal pleasure and

> lust. … That a serpent is stretched from the lower part of my abdomen to the upper is because my lust and pleasure were disorderly and my will wanted to possess and spend everything in many unwise ways. Therefore a serpent now coils in my interior, biting me remorselessly and mercilessly. That my chest is open and corroded by worms is a demonstration of God's true justice. I loved the putrid more than God, and my heart loved the transient.[37]

As creation is interpreted as a sign of God's plan, so the images of the vision are constructed as signs of the meaning of God and existence. The revelations to a large extent transmit their messages through this kind of discourse. Exegetic allegory is a category of imagery which is not treated in the *Poetria* – for obvious reasons, since this does not belong to profane poetry. However, the revelations and their effect are dependent on the two categories of imagery which Mathias labelled *descriptio* and *conformatio*: it is through these that the theological message can be presented.[38]

The question is what can be deduced by these correspondences between Mathias's poetics and the revelations he tutored. On the one hand, scholars have been reluctant to ascribe to Bridget any greater technical consciousness: this has been seen as contrary to the ecstatic, personal, immediate impression they make, and their stylistic unevenness. On the other hand, studies have shown that Bridget used several kinds of inspiration for her revelations.[39] The techniques of visualization were standard in the environment of homiletic practice, within which she was most intimately involved. It goes without saying that the revelations went through considerable revision by learned supervisors: this was even on the admonishment of Christ, who in the revelation where Bridget was assigned the mission said to her:

> Hear my words and go to master Mathias, your confessor, who is skilled in distinguishing the two spirits. Tell him on my behalf that you shall be my bride and my channel and that you will hear and see spiritual things, and that my spirit will be with you all the way to death.[40]

It was Mathias's task to make the revelations known. He initially focused his attention on addressing Swedish audiences and wrote an introduction to Bridget's revelations in Swedish. Subsequently, he nurtured greater ambitions and thus wrote his Latin introduction.[41]

In the *vita* which was composed after her death, two of her confessors described the process: Bridget wrote down her revelation, which was then translated into Latin. While the translation was read to her she would check it against the Swedish version, ensuring that no word was added or removed. If she was ill her confessor and a writer would come to her and she would divulge her revelation as if she was reading it. Then her confessor, in turn, would dictate in Latin for the writer, and finally Bridget would check the Latin version.[42]

According to one of the confessors, Petrus Olavi, Bridget always told Mathias her revelations and followed any decision he made about them.[43] To be sure, a major reason behind the extremely efficient representation of the revelations must have been Bridget's unusual talent for concretion and imagery. But the degree to which she could successfully exploit this gift seems to be attributable to a dedicated commitment from the very beginning by Mathias. Even if he did not edit the revelations, or give theoretical instructions, he may have shown and instigated those ways of persuasion that he had been deeply involved in and that Bridget would employ with such extraordinary success. There is no reason to suppose that Mathias and Saint Bridget discussed Aristotle, but it does seem highly unlikely that Bridget's visions could have reached the same degree of visuality had not Mathias been inspired by Aristotle-Averroës's view on the soul of poetry.

While Averroës used the terms *imaginatio, representatio, imitatio* and *assimilatio* with no great precision, as they all, in a sense, became equivalent to the rhetorical figure of visualization, metaphor held a very special place. While Averroës still admitted room for fiction and the structuring of events when he considerably rearranged the parts of poetry, Mathias, on the other hand, sharpened the terminology. He defined the essence of poetry as *representatio*, dividing it into *descriptio*, distinctly meaning vivid visualization, and simile and trope/metaphor, much in the manner of, but more distinctly than, Averroës. While Averroës took no great interest in mimesis-composition, advising the poet to evade suspicion of lying, Mathias fine-tunes the argument considerably and concludes that lies and fiction are only acceptable insofar as they limit themselves to the figurative significance that constitutes metaphor. In discussing representation of reality, Mathias consequently sees the power of visualization as far more important than medieval commentators on Horace's *ut pictura poesis,*[44] but in a manner quite similar to how Pseudo-Longinus propounds the figure *enargeia* in *Peri hupsous,* as shall be discussed in chapter 8. The *Poetria* of Mathias proposed an extreme redefinition of the soul of poetry and did not influence other poetics. However, the main tendency of mimesis-representation instead of mimesis-composition prevailed for some time in Europe, recurring in new guises. In the following chapters, mimesis-composition can be seen as reconstituting itself, but accompanied with new kinds of reinterpretations.

CHAPTER FOUR

The Italian Renaissance
(16th–17th century)

Aristotle's *Poetics* became an important point of reference in the Italian Renaissance, even though the way to an Aristotelian understanding of it was long. All debate had to start with what was available: Averroës's commentary and those assumptions about poetry which were laid down there. When printing became an option, the Greek Aristotle gradually caught up with the Arabic one. Hermannus's translation of Averroës's commentary was printed in 1481, and in 1498 Giorgio Valla's Latin translation of Aristotle's original appeared. The Greek original was published in 1508 and was widely disseminated through subsequent translations, editions and commentaries.[1] Even though the ideas of the original became more readily available, the rhetorical understanding of it still predominated.

When offering the first Latin translation, Valla established a Latin terminology which became influential even though it was not new:

	Aristotle		Valla
object	plot	*muthos*	*fabula*
object	character	*êthê*	*mores*
object	thought	*dianoia*	*animi sententiae*
medium	diction	*lexis*	*dictio*
medium	lyric poetry	*melopoiia*	*melopoeia*
mode	spectacle	*opsis*	*conspectus*

Valla's division into what we label media, mode and object follows Aristotle's wording of "that through which," "how" and "that which" is imitated.[2] (He also renders Aristotle's words on the soul of tragedy accurately: *fabula* is the main principle and the soul of tragedy.)[3] The Latin term *fabula* comes close to *muthos* but is in danger of being understood in a very wide sense; *mores* obviously invites to a predominantly moral and thus instrumental view on poetry; *animi sententiae* directs "thinking" towards outspoken thoughts; while *dictio* corresponds to *lexis* in a very precise manner. Thus, the distinction between mimesis-composition, *muthos*, the soul of poetry according to Aristotle, and mimesis-representation, *lexis*, the more fundamental but less central instance of mimesis, was made evident in Aristotle's *Poetics* again. This, however, did not mean that the Averroistic poetics vanished – rather, the two attitudes blended, producing new interpretations of the soul of poetry.

In *A History of Literary Criticism in the Italian Renaissance*, Bernard Weinberg studied the rhetoricizing of the *Poetics* in a vast number of texts, demonstrating the complexity of the discussions, and the expansiveness of theories and interpretations deriving from Aristotle's *Poetics*.[4] Restricting the discussion to our questions about the soul of poetry, we may find ample material in Weinberg's extensive explorations on the basis of which conclusions can be made.[5] Weinberg demonstrates the confusion which surrounded the concept of imitation, and points to two main causes for this: first, the parallel meaning of *imitatio* as the imitation of authoritative poets, and second, Plato's uses of mimesis, especially the passage in the *Republic*, book III, where Socrates distinguishes between mimesis, meaning direct speech, and *diegesis*, meaning indirect speech.[6] These distinctions, the latter also at hand in Aristotle, certainly contributed to the confusion.

However, the following discussion will focus on entirely different categories of conceptualization. Weinberg's approach is representative of the Chicago critics: while accentuating the ideas of unity and structure in Aristotle's *Poetics*, much of his work demonstrates how this aspect did not survive in the hands of the Italian commentators.[7] Being apprehended from a profoundly rhetorical view and interpreted in a way which fragmented its different parts, Aristotle's *Poetics* was adjusted so as to account first and foremost for poetry's effect on its audience. Weinberg's approach to the rhetoricized reception of Aristotle's *Poetics* can thus be said to focus on the ideas of effect and audience, while my own perspective focuses on those categories in which poetry and poetics were comprehended.

Weinberg demonstrates how Robortello together with Castelvetro in the 16th century in a sense embody the loss of Aristotle's notion of poetry as a whole:

> As a consequence – or as a corollary – the principles of internal organization of the poem, Aristotle's necessity and probability, are transmuted into principles for relating the poem to nature and to the beliefs of the audience. In this way the requirement of "credibility" becomes a dominating consideration for Robortello. The question is no longer: "How is such or such a part integrated into the artistic structure of the poem?" but rather "Will the audience believe that such or such an action or character is true?" This shift is entirely consistent with the general movement away from the poem and towards the demands or the expectations of the audience.[8]

Still, Robortello did not define the audience as meticulously as Castelvetro would. According to Castelvetro, the objective of poetry is only to amuse an ignoble audience and has to be adapted to that end, a view that is in accordance with Averroës's commentary and which is highly influential of French classicism in Weinberg's historiography.[9]

Weinberg carefully demonstrates the confusion concerning the various uses of the concept imitation, but I think it is possible to better explain parts of the confusion by addressing the issue through the polarities of mimesis as composition and representation. For example, Weinberg says that one sense of imitation which was "not subject to confusion was the 'Ciceronian' meaning of the imitation of earlier poets – the use of a model for matters of language, expression, style."[10] While agreeing that the sense of imitation or emulation of previous poets can to a large degree be separated from the other senses (having left it to the side myself), I think that there is a risk of mistaking it for mimesis-representation, not least when Weinberg tries to clarify the Ciceronian sense by quoting Bernardino Parthenio's *Della imitatione poetica* from 1560:

> [I]t seems to me reasonable and necessary to recall that there are two kinds of poetic imitation. One, which consists in expressing in an excellent fashion the nature and characters of those persons whom we

> undertake to imitate. And this is the end of poetry. … But leaving this type of imitation to Aristotle, we shall treat only the other one, which consists in words and in figures of speech.[11]

Admittedly, imitation of *auctores* involves language and style, but here it is clear that the two instances of imitation which Parthenio discusses are mimesis-composition and mimesis-representation. The first kind is not described in terms of action, but of nature and character (as we shall see, the definitions of the objects of mimesis-composition are a topic of elaboration in the Italian Renaissance). As opposed to this mimesis-composition, Parthenio then describes the kind of imitation concerning *lexis*: representation through words, comprising figures of speech. Thus, Parthenio proves himself to be quite aware of the distinction and furthermore of the fact that it was mimesis-composition which Aristotle considered to be the aim of poetry. Having made that statement, Parthenio feels free to devote his work to the mimesis of *lexis*.

Similarly, Weinberg describes Robortello's words about the end of poetry – to achieve a discourse which imitates as opposed to persuades (*dicimus in poëtice finem esse, sermonem imitantem, sicut in rhetorice sermonem persuadentem*) – as "the Aristotelian end of imitation,"[12] while it is in fact far more Averroistic.[13]

In the following, I will try to clarify the discussion by distinguishing between not only the two instances of mimesis, but also by clarifying what view of Aristotelian *probability* they result in.[14] I will do so by examining only a few statements that concern the aim or duty of the poet or the aim, essence or soul of poetry. The obvious background will be Weinberg's monumental work, and the scope of my investigation is to clarify a perspective rather than offer holistic interpretations.

Robortello

Francesco Robortello's *In Librum Aristotelis de Arte Poetica Explicationes* was published in 1548.[15] Robortello had access to Averroës's commentary, Valla's translation, the edition of 1508 as well as Alessandro de Pazzi's translation of 1536. Accomplishing the first substantial commentary on

Aristotle's *Poetics,* his interpretation became a kind of landmark for the numerous followers.[16] In his treatment, Weinberg has pointed to the pragmatic and rhetorical implications of Robortello's commentary and concluded that his focus on the immediate pleasure and persuasion of a particular audience made him disregard the artistic unity and the plot as a poetic element,[17] a poetological development closely connected to the question of mimesis-composition and mimesis-representation.

In his discussion of tragedy, Robortello rather accurately renders Aristotle's main categories: he describes the parts of tragedy as "fabula, mores, dictio, sententia, apparatus, melodia" (57) and he states that Aristotle considered *fabula* more important than *mores* (64). Robortello does not want to diminish the importance of *mores,* but concludes that they are comprised in the actions: "Therefore, actions and *fabula* are said to be the end of tragedy."[18] He thus accounts for Aristotle's notions rather than those of Averroës. However, Robortello's *Explicationes* amount to a view on poetry which nonetheless slants at mimesis-representation. Robortello curiously describes the three objects of tragedy not as *fabula, mores* and *sententia,* which would be in agreement with Aristotelian *muthos, êthê* and *dianoia.* Instead, he describes *fabula* as mode, and appoints *dictio* as one of the objects of poetry.[19] Aristotle's parts of poetry are thus reorganized as follows:

Aristotle			Robortello	
object	plot	*muthos*	*fabula*	mode
object	character	*êthê*	*mores*	object
object	thought	*dianoia*	*sententia*	object
medium	diction	*lexis*	*dictio*	object
medium	lyric poetry	*melopoiia*	*melodia*	medium
mode	spectacle	*opsis*	*apparatus*	medium

Making diction an object of poetry is in a way consistent with the comparison between the poet and the actor: both can be considered to represent, or present, words. It also accentuates the focus which Robortello places on diction, that is, imitation understood as representation. When he arrives at Aristotle's discussion of *lexis,* he uses the word *dictio* and elaborates on metaphor and other devices, without specifying the relation between *dictio, imitatio, representatio* and *descriptio* (highly reminiscent of Averroës's synonymous use). When he states that the first end of poetry is to imitate, the second to delight (p. 30), it thus seems safe to conclude that the predominant sense of imitation is mimesis-representation, something which is substantiated by the entire framework.

The structure of *Explicationes* is based on that of the *Poetics,* quoting one passage at a time and then explicating it. Before quoting the beginning of the *Poetics,* however, Robortello introduces his own considerations on "what the poetic faculty is like and what force it has, what its aim is, and with which subject matter it accomplishes its work."[20] Distinguishing poetry from rhetoric, dialectics, etc., and referring to that sophisticated and ingenious, albeit Arabic, interpreter of Aristotle, Robortello concludes that poetry's subject matter is that which is false or fabulous. He does not mention fable or actions here, but rather fabulous creatures such as Cerberus, and with this he thinks himself to have spent enough time on the questions of subject matter and wishes to shift to the *end, finis,* of poetry.[21] He then, in accordance with Aristotle, states that horrible things become enjoyable when *represented*: be it in stone, bronze, painting or poetry:

> What other end should we assign to the poetic faculty than to please through representation, description and imitation of all human actions; all motions, all things animate or inanimate?[22]

While Robortello here infinitely widens the array of subject matters for poetry – far beyond *muthos* and its actions, and character and thought – this seems to be nothing more than qualifiers to the real aim of poetry: to represent. The words "representation, description and imitation" do not represent different stages of the poet's craft: they are to be seen as synonymous whereas the creating (as opposed to representing) of subject matter is referred to with "confinguntur" (p. 2, cf. "in effingendis moribus," 183). Thus, the end of poetry is to represent, with the objects of representation being consigned to secondary importance. Contrary to Aristotle's *Poetics,* the essence – end – of poetry is said to be mimesis-representation. In spite of the access to Aristotle's original text, this description is close to that of Averroës, who had redefined the essence of poetry into (forceful) representation with the synonymous use of terms such as *imitatio, representatio* and *descriptio*. Robortello here states that anything can be represented – quite in accordance with the rhetorical idea that *res* are represented with *verba*. The relation to Averroës's view becomes clear when Robortello concludes:

> And since this imitation and representation is made through speech, we say that the end in poetry is imitative discourse, as in rhetoric it is persuasive discourse.[23]

While Averroës labelled poetry *sermo representativus* and rhetoric *sermo persuasivus*, Robortello refers to them as *sermo imitans* and *sermo persuadens*. Thus, even though his work is devoted to Aristotle's *Poetics*, Robortello follows Averroës by holding mimesis-representation to be the end of poetry. Robortello does present the Aristotelian formulations of action and fable, mimesis-composition, in tragedy, but he does so when commenting on the text of Aristotle's *Poetics* and he there proclaims diction instead of *muthos* as object of poetry. In the introduction, where he gives his own view on poetry, he clearly places the soul of poetry in mimesis-representation.

Ulrike Zeuch has interpreted Robortello's *Explicationes* as a reinterpretation of Aristotle's *Poetics*, which created confusion about the ends of literature that would dominate poetological discussions until about 1800.[24] According to Zeuch, Robortello created a definition where "not only human action, but anything can be the object of literary mimesis." His definitions, she argues, depend on a philosophical idea of perception and imply that things are not only represented in words, but also that they are represented mentally. Robortello in this sense would follow the Stoic doctrine of *tuposis*, and therefore his "repræsentationem, descriptionem, & imitationem" would have psychological implications.

It may be perfectly true that Robortello was influenced by current ideas about perception, and even that this changed his view of poetics. Zeuch is without a doubt right in seeing a shift from mimesis of human action to mimesis of any object in Robortello – compared to Aristotle. However,

Zeuch's article demands several comments. First, this shift – which in fact is simply from mimesis-composition to mimesis-representation – was at hand long before Robortello. Second, and this follows from the first, the important thing is not that the represented subject matter changes – Aristotle's mimesis is invention and construction, Robortello's is representation. Third, the difference between these categories was obvious to anyone versed in rhetoric. Fourth, when Robortello advocates effective, persuasive representation, there may be a connection to new philosophical constructions about phantasy and perception, but vivid representation was already part of the discussion in Averroës's account, who as we saw certainly added psychology (from *On the Soul*) when speaking of *imitatio, representatio* and *descriptio* in the same sense as *imaginatio*. Robortello seems to be using Averroës's terms and variants of them, and it should be remembered that *phantasia – imaginatio –* is the term Pseudo-Longinus used when he treated the sublime, mainly identifying it with the rhetorical figure of overwhelming representation. (Pseudo-Longinus's *Peri hupsous* was edited for the first time in 1554 by Robortello.)[25] Finally, the contradictions concerning the ends of poetry which Robortello allegedly created had been part of the poetological tradition for a long time.

Castelvetro

In 1570 the perhaps most influential Italian commentary on Aristotle's *Poetics* was published: Lodovico Castelvetro's *Poetica D'Aristotile vulgarizzata, et sposta.*[26] Castelvetro is known as the one who laid the foundation of the French classicist doctrine of the three unities: Aristotle had spoken of the need for a single plot without episodes, but Castelvetro claimed that an audience could not be pursuaded to believe that the actions presented on a confined space during a few hours actually took place in several settings over a long period time. It has been pointed out that Castelvetro's prescription arose from his notion of audiences being endowed with somewhat limited gifts of imagination. To Castelvetro, the purpose of poetry was solely to please and recreate, implying perhaps that not too much should be required of the audience. His focus on that which is convincing even makes him prescribe "true," historical, events as the subject of poetry.

Weinberg, seeing him as rather exemplary of his tradition, thus describes Castelvetro's view on probability as not focused on "the conditions of the work itself or to preliminary statements within the work, but [on the] reference outside of the work."[27]

As so many others, including Aristotle himself, Castelvetro formulates the organizing principle of poetry in a way which makes it possible to understand it either as mimesis-composition or mimesis-representation: "the proper function of poetics consists in the imitating, through harmonious words, of a human action."[28] Castelvetro, who uses the word *rassomigliare* (resemble) instead of *imitare*, retains much of the obscurity about the soul of poetry. However, he does provide some illustrating definitions of the parts of poetry.

On leafs 73–74, Castelvetro quotes and translates Aristotle's description of *muthos* – *favola* – as the end, *fine*, of poetry. Castelvetro rather often opposes Aristotle,[29] but in this case he feels obliged to defend him. It evinces from his argument that character or customs, *costumi*, is considered more important than action. As Castelvetro deflates the need to legitimate poetry through moral instruction, he is also able to discard character – which to a great extent had become moral didacticism – as the central goal of poetry. Instead, he discusses arguments to demonstrate that Aristotle was right in describing *muthos*, *favola*, as the most important part of poetry (75–76). Poetry should attract men's minds, and thus the parts of poetry can be judged and ranked in accordance with their ability to do this. Since the *favola* contains Castelvetro's versions of *peripeteia* and *anagnôrisis*, "the most attractive things," it is highly important.[30] Thus, while Aristotle's view of the importance of mimesis-composition had been recognized before, Castelvetro is the first to actually defend it.

Castelvetro's terminology is of course not infallible, but he does develop a way of defining the instances of mimesis with rather great precision. He translates Aristotle's words about medium, mode and object as the *con che*, the *come* and the *cvi* of imitation accurately, and translates the six elements "Fauola, Costumi, & Fauella, & Sententia, & Vista, & opera di Melodia" (67). What is more, he clarifies these "qualitative parts" of poetics by comparing them to the parts of rhetoric in a diagram (144). The Italian terms differ from the Latin ones on two occasions: *elocutio* is translated *favella* and *actio* is translated *proferenza*. Without following the graphics of his diagram, Castelvetro's distinctions may be rendered as follows:

Aristotle			Castelvetro	
			parti di qualita della tragedia	*parti di qualita (rhetoric)*
object	plot	*muthos*	*favola*	–
object	character	*êthê*	*costumi*	*inuentione*
object	thought	*dianoia*	*sententia*	*dispositione*
medium	diction	*lexis*	*favella*	*favella*
medium	lyric poetry	*melopoiia*	*melodia*	*proferenza*
mode	spectacle	*opsis*	*vista*	*memoria*

Thus, Castelvetro illuminates what must have been the natural way of understanding the *Poetics*: by connecting "fable," "character" and "thought" with rhetoric's "invention" and "disposition." These are the objects of poetry: according to leaf 68 Castelvetro considers *favella* and *melodia* the media, and his terminology underscores with the utmost clarity that the level of *lexis* is one and the same in rhetoric and poetics: *favella*. *Vista*, finally, is the mode as in Aristotle.

The fusing of rhetoric and poetics has another important aspect, one where Castelvetro does not point back towards Aristotle but forward, even towards romanticism. In the 18th-century development of the fine arts and even romantic thought, as will be discussed in chapter 6, a seminal distinction between *poësie des choses* and *poësie des mots* was made, a dichotomy already formulated by Castelvetro.[31] Since the French concepts occur in a context marked by a certain dissociation from the rhetorical tradition, it should be pointed out here that the distinction is very much a rhetorical one:

> Poetry is similitude, or likening of history. And as history is divided in two main parts, namely matter [*materia*] and words [*parole*], so poetry is divided in two main parts, which are also matter and words. In these two parts, however, history and poetry differ in that history's

> matter is not organized through the gift of the historian but by the course of earthly things or the manifest or hidden will of God, and the words of the historian are of the ordinary kind. Poetry's matter is invented and imagined by the genius of the poet, and the words are not of the everyday kind. For people do not usually speak in verse, but the composition in measured verse is through the genius of the poet.[32]

In a way not entirely agreeing with Aristotle, Castelvetro qualifies the comparison by introducing a new dichotomy: *materia* and *parole*. Aristotle had already suggested such a dichotomy when he said that the poet does not become a poet by making verses but by making plots. However, metre is only one aspect of *lexis*, and Aristotle was not suggesting an opposition between mimesis-composition and mimesis-representation. Castelvetro seems to develop the dichotomy: his interest is in verse, but *parole* becomes equivalent to *lexis* or *favella*. Thus, the differences between poetry and history can be identified in *materia*: the historian cannot invent, and in *parole*, the historian does not use verse.[33]

Muthos is an act of mimesis in itself, but together with character and thought it constitutes the object, or matter if one chooses, of mimesis-representation. The categories which obviously underlie *materia* and *parole* are rhetoric's *res* and *verba*. If one accepts that Aristotle elaborated the six parts of tragedy out of rhetorical categories, and that they have called for such an interpretation throughout the rhetorical tradition, Castelvetro is the one who most succinctly formulates the correspondence.

Towards a new poetics of diction

Being aware of Aristotle's ideal of poetry did not neccesarily mean agreeing with him, as was clear not least in Robortello, whose underscoring of mimesis-representation is much more accentuated in other theoreticians. Similarly, as Weinberg points out, Julius Caesar Scaliger's *Poetices libri septem*, published in 1561, nearly deserves to be described as a grammatical work, in that he defines poetry primarily as discourse and thus treats its relation partly to that which it represents, partly to the audience.[34] In our context, Scaliger is an obvious proponent of the focus on mimesis-representation:[35] although Scaliger lets the poet be the maker of possible worlds,[36] his focus lies on how they will be represented.

While Scaliger in his influential treatise elaborated the rhetorical aspects of poetic diction, the aspect of mimesis-representation was accentuated also in other ways in the Italian discussion. In his *Del bene* (1644), Sforza Pallavicino elaborated a kind of phenomenology which points towards modern aesthetics. He distinguishes between three kinds of human reason: "la prima apprensione," the first appreciation, "il guidizio," the immediate judgement of true and false, and "i discorsi," discursive thinking. Discussing poetry on the basis of these distinctions, Pallavicino is able to define poetry – according to August Buck – through standards that do not have to do with truth or falseness. Instead, the quality of the poet would be dependent only on his "evidenza o energia nel rappresentare," which could be translated as "evidence or energy of representation," but more correctly is to be seen as a direct description of the figure of visualization: *evidentia* or *enargeia*. This Pallavicino equates with Aristotle's demands for "Nachahmung."[37] As Lawrence D. Green has demonstrated in relation to other authors, the Renaissance displays an interest in explaining *elocutio* with the help of the *Rhetoric, On the Soul* and the *Nicomachean Ethics*: "The proper realm of the soul for rhetoric is in the unperfected movement between the sensitive and intellective faculties. The orator uses enthymemes of book 1 [of the *Rhetoric*] to bring distant notions that are *ab oculorum aspectu* and uses *lexis* of book 3 [of the *Rhetoric*] to place them *ante oculos*, before *phantasia* shapes them for their final journey to the higher intellective soul."[38]

While Pallavicino may have elaborated his poetics by considering a new view on the human faculty of perception, there seems to be no need to explain his redefinition of Aristotelian mimesis in terms of an intensified interest in psychology. Rather, to a large extent he draws on the Averroistic identification of mimesis and vivid representation. When he states that "this *evidenza* or *enargia* of representation is that so widely disputed imitation which is proper to the poet and common to all parts of poetry,"[39] he is referring to the rhetorical figure *evidentia*, in Greek *enargeia*. Buck quotes "energia" (as in Aristotle), but it is "enargia" that Pallavicino declares to be the essence of poetry. Thus, his approach is essentially the same as that of Averroës: the soul of poetry lies in *lexis* and consists of visualization. Pallavicino may contribute with additional psychological distinctions, but the focus on psychology, as we have seen, was founded by Averroës.

It is when Pallavicino treats the question of verisimilitude in poetry, and states that history deals with the true and poetry with the fictive, that he asks himself how poetry should be considered and then comes up with an answer that distinctly echoes *On the Soul* and Averroës. Thus, according to Pallavicino, "evidenza o enargia nel rappresentatione" is central to poetry. He speaks of placing "davanti agli occhi" ("before the eyes"), thus translating the conventional words for vivid description: *ante oculos* or *pro ommatôn*. When defining poetry, Pallavicino compares it with painting, which more or less automatically results in the definition of poetry as mimesis-representation. As the painter represents things in a manner which depends on skill and grace, so the poet enables the delight of perception through the vivacity and splendour of his representation – here described as painting and colours. The idea of *colores rhetorici* obviously underlies the description of how similitudes, *prosopopeia* and other figures, but above all metaphors, give an "ultramarine tincture" to the poem. While vivid description is made the main figure, metaphor and simile are, just as in Averroës, mentioned as vital parts, since poetry works by enticing apprehension.[40] Pallavicino also explains that poetry only imitates the real in order to add livelihood to its figments.[41] He is quite aware of the idea of fable, as expounded for example by Castelvetro, but his interest clearly lies in representation – being the object of perception.

Although Aristotle became more and more well known through translations and commentaries, his view on poetics was not taken as the truth of all poetry. We have seen how Robortello, even while he rather accurately explained Aristotle's notion of the soul of poetry, proposes and endorses another form of it. This seems, quite naturally, to have to do with the fact that Aristotle speaks of drama and epic, while lyric is the main interest in the Renaissance discussion. The attention towards lyric directs interest to mimesis-representation instead of mimesis-composition, and this of course is congenial with the rhetorical understanding of poetry. While this appears to mean that the influence of Averroës becomes less evident in the discussions of Aristotle, it may still be considerable in discussions of poetry and poetics on the whole. So, we have seen Robortello develop his ideas of representation and psychological impact in 1548 and Pallavicino stress the issues even more in 1644. Consequentially, we have seen Castelvetro clarify the relation between the poetological and the rhetorical categories in 1570 in a way much more succinct than Averroës. However, the focus on poetry's representational aspects could be elaborated further still, with Emanuele Tesauro perhaps presenting the work that went the farthest in this direction.

Tesauro

As was seen in the case of Mathias, one consequence of Averroistic poetics was that *muthos*, i.e. mimesis-composition, was excluded, boiled down to metaphor. While Castelvetro and others kept close to the focus on mimesis-representation, they certainly recognized – to a greater or lesser extent – that the soul of poetry according to Aristotle himself was mimesis-composition. When Emmanuele Tesauro published his influential "mannerist" poetics in 1654, he summoned Aristotle already in the title: *Il Cannocchiale Aristotelico*. The Aristotelian telescope could be understood as a sign of reappraisal of Aristotle's *Poetics*, but in fact Tesauro very much employs Averroistic notions. The Aristotle in the title of Tesauro's work is not the author of the *Poetics*, but the author of the *Rhetoric*.

Admittedly, Tesauro stresses the illusion rather than the representation of reality, but his focus is entirely on the level of mimesis-representation. The keyword apart from his famous "wit," *argutezza*, is *metafora*. *Il Cannocchiale Aristotelico* is primarily influenced by the third chapter of Aristotle's *Rhetoric* – which deals with metaphor – and it is also there that the foundation of *argutezza* is found: Aristotle here speaks of "smart sayings," *asteia*. The telescope through which one may conveniently examine the virtues and vices of eloquence is precisely Aristotle's *Rhetoric*, even though Tesauro's description of the ocular invention's capacity of revealing the secrets of the world is highly reminiscent of his way of describing metaphor itself.[42] As August Buck notes, Tesauro's use of the telescope as a metaphor is highly typical of baroque metaphoric diction, searching for the unusual and paradoxical.[43] Even more significant, one might add, is

Tesauro's way of attaching an adjectival qualifier to the metaphor. In his theory, metaphor may be at the centre, but its nature, as we shall see below, is such that it more or less requires a contextualizing qualifier.

Tesauro was responsible for bestowing on mannerism theoretical definitions,[44] and he did so by developing *argutezza* – wit which not only surprises but also establishes new connections – into a central feature of poetry. Tesauro, whose theory and practical advice are substantially different from the earlier poetological tradition, is mostly known for his treatment of *argutezza* and metaphor. However, neither of these can be said simply to make up the soul of poetry, and searching for his understanding of the soul of poetry raises a whole series of new questions. The metaphysical and esoteric aspects of Tesauro's poetics have been the subject of several studies, tending between two poles. The connection with a firm religious system of correspondence was the starting-point for J. A. Mazzeo, while Eugenio Donato instead proposed that the conceptual dimension of metaphor and art to Tesauro forms the base for a focus on the poet's more subjective creation of a universe of his own.[45] The focus on poetry's conceptual dimension derives from Aristotle's treatment of metaphor, but it is easy to over-estimate Tesauro's novelty if one does not consider the intervening tradition.

METAPHOR AND IMITATION

The strict definition

Argutezza mainly reveals itself in metaphor: "the great mother of all wit."[46] To Tesauro, metaphor is not merely ornament, but a cognitive tool, and in this he develops Aristotle's words on the cognitive dimensions of metaphor much like he develops Aristotle's *asteion* into *argutezza*. The question is how, exactly, metaphor relates to imitation in Tesauro's world. *Imitatione* is an important concept to him, and even if metaphor is what preoccupies him the most, he must adhere to the view that imitation is the soul of poetry. Imitation is that through which we learn and develop as human beings, and it even achieves the teacher's position:

> Thus, imitation may be called the Mistress of Masters. That is because (as our authority wisely says) it was the first teacher of poetry, whose soul is to imitate.[47]

The soul of poetry thus, as so often, is said to be imitation, but the question is which kind of imitation. Tesauro carefully points out that imitation must not be idle, but creative and novel: "therefore I mean with *imitatione* a wise saying, with which a metaphor or other flower of human genius is intended."[48] Thus, imitation can be said to be the soul of poetry and mistress of masters in that it enables metaphor, which Tesauro elsewhere proclaims as not the soul but the "mother of poetry" (as well as symbol and *impresa*).[49] Aristotle spoke both of mimesis as a means of learning and of metaphor as instructive, but he did not connect the two in the same way as Tesauro.

Aristotelian mimesis, in the sense of *muthos,* is not at hand in Tesauro. Rather, his focus of attention is on diction, but not on everything lexical or stylistic. Aristotle's mimesis-representation, *lexis,* in itself meant nothing but lexical representation, even if it was supposed to be artistic.[50] Tesauro, on the other hand, makes attempts to discard ordinary lexical representation from *imitatione.*

When introducing "Figure Ingeniose," he instead applies the term *rappresentation* for lexical representation:

> The whole power of any signifying word (as we said) consists in representing the thing signified to the human mind. However, this representation can be made either with a bare and proper word that demands no effort of the genius, or it can be made with an ingenious signification, which represents and delights at the same time. Thence arise the two general parts of oration: the one proper and grammatical, the other rhetorical and subtle.[51]

Using *nomina propria* vs. *nomina impropria* is the elementary rhetorical way of defining the difference between literal and figurative speech, and both kinds fall under "representation." However, while "imitation" has conventionally been used for representation in general, although associated with artistry, Tesauro wishes to restrict *imitatione* to figurative and artistic, "rhetorical" speech. He contrives this rather startling notion through one small but important maneouvre – by simply reformulating Aristotle's concept of mimesis. Aristotle maintained that words are mimesis:

> The poets, as was natural, were the first to give an impulse to style; for words are imitations [*mimêmata*], and the voice also.[52]

Tesauro instead advances the notion that words are representation, but not imitation if they are not figurative. This turn is made possible by a redefinition, or perhaps rather a tendentious translation, of Aristotle. Having described imitation as the soul of poetry, Tesauro appends a note which reads:

> The poets, as was natural, were the first to do it. For metaphorical words are imitations.[53]

Thus, Aristotle's "words are imitations" has become "metaphorical words are imitations." This is the hinge of Tesauro's redefinition of the soul of poetry. As we have seen, one can understand Aristotle to have meant that metaphor is the supreme case of mimesis-representation, since it not only represents a thing by means of words, but also redirects the word into another meaning, thus creating not only the word's imitation of the thing, but also using the word as a metaphorical "likening," constituting a kind of double mimetic act. It seems that a similar kind of thinking lies behind Tesauro's way of defining metaphorical words, instead of simply words, as imitation. At the very beginning, he eloquently describes how God's creation consists of metaphors and allegories. Consequently, the poet must be an imitator of God's figurative language, which in turn lends further credence to the notion that metaphor, as opposed to ordinary language, is imitation.

The quotation seems to be from a translation Tesauro had at hand. August Buck surmises, with a reference to Hugo Friedrich, that Tesauro had read Aristotle in a Latin translation which had already reinterpreted the original in a manneristic way.[54] However, the translation he used might simply have been one deriving from the Averroistic tradition.[55] As we have seen, Averroës redefined mimesis into lexical visualization, consisting of two major parts: *evidentia* and figurative speech, essentially metaphor (and his follower Mathias, while holding vivid description to be important, boiled mimesis-compositon down to metaphor).

Metaphor certainly is the quintessential feature in Tesauro, and that in itself enhances vividness. In fact, he approaches vividness and figurative language in the same way as Averroës: through the treatment of metaphor in Aristotle's *Rhetoric,* in which, in chapter III.x, frequent mention is made of setting things "before the eyes," *pro ommatôn*. Chapter III.xi starts as follows:

> We have said that smart sayings [*asteia*] are derived from proportional metaphor and expressions which set things before the eyes. We must now explain the meaning of "before the eyes," and what must be done to produce this.[56]

Tesauro transforms Aristotle's *asteia* into *argutezza,* and visualization thus takes a central position. Tesauro not only repeatedly speaks of the vivacity of the *argutezza* but devotes substantial space to "metaphor of hupotuposis," *hupotuposis* being a traditional term for *evidentia*.[57] In another, particularly pregnant passage, Tesauro describes the visual effect of a metaphor:

> If you tell me that the meadows are delightful, you represent to me only that they flourish. If you say *the meadows are smiling,* as I said you make me see the land become an animated man, with the fields as his face, and their pleasantness as his happy smile. Thus, in one little word appear all these different sorts of notions: land, field, pleasantness, man, soul, smile, and happiness. And the other way around, in a swift turn I can suddenly observe in the human face all the associated notions of an open field, and all the proportions obtaining between the two terms, even though these may have never occurred to me before. And this is the rapid, easy sort of instruction from which delight is born, for when the listener hears a single word, it calls up in his mind a whole theatre full of marvels.[58]

Tesauro's accent on brevity and instruction is unmistakably Aristotelian, but the example, *prata rident* (the importance of which seems great, since it is used also on page 116), derives from Averroës, as was discussed in chapter two.[59]

Already in Aristotle, metaphor and vividness were intrinsically connected, something which would prove essential to Averroës. Like Averroës, but less assertively, Tesauro also speaks of metaphor in the sense of being an instrument for vituperation or praise.[60] In the case of Tesauro one must add that metaphor and vividness were tied together with "smartness," *asteion*: this is what he expands into his description of metaphor as "the more ingenious and sharp; the more strange and wonderful; the more jovial and availing; the more eloquent and fruitful part of human intellect."[61] While Tesauro seems to take his point of departure from Averroistic poetics, in this seed of *argutezza* he certainly adheres to the way of defining poetics through Aristotle's *Rhetoric*. The mannerist programme expounded by Tesauro and heavily promoting metaphor as the vehicle of wit refers to Aristotle, but can be seen as a derivation of Averroës's adaptation of the *Poetics*. While Averroës first and foremost emphasized vividness – either of representation or figurative speech with metaphor as the favourite example – Tesauro emphasizes metaphor more than anything else. So far, one might conclude that Tesauro regards metaphor as constituting the soul of poetry, insofar as *imitatione* is restricted to metaphor. However, his definition of metaphor is not so strict as has been suggested from the above passages; rather, it is in fact remarkably broad.

The lax definition: referentiality

One important trait in Tesauro's system is that it primarily – but not at all exclusively – describes metaphor as consisting of two words, one base-word and one denominator. This is in concordance with Aristotle's examples as well as his statements that metaphor is instructive in both the *Rhetoric* and the *Poetics*. In fact the cognitive character of Tesauro's metaphor is quite simple: basically, metaphor is cognitive because it changes the referent's name and thus the perspective. In order to clarify this perspective, that is, the context in which the referent can be understood, metaphor needs an adjectival determination. Among other examples, Tesauro borrows from Aristotle his description of how "shield of Bacchus" metaphorically represents "beeker," and, vice versa, how "beeker of Mars" means "shield," *tertium comparationis* being that both the shield and the beeker are circular and thus interchangeable, provided the new context is specified.[62] This is only one of Aristotle's examples of metaphor – and one of his favourites, according to Tesauro – and it specifically exemplifies the metaphor of analogy (proportion). This method of explaining the metaphor by placing it in a context can be described as conceptual in that it imposes a "conceptual reality upon the wine through the metaphor."[63]

Tesauro thus delivers numerous examples of metaphors consisting of two words – or, to be precise, metaphors with a determining word – such as different ways of referring to Rome: "the small world" (*Piccol Mondo*), "epitome of the universe" (*Compendio dell'Vniuerso*), "queen of cities" (*Reina delle Città*), "crown of the world" (*Corona del Mondo*) and many others (339–341). The metaphors are ordered in a way reminiscent of *loci communes*: according to action, passion, place, time, etc. They range from highly figurative expressions such as "shipwreck of heretics" (*Naufragio degli Heretici*) to non-figurative circumlocutions such as "the immortal city" (*Città Immortale*). This wide definition demonstrates that figurativeness is not essential to Tesauro – the important thing is to change the perspective of the referent by substituting the literal word with another and defining its new context with a qualifier.

Tesauro's basic definition of metaphor is rather traditional: "to signify one thing by means of another, and not through the proper terms."[64] But he typically speaks of the sign first as a thing, then as a word. In this way, he expands the definitions of the church fathers and applies them to poetry: imitation becomes not verbal representation, but any representation of the kind that imitates the language of God: poetic, above all metaphoric (in Tesauro's very specific sense). Thus, the definition of the sign is widened. On the other hand, also the definition of metaphor's referentiality is widened. As we have seen, substituting the name of Rome with "the city" may be sufficient for it to become a metaphor, although such a circumlocution is not really figurative. There is precedence in the grammatical-rhetorical tradition for this sliding in grammatical categories: a metaphor is principally produced when the *nomen proprium* is substituted with a *nomen improprium*: a warrior is called a lion, which is not a proper description. However, *nomen proprium* is also used as opposed to *nomen commune*, that is, personal name vs. common denomination: the *nomen proprium* of Achilles is "Achilles," while a *nomen commune* designating him is, for example, "warrior." The definition of metaphor as the exchange of the *nomen proprium* into another word thus made room for substituting the referent not only with a metaphorical word, but also with a word which simply designated a more universal class.

The lax definition: sign

This analysis has no ambition to clarify the subtleties of *Il Cannocchiale Aristotelico* – only to address the basic conceptions – and obviously there are contradictions to be found in Tesauro as in the other theoreticians. One aspect of his metaphysics, however, is directly connected to the question of representation. Tesauro's definition of the sign differs not only from Aristotle, but from all hitherto discussed theories.

Metaphor is essentially *imitatione* because it imitates the language of God. *Argutezza* is the principle of explaining the world, the trace of God in the spirit of man. At least this seems to be part of Tesauro's way of legitimizing his project:

> [T]he angels themselves, nature, the great God, in communicating with the human beings, have expressed the most abstruse and important secrets with *argutezze*, either verbal or symbolic.[65]

Tesauro's poetics may have been radical and provocative, but he is very cautious in claiming authority from the highest place. He thoroughly explains how poetic style is construed in exact analogy with God's word, with reading poetry corresponding to the exegetical interpretation of Scripture and the world. The three levels of scriptural exegesis above the literal level, the tropological, allegorical and anagogical, are all described as metaphorical (rather than allegorical, the more conventional description).[66] Thus, metaphor must be seen as a vital tool of truth. But this is also of great consequence for the definition of the sign. Rhetorical theory always assumes that one chooses a word for a thing (*verbum-res*), but when the church fathers, foremost St Augustine, applied rhetorical theory to the Bible they needed to expand the definition of the sign. In profane allegory, as in all tropes, the sign was a word. In Biblical allegory, however, the typological sign was a fact or a person. Augustine thus had to distinguish between *allegoria in verbis* and *allegoria in rebus*.[67] Tesauro is faced with a definition that serves him very well when he ties poetics to exegetics. In the above quotation he speaks of both "verbal" and "symbolic" *argutezze*, and the connection between verbal and factual sign meets again and again, which in the end assists him in treating the old issue of the sister arts.[68] Music, painting and acting have long been said to be mimetic arts, analogous to poetry, but Tesauro needs not dwell on the question of imitation. Rather, he can define dance, theatre and painting – all arts that are "represented before the eyes" (*ocularmente rappresentato*) – as metaphors which convey their referents by way of factual signs: *simboli in fatto* (731–734).[69]

Thus, the sign of the metaphor is expanded into much more than the "improper" word. On the other hand, metaphor's referentiality is also made very wide and in fact comes to include ordinary representation. As we have seen, Tesauro uses the word *rappresentation* to define the sense of mimesis-representation as opposed to the wider concept of "imitation." However, his definition of metaphor in other places becomes more or less equivalent to "representation." Beginning to distinguish poetry from the other arts, he says that "metaphor is nothing but poetic imitation, be it representing through words, objects or animated actions."[70] The difference between metaphor and representation becomes even more obscure as picture and sculpture are said to be "metaphors representing an object by means of imitation of colours in a picture or features in relief."[71] Tesauro significantly elevates metaphor, but his definition of it becomes extremely wide. His definition of metaphor and *argutezza* allows him to include the sister arts as well, which in a sense can be regarded as preceding the 18th-century ideas of the fine arts. His basic principle, then, is not really metaphor but mimesis-representation with an enlarged array of signs. Significantly, Tesauro continuously comments upon the visuality and vividness of the different kinds of signs, which, rather than metaphoricity in a traditional sense, constitutes the common denominator of the arts.

The focus on visuality is explained early on in *Cannocchiale*, where Tesauro refers to Aristotle's *On the Soul*: "The same thing occurs in the mind as in the painters' canvasses, where nothing is painted but anything can be painted."[72] Every notion of the cognitive aspects of metaphor and representation draws on the idea that the mind is dependent on images.

As imitation – in the wider sense of "representation" which in reality dominates *Cannocchiale* – constitutes the soul of poetry as well as of the other arts, it is tightly connected to visualization. The question, then, is what is really meant with the name *Cannocchiale Aristotelico*? Tesauro comments on the telescope which

> with two glass windows, carries human sight through a hollow tube to where the birds cannot reach. With these you can cross the sea without a sail: you can see the pupil of the eye up close: even fly to the heavens in a flash, observe the spots in the sun; descry the horns of Vulcan in the forehead of Venus: measure the mountains and seas in the globe of the moon: number the children [i.e., the moons] of Jupiter: and what God conceals there, a little glass reveals to you.[73]

Tesauro himself explains the title of his work as expressing his best help in studying the sources of the art of poetry: Aristotle's *Rhetoric* is "a most bright [*limpidissimo*] telescope for examining the perfections and imperfections of eloquence."[74] It has also been suggested that the Aristotelian telescope might be understood to be the metaphor, which shifts perspectives and points of view, reveals new relations between things and makes "short-circuits across rational boundaries."[75] As the astronomer scrutinizes things impossible to discern with the eye through the telescope, so Tesauro scrutinizes things impossible to discern with common language through the metaphor. However, even though metaphor dominates Tesauro's discussion, it is a metaphor remote from traditional descriptions. As visualization of the Averroistic kind lies at the heart of Tesauro's view on metaphor, poetry and the arts, one may well suspect that the basic telescopic function simply concerns enhancing the brightness of discourse. That is, the visualizing techniques make poetry "most bright," thus enhancing not only pleasure and astonishment but also cognitive reception.

In effect, Tesauro widens the definition of metaphor drastically in order to include art as a whole and any kind of signs. He adheres to the notion that imitation is the soul of poetry, but to him it is not the mimesis-composition of Aristotle. Rather, it is the mimesis-representation of the Averroistic tradition, with a strong accent on visualization, but also with an accentuated – if not entirely consistent – focus on metaphor. Metaphor is traditionally an instance of diction, mimesis-representation, but it seems that to Tesauro the definition of the soul of poetry applies because it is possible to construe a metaphoricity of the same kind as God's language through metaphor. Tesauro relies on a rendition of the *Rhetoric* which is much closer to the original than to Averroës, but his understanding was Averroistic and there is little doubt that in this respect his baroque poetics is a development of the Arabian Aristotle. He also proposes to offer a very strict definition of *imitatione*, which makes the soul of poetry more or less exclusively the same as metaphor.

That specific aspect of mimesis-representation which Tesauro develops distinctly focuses on the *how*, but in fact extends into the question of the objects of poetry, since not only words, but also things signify. The influence comes from scriptural exegesis and the wish to find a common denominator for the arts, and with this Tesauro takes an early step towards symbolism, an aspect that will be further studied in chapter 9.

The ambiguity of imitation – the ambiguity of verisimilitude

At this stage, it has become evident that not only the definitions of "imitation" are very vague, but also that this effects the different authors' notion of verisimilitude. The definition of plot, *muthos*, as imitation and the soul of poetry is explicit in Aristotle (ch. 6, 1450a4) and has to be accounted for by the 16th- and 17th-century theoreticians – even if they do not in fact share Aristotle's preferences. The definition is important in relation to Aristotle's comparison between poet and historian. When, for example, Castelvetro compares poetry to history, imitation is held to mean fiction. This is a more or less automatic result of the point of comparison: the relation between poet and historian usually directs attention towards content, not diction. Another eloquent example of how imitation comes to mean not "represent" but "feign" is offered by Dionigi Atanagi in a description of historiography from 1559:[76] the historian, he says, does not imitate, whereas the poet does. (While the historian may not write as artistically as the poet, his discourse must not be artless; rather, it is required to represent things vividly, i.e. using *evidentia*.) Thus, imitation here does not seem to mean "artistic representation" (as opposed to artless representation) but rather the imitation of the world which results in *muthos*. Following Aristotle, Atanagi defines imitation as mimesis-composition.

One of the most lucid interpreters of Aristotle's *muthos* is Jacopo Grifolo, who in 1550 stressed the importance of Aristotle's view that it is not verse that constitutes poetry:

> As the poet (as Aristotle confirms) makes fiction, he is a poet of things, not of metre. Thus, a remarkable invention and constitution of the fable, with a careful instruction of ethics, seizes the spectators more than inane verses, forcefully projected on stage.[77]

Grifolo not only defends mimesis-composition in a most unusual (and uninfluential) way; by speaking of the "poet of things" he also phrases the different kinds of poetry in a manner which anticipates later discussions: the distinction between poetry of things and poetry of words. Aristotle had already made this distinction, which is self-evident in any rhetorical way of thinking, but Castelvetro, as we have seen, twenty years later formulated it in the more rhetorical categories *things-words*, a distinction which eventually turns into an ideological standpoint.

However, these expressions of mimesis-composition are rare, overshadowed by the interest in mimesis-representation. As we have seen, even when rendering Aristotle's words rather precisely, Robortello frames the master's notions with his own ideal of poetry: mimesis-representation. This is the heritage not only from the rhetorical tradition as such, but also from the Averroistic *Poetics*. "Imitation," widely acclaimed the soul of poetry, usually means mimesis-representation, only occasionally mimesis-composition.

The rhetorical approach implies a clear distinction between mimesis-composition and mimesis-representation, i.e. between *res* and *verba*. One apparent example is when Alessandro Lionardi indulges in poetical invention: in his *Dialogi della inventione poetica*, from 1554, he writes that "every oration and speech consists of form, which is eloquence, of matter, which is the thing proposed, and of the end, which is the listener."[78] He exemplifies the distinction more accurately than usual, perhaps because his subject is invention, concerning *res, logos*.

The writers of commentaries and treatises are mostly interested in diction, concerning *verba, lexis,* and do not elaborate the difference between what is said and how it is said clearly. This ambiguity is inherent in the poetological tradition: every theoretician naturally distinguishes between *res* and *verba,* but the definition of the soul of poetry regularly obscures the distinction. When Vincenzo Maggi in his *In Aristotelis librum de poetica communes explanationes* (1550) states that poetry aims at "imitating human actions through pleasant language, to ennoble the mind," he clearly exemplifies the vagueness (while subjugating imitation under Horatian aims).[79] To imitate actions through diction *can* be understood as first creating a *muthos,* content (mimesis-composition), and then representing it with words (mimesis-representation). But it does not have to mean more than representing things with words, that is, mimesis-representation. The distinction is thus obscured and the wording lends itself to being understood as regarding only representation, mimesis-representation. This obscurity was, as we have seen, at hand already in the original *Poetics,* but there the discussion forcefully stressed mimesis-composition. The obscurity recurs regularly and is vital to practically any discussion of mimesis.

In the Italian Renaissance, the Aristotelian distinctions concering *muthos* and even its position as the soul of poetry are often asserted. Robortello is one example of this, Antonio Sebastiano Minturno in his *L'arte poetica* (1564) is another.[80] The point is that even if *muthos* is declared to be the soul of poetry, it is very seldom seen as the important part of poetry – or even as imitation. *Imitatione* often melts together with *rappresentatione* and other terms, and comes to mean, foremost, poetic diction. The background for this assessment is, of course, Averroistic poetics and the general rhetorical slant, but the renewed interest in genre theory also contributes to this development. While it is clear to the Italian theorists – of which, as we shall see, Minturno is an especially good example – that Aristotle was most interested in tragedy and also epic poetry, they very much needed to reach a definition of poetry which included lyric. This resulted in a theoretician being able to render Aristotle's view on tragedy and the soul of poetry rather truthfully, but at the same time offering another definition of the essence of poetry generally, where imitation meaning representation becomes central.

While mimesis-composition is actualized by the comparison between poet and historian, mimesis-representation is actualized as soon as comparison is made between poetry and the other arts: simply because the image represents in a way corresponding to words. In addition, any time mimesis-representation, diction, is discussed, it is not in the sense of pure and simple verbal representation; rather, it is understood as artistic. This is a natural point of departure in any discussion of poetics or rhetoric, but it deserves to be pointed out, since it is important to the aesthetic concept of *belle nature* later on. Above all, the ambiguity of "imitation" results in an ambiguity of "verisimilitude."

VERISIMILITUDE

The distinction between mimesis-composition and mimesis-representation implies different ways of achieving plausibility – from the Latin tradition onwards referred to as *verisimilitudo*. The problem is that *verisimilitudo*, and any vernacular translations, is nearly as vague as the concept of imitation.

When mimesis-composition dominates, verisimilitude is inherent in *muthos*; actions and events need to be probable – would a person of that position do this or that? – and necessary – is this event a consequence of the preceding events within the fable? This is what Aristotle discusses as *eikos* and *anankaion* respectively. Verisimilitude in mimesis-composition is partly sequential and mainly related to content: it regards actions and the course of events.

When mimesis-representation, on the other hand, dominates, verisimilitude inheres in verbal representation. Credibility and engagement are created through depiction and evoking of sceneries. Analogously to painting, verisimilitude depends on how things are depicted: lifelikeness, overwhelming images, etc. This kind of verisimilitude is mainly spatial and does not concern a course of events, with visualizing techniques such as *enargeia/evidentia* and any kind of imagery thus becoming central. Aristotle barely treats this aspect in his *Poetics*, but in his *Rhetoric* these techniques of persuasion are of the essence.

A seminal problem both in historical discussions and in modern scholarship is that this distinction tends to be obscured, mainly because both aspects are labelled *verisimilitudo* or *verisimilitude*, a diffuse word embodying a wide range of meanings. When mimesis is discussed in comparison with the other arts, the aspect that dominates is *lexis*, representation, which is also usually the case in rhetorically influenced discussions. In the Italian context, the Averroistic conception is the starting-point, but gradually Aristotle's view on the important instance of mimesis – *muthos* – surfaces. The focus on persuasive detail in the Italian Renaissance is in line with the rhetoricized Aristotle transmitted by Averroës. The verisimilitude caused by verbal representation is fundamental to the theoretical discussions from the 13th century onwards, even though Aristotle's own ideas eventually emerge more clearly.

CHAPTER FIVE

French classicism and the necessity of probability (17th century)

It is well known that Aristotle's *Poetics* within French classicism was developed into a rigorous set of rules. The most well-known expression of this is the idea of the three so-called unities of action, place and time (*l'unité d'action, de lieu, et de jour*). Of these, Aristotle himself had only spoken about action, stating that the tragedy should confine itself to one sequence of events without episodic aberrations. The unity of time and space can be considered aspects of the unity of action: the whole story should develop within 24 hours and in a single place. The unities were not really a French invention, but were developed as a means of persuasion already by Castelvetro in his *Poetica D'Aristotile vulgarizzata, et sposta*. Castelvetro believed that it would be asking too much of an audience to imagine that what took place before them on stage in fact happened at several different points in time and in different places.[1]

The issue of persuasion was usually codified in the demand for *vraisemblance*, which, beside taste, *bienséance*, was a keyword of French classicism. The French classicists focus not on mimesis-representation but on mimesis-composition, so the "verisimilar" here comes close to that of Aristotle, but developed in a special way. Aristotle had stressed that *muthos* had to possess probability (*eikos*) and necessity (*anankê, anankaion*), but it was not clear how this should be interpreted. Probability of the plot was central to the French classicists, but how was it defined, and how was it to be achieved? To a great extent, the answer lies in the three unities, but I will primarily seek it through the notion of necessity. The question will be pursued through the treatises on drama (published in 1660) by Pierre

Corneille – who was not the most rigorous theoretician, but viewed the issues also from the author's practical horizon – and through Jean Racine's *Phèdre* from 1676, often hailed as the ideal French classicist drama.[2]

Corneille

The opening performance of Corneille's *Le Cid* in 1637 was followed by an animated debate as to whether it followed the rules of Aristotle. On behalf of the French Academy, Jean Chapelain, prominent defender of "Aristotelian" rules, contributed with *Les Sentiments de l'Académie Française touchant les observastions faites sur la tragi-comédie du Cid* (1638).[3] In spite of the critique, *Le Cid* was a great success and Corneille would become a recognized playwright of his day. He would later collect his reflections on drama in three treatises which were published in 1660. Especially interesting here is his discussion of probability: the critics of *Le Cid* had laid much emphasis on its lack of probability, an issue he therefore treats carefully.

In the first treatise, *Discours de l'utilité et des parties du poème dramatique*, Corneille wishes to underline the moral and social use of drama, but he does so by discussing its constituent parts. The drama has two kinds of parts: the quantitative – consisting of prologue, episode, exodus, etc. – and the "integrated," consisting of "fable, customs, thoughts, diction, music and decoration of the theatre."[4] These are of course Aristotle's six parts, which are not relocated so radically as we have seen in previous chapters, but still with some adjustments. "Thought" and "character"/"customs" have changed place: *moeurs,* Corneille's word for "character," forcefully implies ethics and morals, while *sentiments* corresponds to "thought" and those expressions of thought and emotions that are made, but is expressly defined as subordinated to *moeurs.* (The description of Aristotle's *opsis* as decoration of the theatre does not concern this argument.)

Initially, Corneille establishes that the three unities must be observed. This, he admits, is a difficult if not impossible task, as the unities are linked to the demand for *vraisemblance* (which I will translate "probability"):

> Nobody doubts that one must observe the unity of action, space and time, but it is no small difficulty to know what this unity of action is, and how far the unity of time and space reaches. The poet must treat his subject according to the probable and the necessary, Aristotle says. All his interpreters repeat the same words and find them so clear and intelligible that not one of them has deigned to tell in a more lucid way than he what the probable and the necessary really are. So little have they considered the latter, which always follows the former in the philosopher (except once, when he speaks of comedy), that they have established a very false principle, namely that *the story of a tragedy must be probable*: in that manner they only apply onto the story half of the conditions which Aristotle says must be applied to it.[5]

What Corneille wants to stress is necessity, neglected by previous interpreters. *Vraisemblance* is central, but *nécessité* is its overlooked aid. It cannot be defined as probable that Medea kills her children or that Clytaimnestra murders her husband, Corneille continues, but those are the stories related and cannot be changed. In the three treatises he demonstrates how probability can be strengthened, or compensated, by necessity. The first treatise puts forth utility, *l'utile*, as a necessity which renders legitimacy. The morally edificational aspects of the drama legitimize the lack of probability, or, rather, strengthen probability. Corneille does not use the word "universal," but his idea could be rephrased allowing for utility to make the drama universal, causing it to leave the particular. Moral utility is necessary, and "even if utility only makes its entry in the form of the agreeable, it never ceases to be necessary there."[6]

Utility is moral edification and so central to Corneille that he modifies Aristotle's description of *muthos* as the soul of poetry. He agrees that action is the soul of poetry, but proclaims that *moeurs*, customs and ethics, constitute the principle and justification of the actions.[7] That is, the soul of poetry is still the sequence of actions, but it is governed by a higher principle: ethics. Ethics thus provide a new form of necessity, which strengthens or compensates the probability of the story. Utility is thereby tied to the construction of action – which is governed by ethics. These parts are connected to probability and Corneille's own contribution: necessity. In the treatise, other rules are also described as necessary in different respects, thereby strengthening the story. But in the second treatise the question of necessity is analyzed in a way which is more directly relevant to the composition of action.

As appears from the title, *Discours de la tragédie, et des moyens de la traiter, selon le vraisemblable ou le nécessaire* specifically treats the relation between probability and necessity within the plot. Corneille returns to Aristotle's repeated combination of the words probability and necessity, concluding that they are never explained. He now takes this task upon himself, because it is a freedom which Aristotle has bequeathed us: "if we can treat the things according to the probable or necessary, we can leave the probable in order to cultivate the necessary."[8] An argument for this, according to Corneille, is that Aristotle sometimes reverses the order, placing necessity first, and thus leaves the decision of priority to us. Probability primarily concerns whether events appear feasible in relation to "outer" criteria, necessity primarily whether they appear feasible in relation to what has previously taken place in the plot.[9] Corneille follows the same lines as Aristotle's here: necessity lies in the composition of action and the inevitable development of one event into another.[10] However, he also relates the compression of the story to the unity of time and space, maintaining that these rules are what gives us the freedom to leave probability: observing the unities is described as a *nécessité*.[11] In order to persuade the audience, confined in the theatre during a few hours, it is necessary to observe the unities.[12]

That the events of the story must be generated out of one another is inherent in the idea of the unity of action, and Corneille underlines it in the very beginning of his third discourse, *Discours des trois unités, d'action, de jour, et de lieu*. He here discusses how expositions can be made, treating *noeud* and *dénouement* (the Greek *desis* and *lusis*): the "knot" or complication and its disentangling, concepts so vital to the composition of drama.[13] The focus of his attention is constantly on the question as to how the probability of drama can be maintained and how probability must be subordinated not only to the necessity of story, but also to that necessity which the three unities constitute. In the end, this means that all rules of French classicism constitute necessities which on the one hand regulate probability, on the other hand justify violations of probability.

Corneille's treatises are polemical, instigated by the old critique directed towards his *Le Cid*. His theory is radical, calling into question and criticizing the simplified tributes to *vraisemblance*. The solution Corneille puts forth is *la nécessaire*, defined through a number of different categories but, as in Aristotle, founded in mimesis-composition. An extraordinarily consistent application of necessity in drama was made not by Corneille himself, but by another French playwright, Racine.

Racine

Racine did not write theoretically as Corneille did, but he did not pay less attention to necessity. While Corneille referred to Castelvetro's translation of the *Poetics*, it is known that Racine also consulted the Latin translation of Vettori, as his copy, containing translated passages in the margins that he considered especially important, has been preserved.[14] Racine agrees that *muthos* is the soul of poetry,[15] but much like Corneille he makes ethics a dominant feature of it: while Aristotle in the sixth chapter of his *Poetics* points out that character helps us ascribe qualities to actions (1449b30), Racine, inspired by Vettori, says that

> it is the ethics and inclination [equivalent to character, according to Racine], that is, the mind's disposition, which make the actions so or so. Consequentially, the ethics and thought, or the mind's disposition, are the two principles of actions.[16]

More importantly, Racine develops the notion of necessity and probability in a most stringent way, transferring into French the passage where Aristotle so strongly emphasizes the importance of necessity and probability:

> In customs, as well as in the composition of the fable, one must always search for the necessary, or the probable: that is, who says or does something must do so through necessity or probability, and one thing must only take place after the other if it is necessary or probable that it happens.[17]

Aristotle himself repeats the pair necessity-probability twice within the space of a few lines, and here, in chapter 15 of the *Poetics*, he places necessity ahead of probability, with the composition and linearity of events thus being highlighted as central. Racine, subscribing to every word, continues to render Aristotle: "Thus, it is obvious that the denouement shall be drawn from the fable itself."[18] It is Aristotle's *lusis* which Racine verbalizes, and we can conclude that the necessity of action is vital to him. As we shall see, in *Phèdre*, he employs it in practice by means of a very special technique which can be called "double motivation."

It has often been said that *Phèdre* connects to the ancient idea of destiny. Phedra, who takes a much more central role than in the plays it is modelled on, Euripides's *Hippolytos* and Seneca's *Phaedra*, is driven by a passion she can only detest but not change. Racine's *forte*, psychological characterization, here manifests itself in the fact that it is very much in Phedra's realization that the necessity of the drama emerges as inexorable. In the preface, Racine stated that he had striven to make her less unequivocally evil, but more complex, at the same time as making Hippolytos less unequivocally good.[19] Racine combines the notion of destiny with psychological necessity, but he also strengthens psychological necessity with other techniques.

Phedra's motive force is of course her emotions, but they are strengthened in the drama with the mythological "heritage" in the event they might be deemed improbable or unnecessary. Being the daughter of Minos and Pasiphaë, Phedra is doomed to illicit love – her mother fell in love with a bull, resulting in the birth of Minotaurus, and she herself falls in love with the son of her husband. In this sense, as Racine remarked in his preface, the will of the gods thus governs the events. Halliwell here sees a conflict between the rational demand for probability and the religious myth, which Racine inherits from Aristotle: divine destiny both seems to rule the human passions and to be a punishment for them.[20] But one could also say that myth and destiny actually strengthen the motivation of both actions and emotions, and in addition that they strengthen necessity (albeit not probability) in the course of events. This interaction between necessity and probability seems to be congenial with Aristotle's way of treating them together. There is no doubt that Racine held them to cooperate rather than be opposed, judging by his careful mention of the family's heritage.

In the preface to *Phèdre* Racine further explains that his introduction of the character Aricia in the drama rests on Virgil. Aricia is the last surviving member of the Athenian royal family, the enemies of Theseus, and she is kept prisoner so as not to propagate the family. Racine thereby achieves several things: it is through his love to Aricia that Hippolytos becomes a more human character, an ambition formulated in the preface. Aricia enables a second doubling of the illegitimate love: besides that of Phedra and her mother, the love between Hippolytos and Aricia is seen as treasonous since their respective families are enemies. Aricia adds to the dramatic tension: about to confess her feelings and save the life of Hippolytos, Phedra finds out that he loves Aricia, and jealousy makes her change her mind (IV.5). The presence of Aricia gives the drama an extra dimension of necessity: Phedra's struggle to overcome her feelings for Hippolytos can now be mirrored in Hippolytos's struggle to overcome his feelings for Aricia, and in Aricia's relation to her own emotions. However, the most obvious effort of Racine is to motivate the actions of the characters, that is, to strengthen the necessity through which one event leads to the next. He does this by doubling the emotional motives of the characters not only with mythological determination, but also with political motives. Aricia loves Hippolytos – but the association with him is also her only political opportunity to be released, and even regain the power of her family (II.1–2). Phedra loves Hippolytos but the association with him is also her only political opportunity to save her children, and even see her son gain power (I.3, I.5). When it turns out that Theseus is alive and Phedra's feelings for the son of her husband are acknowledged as reprehensible, she first of all reflects on her reputation, but she also mentions her children, whose future now – implicitly – can only be salvaged by the death of Hippolytos – doubling her motives of jealousy (III.3).

* * *

Pragmatic motives are apt to be considered probable, but the fact that the motives of the different characters are doubled and even tripled with such consistency is hardly probable, although it does impose a sense of necessity on the events. This necessity was the subject of Corneille's careful considerations and development of Aristotelian theory. In practice, Racine develops necessity in *Phèdre* to the utmost degree, even in accordance with that demanded by Corneille's rules: *Phèdre,* like no other drama, observes the unity of time, space and action, the placement of complication and denouement, exposition, *peripeteia,* etc. The necessity of the drama becomes maximized as its probability is dominated and doubled by necessity.

French classicism is primarily associated with the demand for *vraisemblance.* However, this concept was subject to constant negotiation and the urge to achieve this probability resulted in several methods, the most efficient of which seems to have been double motivation: improbable, but yet strengthening probability. The intense focus on probability and necessity keeps the discussions within the framework of mimesis-composition: the fable, or actions, are again seen as the soul of poetry (although governed by character and thought), with mimesis-representation again being consigned to its marginal position. Averroës held persuasion to be of the essence, but while his point of departure was written or spoken poetry, the means of persuasion were sought within diction, mimesis-representation. In turn, the point of departure for the French classicists is drama, and the means of persuasion is sought within *muthos,* mimesis-composition.

CHAPTER SIX

The principle and polemics of the fine arts (18th century)

While mimesis or *imitatio* was subject to continuous redefinition during the preceding centuries, in the 18th century the concept was challenged. The doctrine that art should imitate nature was elaborated by classicists but called into question by emerging romantic theories. Although it is clear that substantial changes took place as aesthetics was developed and romanticism entered the stage, the critique of the theory of imitation calls for being understood through a refined definition of the term and the concept.

The idea that art imitates nature dominated in what is usually called classicist doctrine, and the object of poetry was specified as beautiful nature, *belle nature*. Such an object would inevitably prove problematic, since it would be an idealized and embellished one. But focus was also shifting from the object to the mediating subject. The emphasis on imagination and the evolving aesthetics implied that imitation could no longer be the essence of poetry. One remarkable example of the conflict between different paradigms is the reception of Charles Batteux's *Les beaux arts réduits à un même principe*, first published in 1746. The work codified a rather traditional classicist approach to poetry, but Batteux, who had even returned to Aristotle himself in order to find the uniting principle of the arts, offered a synthesis that was a remarkable piece of theory. Batteux distinguished the merely useful arts, such as the mechanic ones, from *les beaux arts*, the "fine" arts which give pleasure: poetry, painting, etc. A third class, both useful and pleasurable, comprises rhetoric and architecture. In launching pleasure in this way, Batteux departed from older traditions and in at least one respect formed part of the emerging aesthetics.[1]

Batteux's work attracted much attention in Germany.[2] It was published in German several times, the most interesting translation being the one by Johann Adolph Schlegel, father of the more illustrious August Wilhelm and Friedrich. His translation was first published in 1751, then again in 1759 and 1770. These editions grew more and more voluminous, as Schlegel filled them with footnotes questioning and contradicting Batteux's propositions about poetry. In subsequent editions of the French original, Batteux would respond to some of the criticism in footnotes of his own, which Schlegel would then translate and comment upon yet further. The translator also expands his considerations into treatises, which he appends to the translation: in 1770 they constitute a whole second volume. Thus, the 1770 edition of *Einschränkung der Schönen Künste auf einen einzigen Grundsatz* conveys the conflict most fully.[3]

As is evident from the title of the work, Batteux took great pride in having found the unifying principle of the arts. This principle is "imitation," that form of mimesis which had so often been discussed in connection with poetry and art through the centuries. But Batteux believed that he had found a way of systematizing the principle so that it covered the arts. In Germany imitation was defended by among others Johann Christoph Gottsched, but considerably more progressive ideas were on the move.[4]

It is commonly recognized that Schlegel demanded authenticity, which Batteux did not find necessary. It has also been recognized that the differences between them on the whole were not so great after all.[5] Still, the question is what definitions of poetry were actualized, and how Batteux actually defined imitation – not to mention how others defined it. The definition of imitation and mimesis is always uncertain and expansive, but in this quarrel, at this point in history, the definition of imitation is crucial. Here, it also becomes especially apparent how definitions grow even more complicated when different languages are involved.

With Schlegel's critique of Batteux's poet as a dissimulating actor generally being in focus, later commentators have stressed the contradictions in Batteux's system: Manfred Schenker concluded that only the poet's mimicking another person is pure imitation;[6] Hugo Bieber made an exposition into the tradition of debate on direct and indirect speech;[7]

Lars Gustafsson concludes that lyric poetry in Batteux belongs to imitation because it consists in a kind of "figuration dramatique de sentiments" and displays the tradition of comparing the poet to an actor. Gustafsson concludes that this aspect, which was most forcefully pronounced by Plato and resonated strongly even in the 18th century, was essential to Batteux but unacceptable to Schlegel;[8] Klaus Scherpe claims that Batteux used the terms *Nachahmung, Erdichtung, Handlung* and *Fiktion* indiscriminately – but it is not Batteux's original text he identifies with Batteux, only the German translation;[9] Tzvetan Todorov comments on how "Batteux's reasoning is remarkable in its blindness";[10] Irmela von der Lühe states that Batteux's strict demand to stick to imitation of nature conflicts with his simultaneous demand that nature should be improved;[11] and finally Anna Cullhed asks in what way the art of lyric poets is considered an imitation, following Gustafsson's discussion of the poet as an actor.[12]

Batteux did not manage to create a waterproof system, but his definition of the arts is more consistent than has conventionally been suggested. Evidently, the analogy between the poet and the actor is a recurring issue throughout the history of poetics, and there are obvious grounds for rejecting the poet who simulates emotions – especially so with the emergence of new theories of authenticity and originality in the 18th century. What needs to be pointed out, however, is that this assimilation of poet and actor is *not* Batteux's definition of poetry. His principle of imitation is customarily reduced to this, but Schlegel's critique, and its modern echoes, do not actually concern Batteux's basic conception. In fact, Schlegel is only able to express his critique through a persistent misreading of Batteux. This misreading, founded on the ambiguity of the concept of imitation, seems to have given rise to problems enhanced through the German translation *Nachahmung*.

In the following, I shall demonstrate how consistently Batteux did in fact rework Aristotle's theory. My intention is not to claim that Batteux's argument is valid as a whole, but to lay bare his principal idea.

Charles Batteux: The fine arts reduced to a single principle

In his preface, Batteux states that he has searched the ancient authorities for a precise definition of poetry, and that this is his starting point. To begin with, he asks and then answers a central question: "What is, then, the function of the arts? It is to transfer traits which are in nature, and present them in objects which are not natural for them."[13] This is a formula of imitation which accords with Aristotle's comparison of poetry with the other arts, and it corresponds to Plato's view on mimesis: this is the instance of imitation that we have defined as mimesis-representation, analogous to the painter's colours. The transfer is achieved through imitation:

> To imitate is to copy a model. This term comprises two ideas: 1. the prototype which carries the traits which one wishes to copy. 2. the copy which represents them. Nature, that is, everything which is or which we can easily conceive as possible, is the prototype or the model of the arts.[14]

In accordance with this overarching definition, Batteux points out that the only difference between the arts is the means, *moyen*, by which they achieve imitation:

> In the first [part], the nature of the arts, their essential differences and parts are examined. It is demonstrated through the very quality of the human mind that imitation of nature should be their common object, and that they only differ through the means which they employ to achieve this imitation. The means of painting, music and dance are colours, sounds and gestures: the means of poetry is discourse.[15]

It is essential to recognize that when Batteux speaks of imitation as the unifying principle of the arts, it is the means he focuses on. He uses imitation in other senses as well, but in perfect accordance with Aristotle he regards the arts as constitutively representational. In less accordance with Aristotle, Batteux makes mimesis-representation the main instance of poetry. His whole system starts from the notion of imitation as representation, which basically constitutes his understanding of the fine arts. As we have seen, this is the default definition when mimesis is discussed by comparison between poetry and the other arts, and Batteux is no exception. While Aristotle took mimesis-representation for granted but considered the fable, i.e. mimesis-composition, to be the soul of poetry, Batteux defines the unifying principle of the arts as representation. He discusses mimesis-composition as well, but only as a consequence of his overarching principle.

Defining the fine arts as imitation was easy, since Aristotle had already spoken of painting, music and dance as imitative. The real challenge for Batteux was lyric poetry, since it was not one of the main genres in Aristotle's *Poetics*. By the middle of the 18th century there was an apparent need for defining lyric poetry as a genre of the same authority as drama and epic: the tripartite genre description had evolved in the Italian 16th century and was fairly well established by 1700 – presented in Germany by Alexander Gottlieb Baumgarten in 1735 – but its legitimation and theoretical system were in need of being developed.[16] Aristotle's *muthos* was the composition of actions, which could not possibly cover lyric poetry. In accordance with Aristotle, Batteux views drama and epic as representation, through diction, of action – and, to a lesser extent, of character and thought. In order to define lyric poetry as a genre of the same authority as drama and epic, Batteux therefore simply concludes that they have the same medium, diction, but different objects: lyric does not represent actions but thoughts and emotions:

> Just as one imitates actions and customs in epic and dramatic poetry, so one sings of imitated emotions or passions in lyric.[17]

Thus, Batteux introduces a new object, emotion, and fits it in on the same level as traditional action and character (seemingly replacing thought).[18] He adheres to Aristotle's categories, but rearranges the category of object and achieves a coherent adaptation of Aristotle's system. This means that his proposed principle of the fine arts is simplified and strengthened at the same time: the arts, as well as lyric, all *represent* – through different means – objects, the foremost of which are actions and emotions.[19]

Batteux expands Aristotle's categories in a congenial way – even the maneouvre of elevating emotion as a central object of poetry is in fact in accordance with Aristotle. Although he does not mention this in his definition of the different parts of tragedy, Aristotle explicitly states, in the very first chapter of the *Poetics*, that emotion can be the object of arts:

> [R]hythm on its own, without melody, is used by the art of dancers (since they too, through rhythms translated into movements, create mimesis of character, emotions [*pathê*], and actions). (1447a25–26)

Interpreting *pathê* as "emotion" is not uncomplicated, as we shall see in chapter 10, but this is what Batteux does here, as well as in his translation of Aristotle's *Poetics*: "the dancers express customs, emotions and actions."[20] That is, emotions have been mentioned as an object, in connection with melody and rhythm, by Aristotle, and what could be more appropriate than developing his argument when placing lyric among the main genres. Batteux sensitively adjusts the objects of poetry, subordinating them under medium as the common definition – since the medium is the unifying principle of the arts. The medium, diction, defines poetry: the object, emotions, defines the lyric genre. This is the main principle of the fine arts and poetry, and to it is connected a set of *rules* formulated by good taste, "le bon goût" (53–56), that imply certain adjustments of selection and style. However, Batteux was not pedagogical enough, since his readers have constantly interpreted his principle of imitation as fiction, invention, fable, feigning and acting, thereby describing his principle of poetry and the arts as something it was not. Part of the pedagogical problem is that Batteux himself does not always uphold a clear distinction between the different instances of imitation, or the rules that follow the principle.

Fiction – representation

In a chapter where Batteux rejects previous views on the essence or principle of poetry, he dismisses the idea of fiction as the essence, at least if it is defined as the introduction of gods into the story, or as allegorical representations of abstracts (135–136). However, if one understands fiction in accordance with Latin *fingere*, the word means artful imitation of characters, actions and such. And if it thus means the same as representation or as counterfeit, then this notion fits with that of Batteux:

> If they mean the same thing with *fiction* as *feign*, or Latin *fingere*, the word *fiction* should only signify the artificial imitation of characters, customs, actions, speech etc. So *feign* is the same thing as *represent*, or, rather, *counterfeit*: and so this opinion suits the one we have established.[21]

This passage could possibly be understood as a declaration that invention and plot are the essence of poetry. In fact, however, Batteux does mention traditional objects such as action and character, but it is the technique of representing them that constitutes the essence of poetry: only if "feign" is understood as "represent" can he agree with that definition of poetry. To Batteux the term fiction is congruous with his notion that art represents nature: the artist can only represent and combine in new ways. If fiction were defined as mimesis-representation and not mimesis-composition, Batteux would be able to proclaim it the most important principle of poetry. But he prefers imitation.

Batteux certainly speaks of fiction in the sense of the invention and organization of events in epic. However, this is not the primary meaning of imitation to him, but rather a related issue which must also be addressed since it concerns, but does not consist in, the kind of imitation which constitutes the familiarity of arts. Such related issues he calls rules – of taste (148–167).

This notion of fiction and *feindre* is important to bear in mind: when Batteux speaks of deceiving and counterfeiting, he means that kind of deception that occurs when one shows not the object proper but a representation of it. This representation has nothing negative about it: it is pure artifice.[22] When a painter paints a lion or, analogously, the poet describes a lion, they transfer the form of the object onto something else, a matter which does not belong to the object.[23] This is the deception that Batteux speaks of, for example, when he exclaims that art is intended to deceive ("L'art n'est fait que pour tromper"; 261): art represents things that are not what they seem, that are not the actual objects. Deception is here used in the same way as in "trompe l'oeil," when a painting is so naturalistic that the observer thinks it is the real thing. It has nothing to do with invented actions or stories.

Thus, literary imitation is pure mimesis-representation, and also fiction is closer to mimesis representation than mimesis-composition when Batteux speaks of fiction or artificiality in this context. The sciences deal with the true – the arts deal with the verisimilar.[24] Verisimilitude here is, of course, likeness with nature. However, as we shall see, verisimilitude also verges on universality, that which is applicable not to one but to many.

Poësie des choses *and* poësie du style

According to Batteux fiction thus belongs to representation. But if the arts are defined by imitation in the sense of representation, what makes them different from ordinary speech? The answer is that in imitation Batteux reads artistic representation, not just any representation.[25] This is the common way of viewing *lexis* or *elocutio*, but the consequences are more important in Batteux. When he describes the function of the arts as the transfer of traits of nature onto other materials, he says that the poet does so by "invention" and "harmony of his verses":

> What is the function of the arts? It is to transfer traits that are in nature and present them in objects to which they are not natural. This is how the sculptor's chisel shows a hero in a block of marble. With his colours, the painter makes all visible objects appear on the canvas. With artificial sounds, the musician makes the storm thunder while everything is calm. The poet, finally, with his invention and the harmony of his verses, fills our mind with feigned images and our hearts with artificial emotions, which are often more charming than the true and natural ones.[26]

Again, as before, the poet uses words to represent emotions in the same way as the painter uses colours: the final result is thus feigned and artificial, as is the case with all art. The poet's invention concerns the material and corresponds to mimesis-composition, while "l'harmonie de ses vers" seems to correspond to mimesis-representation. The latter should not be understood as "beautiful verse" but as "beauty within the verses," that is, the artistic diction that is in the lines of the poem. In much the same way as Aristotle placed his chapters on *lexis* towards the end of his *Poetics*, so Batteux devotes pages 167–192 to stylistic issues: what he calls the rules of *poësie du style*. Here, diction is treated according to harmony of different kinds.

In fact, Batteux contributes a succinct way of distinguishing invention from representation, mimesis-composition from mimesis-representation. While attempts at such a distinction were made by Grifolo and Castelvetro as a way of adapting poetics to rhetoric, Batteux develops the distinction in a manner which is adapted both to rhetoric's categories and to those of Aristotle himself.

The whole of the third chapter of the section on poetry is devoted to what Batteux calls *poësie des choses* and *poësie du style* respectively (*Les beaux arts*, 148–224). The former consists in the creation and disposition of the objects, while the latter concerns diction (including thoughts):

> That which is called poetry of style, as opposed to poetry of things (which consists in the creation and disposition of objects), has four parts: 1: thoughts, 2: words, 3: expressions, 4: harmony.[27]

Poësie du style, as we have seen, concerns all aspects of diction. In connection with *poësie des choses*, Batteux discusses how actions should be arranged and characters portrayed. He furthermore discusses how epic and drama should be built up, mentioning fable as the craftsmanship of the epic.[28] Although Batteux devotes considerable attention to the fable, it is obvious that to him fable is not the essence of poetry but a consequence of the fact that imitation always requires an object. If fable were considered the essence of epic and drama, lyric could not possibly be defined as a genre. As we have seen, representation instead is the essence, and thus lyric is separated from the other genres precisely by the shift of object.

Batteux thus follows Aristotle's system with unusual precision, at the same time redefining his categories into a new system. From the above quotation, it appears that he places thought within the category of *lexis*, his imitation. The objects of epic and drama he calls *action* and *mœurs* (the former meaning actions and events rather than plot). Batteux does speak of the harmony of verse as a medium, and lyric as such is elevated into a genre on the level above the parts of poetry. The poet's performance could perhaps be equated with Arisotle's *opsis,* but it appears natural for Batteux to keep physical performance out of the parts of poetry proper. His equivalent to Aristotle's six parts can thus be set up as follows:

	Aristotle		Batteux
object	plot	*muthos*	*actions*
object	character	*êthê*	*mœurs*
object	thought	*dianoia*	*sentimens* (instead of thought)
medium	diction	*lexis*	*imitation* or *discours* (including thought)
medium	lyric poetry	*melopoiia*	*harmonie des vers*
mode	spectacle	*opsis*	(not discussed as poetry)

The central issue here is that emotions are introduced as an object and function as a qualifier of genre, belonging to lyric. This means that although Batteux moves within Aristotelian categories, he is able to make mimesis-representation, not mimesis-composition, the governing principle of poetry: a principle that is common to all the fine arts. Batteux's categories *poësie du style* and *poësie des choses* correspond precisely with these instances and his discussion of them concerns *rules* of imitation – established on the basis of taste. The principle or essence of imitation is that poetry *represents,* through diction. When establishing *poësie du style* and *poësie des choses,* Batteux is actually clearer than Aristotle, probably because he can lean on a long discussion of poetics from the view of rhetoric in the preceding centuries. However, Batteux does not speak of these two categories in terms of imitation. Had he done so, there would have been much less grounds for Schlegel's objections.

Schlegel's critique

In one of those footnotes which leave only a couple of lines for the translation itself on the page, Schlegel summarized the points where he does not agree with Batteux:

1 Imitation cannot be the governing principle of poetry, since an equally important principle must be "improved nature," and both of these must be subsumed under a higher principle.
2 Lyric cannot be defined as imitation, since it must have its origins in authentic emotion.
3 Truth is often *not* restricted by a "mask of imitation," and the readers should not apprehend poetry as imitation.[29]

Imitation cannot be the governing principle of poetry
Two issues of translation seem to be connected to this objection. Schlegel translates *Les beaux arts réduits à un même principe* into *Einschränkung der schönen Künste auf einen einzigen Grundsatz.* The French *réduire* means "reduce," "restrict, "confine," as does the German *einschränken,* but in *réduire* (Lat. *reducere*) the "reducing" originally means precisely "leading" or "tracing back." *Réduire* thus implies searching for the origin as well as simplifying the fine arts, narrowing them down to one common principle. *Einschränkung,* on the other hand, has a much more precise meaning of forceful "delimitation," "restriction" and "simplification." In addition, the French title places the fine arts before the verb, while the German translation turns the restriction into a noun which dominates the title completely (even though it was preceded by a lengthy description of the author, "Herrn Abt Batteux, königlichen Professors ..."). This can be compared with Ramler's translation, which was neutrally titled *Einleitung in die Schönen Wissenschaften.*[30] Significantly, when Batteux points out that there is one unifying principle, Schlegel reacts strongly, as if it were a constriction: "he cannot adduce one single argument for his main thesis, that all poetry, even the ode, must reduce itself to imitation."[31] Thus Schlegel converts Batteux's unifying principle into a reduction, and then makes this a point of criticism.

The other, and greater, terminological problem is the use of *Nach-*

ahmung as a translation of *imitation. Imitation* obviously goes back to mimesis and a long tradition of deliberation on the relationship between art and nature. *Nachahmung*, on the other hand, was a relatively new word which implied simulation, even mimicking, much stronger than either representation or *muthos* (mimesis-representation and mimesis-composition). As we shall see, the translation obscures Batteux's idea of representation as the unifying principle of the arts, which in many instances is the reason for Schlegel not following Batteux.

Schlegel criticizes Batteux for placing the principle of *imitation* above the principle of "improved nature." Batteux's overarching formulation is that the arts imitate beautiful nature, which means that they represent it. Even though Batteux's principle concerns the means or media of representation, not the objects, he also has ample reason to speak of *invention*, that is, the objects. Only, they do not constitute the overarching principle: they are a subdivision of it, that which defines the genres. As Gustafsson has pointed out, when Schlegel says that Batteux should bring in "ausgebesserte Natur" into the definition of poetry and the arts, he in effect arrives at a position close to that of Batteux.[32] When Schlegel makes this suggestion, he in fact shifts from mimesis-representation to mimesis-composition. "Ausgebesserte Natur" is included within Batteux's description, since he has stressed that *imitation* is not slavish copying of nature but representation of a very select choice of objects.[33] His concept of *belle nature* does not mean copying nature but selecting in order to improve upon it:

> What did Zeuxis do when he wished to paint a perfect beauty? Did he portray a particular beauty, making his painting her record? No: he collected the separate traits of several existing beauties.[34]

In one of his series of questions, Schlegel asks if Batteux by imitation means "improvement of nature," but concludes that this cannot be the case since Batteux eliminates "Ausbesserung der Natur" from imitation.[35] True, Batteux did not think of improving nature as a unifying principle, but to him artistic representation always focuses on the artistic and beautiful, thus necessitating an "improved nature." And instead of making philosophical definitions of nature, his notion of *belle nature* could be seen to rest on the following dictum in Aristotle's *Poetics* (chapter 25):

> Since the poet, like a painter or any other image-maker, is a mimetic artist, he must represent, in any instance, one of three objects: the kind of things which were or are the case; the kind of things that people say and think; the kind of things that ought to be the case. (1460b8–11)

Finding and selecting the beautiful – how things ought to be – do not constitute Batteux's principle of the arts, but they necessarily follow from it. Schlegel's critique implies that the governing principle of poetry cannot be equated with pure mimesis-representation but that the object of poetry is equally important. This is not the same as saying that mimesis-composition is equally important, but it is a gesture in that direction, turning towards invention and the objects of poetry.

Lyric cannot be defined as imitation

To Schlegel, the lack of imitation in the oldest poems, such as the truly authentic psalms of David, must mean that the principle of imitation is untenable.[36] However, the objection seems mostly to amuse Batteux, who in the edition of 1764 replies that they cannot dominate, whatever the beginnings, the definition of the art of poetry.[37] According to this view, an ancient poem with no imitation is possible – meaning that the emotions are authentic, that there is verity instead of verisimilitude and that there is artless expression instead of artistic diction.

However, the issue of authenticity in the object of lyric is not entirely clear in Batteux's view. In accordance with the definition of drama and epic as representing actions, he holds the imitation of emotions to mean the (artistic) representation of emotion, but the distinctions are not unequivocal. Starting with the origin of lyric, he foresees the objection that the oldest lyric, such as the psalms, were mere emotion and thus could not be seen as imitation. Batteux sees no conflict in this: notwithstanding whether the emotions represented are authentic, the important thing is that they must always be presented as if they were imitations, that is, the poem must be artfully shaped in accordance with the rules – and the emotions must become universal:

> Moreover, why do the sacred songs appear so beautiful to us? Is it not precisely because we there find, perfectly expressed, the emotions that it seems to us we would have experienced in the situation of the prophets? If these emotions were only true, and not verisimilar, we should respect them – but they would not be able to please us. So, in order to please people, even if one is not imitating, one has to make it as if one were imitating, and endow truth with the traits of verisimilitude.[38]

The hymns are beautiful to us not because they express authentic emotions, but because these emotions are possible to adapt to ourselves. The emotions are subjective and true, but at the same time universal and thus verisimilar. If they were true but not universal, they would not please us. Thus, even if the poet's object is his own true feelings, he must see to it that they are universal – by treating them as he would any other poetic object. The old hymns were not made with artistic intentions but manifest pleasure and universality all the same.[39]

Schlegel's objection implies that authentic emotion has no place in Batteux's system, which in turn implies that Batteux's poet feigns and pretends. On this point of criticism, he thus tries to change mimesis-representation into the actor's performance, which does not form part of Batteux's definition of the arts. In his following remarks, Schlegel further develops this histrionic aspect of imitation.

Truth is often not restricted by a "mask of imitation"

In the discussion of emotions as the object of imitation, then, Schlegel comes to understand Batteux's imitation as acting and simulating. This is abhorrent to his own idea of authenticity, as it causes the reader to lose confidence in the poet. This is apparent when Schlegel speaks of a "mask of imitation," having touched upon the idea previously, asking whether the poet should be like the actor who feigns to be what he is not, just as the irreligious Voltaire who wrote Christian tragedies.[40] To Schlegel's mind this is hypocrisy, but, he states, even if one accepts this, expressing one's own feelings cannot be considered imitation: "Aber seine eignen *Empfindungen auszudrücken*, das kann ohnmöglich so viel heißen, als nachbilden, fingere, *hypokrinein*" (376).

Here it is obvious that Schlegel considers the three words "nachbilden, fingere, *hypokrinein*" to be synonymous with *nachahmen*, which thus must mean that imitation is acting, mimicking. *Nachbilden* has more of the meaning "copy" to it than *nachahmen*. *Fingere* and especially *hypokrinein* – *hupokritês* is Aristotle's word for "actor" – lead the mind towards "impersonating." Schlegel has thus left the field of poetry and moved to the field of performance. Batteux does open for this kind of connection by comparing the poet to the actor. However, this comparison should not be confused with the principle of imitation. In a chapter on the character of lyric poetry he says:

> The monologues of Polieucte, Camille and Chimene are lyrical pieces, and if this is the case, why would not the emotion which is the object of imitation in a drama be the object of an ode? Why should it be impossible to imitate the passion in a song, when one imitates it in a scene?[41]

Asking whether there should not be imitation of emotions in a song when there is such imitation in a drama or an ode can lead the thoughts towards rhetorical *prosopopeia* and Plato's discussions of the poet's acting.[42] But that is not Batteux's errand here since he treats the object of lyric, not performance. He has stated that lyric, as drama and epic, is verbal representation, and now he wishes to show that the object of this representation is emotion. He does not discuss what happens *on* the stage, but *in* the scene of the dramatic text. That is, he speaks of mimesis-representation and its object.

However, Batteux also speaks of the performance of the poet, as well as his enthusiasm. But that discussion follows as a consequence, it is one of the rules of taste that follow the principle of imitation. He discusses ways for the poet to be inspired and to achieve emotions corresponding to his subject matter:

> Thus, poetic imitation can be reduced to thoughts, expression and harmony, which should intrinsically conform with the objects. If the emotions are not true and real, that is, if the poet is not actually in the situation which produces the emotions he is in need of, then he

> should excite such emotions, similar to the real ones, and feign them accordingly to the object. And when he arrives at the degree of fervour which suits his topic, then he is inspired.[43]

The parallel between actor and poet is here in focus, a parallel, however, that is not the governing principle of poetry. Aristotle kept the actors' imitation away from the mimesis of poetry, and so does Batteux. He considers enthusiastic delivery to be important, but he does not confuse the actor's or the poet's feigning with the essence of poetry, the unifying principle of the arts. At the end of the chapter he ties things together and concludes that lyric represents emotions instead of actions and characters/customs. If there are real emotions it is an asset, since that strengthens credibility.[44]

Batteux does not describe David's psalms, for example, as imitation, but he regards the contemporary poet as an imitator. This is the foundation of his theory: the lyric poet chooses his object, emotions, and represents it, artistically. The psalmist did not choose his object but expressed his own, true, emotions, and he did so without making his representation artistic according to rules (which did not then exist). The argument is not waterproof, but the important thing is that it is derived from the idea that poetry is representation, and lyric is representation of emotions. This principle does not comprise the poet's inspiration or performance, although it leads to those questions as well. Since the objects are emotions, the issues of inspiration and performance will follow. Thus, the poet may be compared to the actor, but this is not pertinent to Batteux's principle of imitation. The poet's performance belongs to the rules of imitation, i.e. the rules of taste. As Batteux says in an attempt to clarify the matter:

> I needed to demonstrate only two things: First, that emotions can be feigned and imitated just like actions – I think M. Schlegel would agree that this is true. Second, that all emotions expressed in lyric, feigned or true, should be subject to the rules of poetic imitation, that is, they should be verisimilar, selected, elevated, as perfected as their genre allows, and finally rendered with all grace and all the force of poetic expression. That is the meaning of the principle of imitation, that is its spirit.[45]

The main principle in his poetics is that poetry is verbal representation (mimesis-representation) – on the background of which Batteux has tried to demonstrate that the objects (mimesis-composition) may be real or fictitious. That *les sentimens* are *imitées* does not mean that the poet imitates feelings: the parallel with actions, the objects of epic and drama, proves that. Imitated emotions, then, are represented emotions. Batteux's second issue concerns the *rules* of poetic imitation: the objects have to be verisimilar, i.e. universal, chosen, i.e. omitting that which is not beautiful, elevated, perfected and rendered in a graceful way. This, however, does not constitute the principle of imitation, it is a consequence of it. As Batteux says in the first pages of *Les beaux arts*: "the rules of taste are nothing but consequences of the principle of imitation."[46] Thus, it seems that Batteux keeps the principle of imitation rather strictly apart from the rules of imitation: the former is the trunk, the latter the branches.[47] The principle is that art is representation, in the case of poetry verbal. This principle makes it possible to separate the genres according to their objects. The rules of imitation follow from the principle: the objects are to be chosen carefully, and the language used to represent, render, them is to be artistic. At yet one remove come matters such as the poet's or the actor's performance. This, then, should be kept apart from Batteux's introductory words that poetry feigns – which are only meant to clarify the difference between nature and the fine arts. The arts feign in that they are not real nature, but artifice.

* * *

In his critique of Batteux, Schlegel concluded that there must be a higher principle, governing both *Nachahmung* and *ausgebesserte Natur*, a principle he would first define in his own theoretical treatises which he began to append to the translation. Schlegel here elaborated his own definition of poetry, and in "Von dem höchsten und allgemeinsten Grundsatze der Poesie" he established:[48]

> Poetry thus will be the most sensual and pleasant expression of the beautiful, or the good, or the beautiful and good at once, through language.[49]

In the 1751 edition Schlegel had used "Vorstellung" instead of "Ausdruck," but the most interesting part of the definition is "through language" (*durch die Sprache*). Obviously Schlegel's definitions of the sensual, the good and the beautiful are not the same as Batteux's, but the question is how far apart their definitions are from each other. The essence of Batteux's definition of poetry is representation, *through diction,* of beautiful nature, a definition Batteux had clearly stated in his preface, using the word *discours,* which Schlegel had translated as *Rede.*[50] *Discours* and *Rede* have a stronger association to artistic language than *Sprache,* but so does Schlegel's qualifier *angenehmste* to *Sprache.* In his footnotes, Schlegel had managed to rid from Batteux's concept of *imitation* its essential meaning as medium, language – even to such a degree that he could himself describe the *Grundsatz* of poetry as pleasant expression through language – thus describing the soul of poetry in the same way as Batteux but altering Batteux's definition so as to be able to contest it.

Since Aristotle himself launched the distinction of direct and indirect speech as a criterion for distinguishing between the genres, the poet's simulation of persons is included in the question of poetry as imitation. Drama is enacted only in direct speech, while epic combines direct and indirect speech, a distinction constantly taken up in the tradition. What is important to discern is that the issue of direct and indirect speech (mimesis vs. *diegesis*) is on a sub-level of the question of poetry as imitation: even though the word used for direct speech is mimesis, it is neither mimesis-composition nor mimesis-representation, but mimesis in yet another sense. It is clear both in Aristotle and Batteux that the physical performance of an actor, or even poet, is not essential to the art of poetry. To the latter, poetry is imitation in the sense of representation: in drama and epic, actions are represented through the medium of words, and in lyric emotions are represented. At a lower level, *within* the representation of words, *lexis,* it is possible to distinguish between direct and indirect speech. The actor's or poet's physical performance is further removed from the definition of poetry.

Batteux and Schlegel can be seen to continuously qualify their arguments, thus coming closer and closer to each other.[51] However, while Batteux offers more and more detailed explanations, he does not change his basic definition.[52] He does not manage to keep the distinctions clear when Schlegel blurs them, but he does – unlike Schlegel – hold onto his original definition, even though his distinctions are not ideal. Batteux's comments in the new editions are to a much larger degree pedagogical enhancements (which does not mean that his system is unproblematic). From the beginning, in the *Avant-propos* of 1746, he stated that the *moyen* of poetry for achieving imitation is *le discours*, and while the object of the fine arts is *belle nature*, the object of poetry also qualifies the different genres: the objects of epic and drama are actions, the object of lyric is emotions. Through the years, Batteux tries to explain this principle again and again, but while it is easy to find obscure or contradictory passages in his system, his main idea is consistent and quite apparent. Schlegel, on the other hand, after constantly misinterpreting Batteux's idea of artistic representation in words being the soul of poetry, in his own treatise on poetry finally reached just about the same conclusion.

Batteux thus makes mimesis-representation the soul of poetry, and its objects, including mimesis-composition, subordinated qualifiers. To be sure, Batteux does not always keep his definitions and categories distinct: the various dimensions of the concept of imitation were not entirely controllable, and his definition of *belle nature* was not precise. His discussions of the poet's inspiration seem to have invited readers to misunderstand the principle of imitation: the critics were no less confounded by the dimensions of the concept. The foundation of Batteux's theory is that imitation is representation, through words in the case of poetry, and that representation, as opposed to nature, is artificial. Schlegel pushed the meaning of imitation into mimicking and acting, but he also pushed it in the direction of "invention" when he wondered whether Batteux with "imitation" meant "Ausbesserung." These instances of imitation do not constitute Batteux's principle of imitation, only rules deriving from it. Interestingly, when Schlegel launched his own alternative highest principle of poetry, he in fact seems to revert to Batteux's pure artistic representation, speaking of "Ausdruck ... durch der Sprache." In his discussion of "the misfortunes of imitation," Todorov effectively comments that "[a]rtistic imitation is, as it happens, a paradoxical notion: it disappears at the very moment that it achieves perfection," and that "[i]f imitation were the only law of art, it ought to bring about the disappearance of art: the latter would differ in no way from 'imitated' nature."[53] While the argument is in essence correct, it is not valid when one counts in that "imitation" means "representation": it is perfectly possible to regard artistic representation, even at perfection, as not only remaining but even triumphing – albeit the representation would for obvious reasons differ from its object. This is how Batteux views poetry and all the arts.

Batteux himself opened up for these misinterpretations, but the foundation of his theoretical construction is a very consistent adaptation of Aristotle's categories. The kernel of this quarrel over the soul of poetry is the difference between imitation and *Nachahmung*. The word *Nachahmung* leads both towards *invention* and the actor's mimicking. It could be added that the barriers of language were not impossible to overcome: it was possible to distinctly define the instances of German *Nachahmung* as well. So, Johann Christoph Gottsched distinguished between three kinds of *Nachahmung*: one is "bloße Beschreibung," what we have termed mimesis-representation, the second is the poet's impersonating imitation, and the third is "Fabel," what we have termed mimesis-composition. The addition of the second category as a main category does not correspond to Aristotle, but Gottsched in turn demonstrates a more congenial interpretation than either Schlegel or Batteux. As opposed to Batteux, Gottsched is also quite clear about mimesis-composition being the soul of poetry.[54]

Towards the end of the 18th century and especially with romanticism, the principle of imitation is known to have waned and more or less disappeared. However, as was seen in the case of J. A. Schlegel and will be further discussed in the following chapter, in the light of the distinction between mimesis-composition and mimesis-representation, it appears that the principle of imitation, meaning representation, actually did not disappear. It was renamed and new associations were tied to it, but – depending on the point of view – the focus on mimesis-representation was enhanced rather than dismissed by the romantics.

CHAPTER SEVEN

The nachleben *of imitation*
(early 19th century)

The idea that poetry in one way or another consists in mimesis proves fruitful to theoreticians and scholars even in our day. Just as in the material hitherto discussed, one reason for this seems to be the latitude of the concept. The concept of mimesis certainly was challenged by theoreticians after Batteux, even though it has been demonstrated that several romantics displayed a much stronger theoretical continuity than has been recognized.[1] There is reason to sketch one aspect of the nature of this shift in ideals and aesthetics.

Any critique of the principle of imitation seems doomed to redefine "imitation" in order to assert the critique. Batteux's basic proposal, that the common denominator of the arts is that they represent, is rather unchallenging. His conclusion that (artistic) language is poetry's medium of imitating, i.e. representing, is so truistic that hardly anyone could object to it. But one objection could be that the definition is too wide, although the problem seems not to be the principle of imitation itself, rather those associations which are layered around it. Batteux connects the *principe* with a set of *règles,* which are objectionable. In addition, his critics understand imitation and, even more, *Nachahmung,* with stronger associations to falsifying, mimicking, feigning and deceiving. To be sure, Batteux spoke of feigning and deception, but in discussing poetry, he did so in order to distinguish art from nature and science, not to pass moral judgement.

The principle of imitation was often dismissed by theoreticians after Batteux, but this dismissal was made in a way which did not really concern the nucleus of the principle. Cullhed shows how imitation recurs in several works and how it in its different manifestations may be deemed bad or good. She finds no clear opposition between imitation and *poiêsis* in the material, although imitation often appears as a contrast to authenticity.[2] A conclusion which remains to be drawn is that if one wishes to examine what happened to the principle of imitation, one must address not only the discussions of terms such as imitation, *Nachahmung*, etc., but also the discussions of language as such, especially in relation to poetry. Such an extensive examination cannot be performed here, but the argument will be put forth briefly.

As Cullhed points out, J.A. Schlegel's son A.W. Schlegel was rather more appreciative of Batteux's description and did not accuse it of falsehood but rather condoled the antiquity of terminology:

> Either one imitates nature as one finds it, and then it may not turn out beautiful, or one makes it beautiful, and then it is no longer imitation [*Nachahmung*]. Why do they not say: art shall represent [*darstellen*] the beautiful, and leave nature out of consideration? Then one would be rid of the problem that appearances of art have to be reinterpreted into nature, something which is only possible with extreme violence.[3]

Cullhed describes A.W. Schlegel's solution as "a kind of translation" which diminishes the distance between the theories represented by Batteux and J.A. Schlegel.[4] However, A.W. Schlegel's own suggestion, *Darstellung*, does not in essence differ from Batteux's imitation: he changes Batteux's *imitation*, which in the case of poetry meant verbal representation, to the more precise and less evocative synonym *Darstellung*. He refers to Batteux as a proponent of the idea that art should copy nature as accurately as possible, and concludes that such an ideal must make *Täuschung*, deception, its goal. While Batteux does speak of deception, it is in order to distinguish art from reality and from science. It is not requisite that the verbal representation which Batteux calls imitation needs copy or attempt to accurately portray nature's external objects. Only, A.W. Schlegel states that only slavish verbal representation is *Nachahmung*. Thus, he too has forced Batteux's definition of representation into a slavish and yet fraudulent copying of nature.[5] A.W. Schlegel's *Darstellung* is a more congenial term for that representation in which Batteux saw the essence of poetry. "Art is representation of beautiful nature" and "Art should represent the beautiful": although the philosophical distance between Batteux and A.W. Schlegel was considerable, to say the least, their definitions of art and poetry in its essence were very close to each other.

A.W. Schlegel's words demonstrate that there is no specific limit to the principle of imitation: in fact he even stated that "art shall imitate nature" – but then his definition of *Nachahmung* was a creative one, opposed to *Nachäffung*.[6] It continues with the romantics, who of course continue discussing art as representation. The theory of art proper, at least according to Batteux, defines art as representation but is always more or less intermingled with the other, albeit secondary or tertiary, senses of "imitation." What happens with A.W. Schlegel is that terminology is connected to a new philosophical framework, but the main definition of poetry as verbal representation still applies. In fact, the notion of poetry as verbal representation is elevated to the highest degree by A.W. Schlegel and his contemporaries, with language and humanity becoming closely connected. He combines the old notion that words are imitations of things – the original sense of mimesis-representation – and the suggestion that language is originally the expression of emotions, as in this example from 1795:

> Language originates either from sounds of feeling alone, or from imitations [*Nachahmungen*] of objects alone, or from both of these together.[7]

It thus seems that Schlegel might find verbal representation as such to be a rather base exercise. However, it is not really the act of representing – but rather representing objects superficially – which is base. In Schlegel's view, the *Ursprache* was directed not to understanding but to imagination. Words evoked mental images of their referents, and thus imagery, *Bildlichkeit*, was fundamental to that original language which was truly poetic. With time, language became more directed to understanding, *Verstand*, and thus lost much of its poetry. The *Ursprache* was characterized by the same unity of the mental faculties that Immanuel Kant found in the aesthetic experience. Language in itself always keeps a poetic potential, and the poet restores language into that imaginative poetry. Language's representation is not direct: it is "a transforming representation" ("eine umbildende Darstellung"), which represents not the object *per se* but the perception of it.[8] That is to say: poetry *is* language. As Batteux would have said, poetry as imitation equals verbal representation. But not only is verbal representation at the centre of poetry, it is even the means by which we think. Language, as part of *Poesie*, is part of all thinking and of all arts:

> Language, the most wonderful creation of human capacity for poetry and at the same time that grand, never completed poem, where human nature represents itself.[9]

Provided that nature is defined as intelligent and productive, art imitates nature:

> If nature is understood in this most worthy sense, not as a mass of products but as the producing itself, and if the expression *Nachahmung* is also understood in a more noble sense, meaning not mimicking [*Nachäffung*] the superficial aspects of a man, but appropriating the principles of his actions – then there is no objecting to the principle, only to add: art shall imitate [*nachahmen*] nature.[10]

Schlegel here uses the derogatory *nachäffen* for *nachahmen*, and he does so to describe the kind of representation which focuses on the superficial. Discarding this mimesis-representation, he instead directs focus towards the fundamental principles of human behaviour. In addition, the fictional world in Schlegel's thinking establishes its own rules, and when discussing the organity of art he stresses that the work of art should be conceived as a whole,[11] that is, he tends to prefer mimesis-composition. However, there is one problem. In order to represent the essence of life, one is obliged to depict the objects of nature – for things reveal their inner nature through their outer nature, and it is the outside which gives clues to the inside.[12] In nature, all things refer not only to their own essence, but also to each other. In that capacity, everything shall be connected in art as well:

> The mutual chain formed by all things in an uninterrupted symbolizing, on which the first creation of language is founded, should be produced in the recreation of language, of poetry.[13]

This means that poetry becomes practically tantamount to imagery. Schlegel speaks of metaphor, simile, tropes, *Bildlichkeit* and symbol. The imaginary is the subconscious part of the work of genius, arising from and speaking to imagination: the basic power of human spirit ("die Grundkraft des menschlichen Geistes"). The images amount to fictions, following their own rules, but still the question remains as to what distinguishes the kind of representation of sensual things used in order to symbolize poetic truths from the kind of representation of the superficious which is called *Nachäffung*, mimicking like a monkey. Schlegel formulates the question:

> Now, how can the infinite be brought to the surface, to the appearance? Only symbolically, in images and signs. The unpoetical aspect of things is the one which regards everything as settled with the mind's perceptions and the intellect's definitions. The poetical aspect is the one which continuously interprets them and sees a figurative inexhaustibility in them. ... Only thereby will everything become lively to us. Making poetry [*Dichten*] (in the broad sense of the poetical which is the foundation of all arts) is nothing but eternal symbolizing: either we seek an outer cover for something spiritual, or we apply a surface on something inner which cannot be seen.[14]

One can easily imagine that Schlegel would wish for no traditional allegories and personifications of intellectual concepts, but apart from that it is not uncomplicated to define the referentiality of different parts of a poem. The final criterion seems to be its effect: when the meaning is as it should be, everything becomes lively, *lebendig*. Thus, the imaginative and vivid description that becomes lively in the right sense is poetry. This raises the question of those devices for enhancing vividness which were stored in the treasuries of rhetorical tradition. Even though rhetoric was increasingly questioned, these devices as such were not discarded.[15] Rather, as shall be seen, they could be raised into new, metaphysical esteem.

Evidently, the differences between A.W. Schlegel's and Batteux's philosophical and normative approaches are considerable, not to mention the practical poetry with which they are dealing. But one could say that Schlegel elevated Batteux's principle of poetry – imitation, i.e. representation, mimesis-representation – into a higher sphere. Although privileging mimesis-composition, the fictional world, he also thought mimesis-representation to be essential. And by claiming that poetry is eternal symbolizing, through language, he seems to have transferred the soul of poetry to this new, metaphysical, definition of mimesis-representation. One could also say that the symbol has become the soul of poetry, which raises new questions. A.W. Schlegel speaks of the symbol together with vividness, figurative speech and language, but the symbol itself is a matter of content rather than of form (a separate chapter below will be devoted to this issue). Here, the conclusion must be that the kernel of Batteux's doctrine of imitation – that poetry represents through language – was certainly not dismissed but on the contrary developed into the essence of romantic aesthetics as presented by A.W. Schlegel.

* * *

The following chapters will not study adaptations of Aristotelian theory proper. Instead, they will treat three issues that are indirectly connected to the questions of mimesis-composition and especially mimesis-representation in the development of aesthetics. The first issue is that of the sublime, the second is the symbol, and the third is the place of emotions in the historical development of genre theory.

Beyond Aristotelian concepts

CHAPTER EIGHT

The technique of the sublime
(3rd–18th century)

The sublime is clearly an inexhaustible source of discussion, although the intensity of interest in the topic may wax and wane. It has even been incorporated in modern text theory.[1] The interest in the sublime can be traced to the 3rd-century treatise *Peri hupsous* by an unknown author usually dubbed Longinus. Although this work is no longer at the centre of the discussion about the sublime, the contribution of *Peri hupsous* to the rhetorical tradition has been extraordinary, not only in associating the literary sublime with the grandeur of its sources, but also in opening for wider considerations about the impact of art on its audience. The readers and translators initially most interested in the treatise (Boileau, for example) focused mainly upon the literary aspects of the sublime. However, when Edmund Burke published his theories on the sublime in 1757, he hardly treated literary aspects at all,[2] and his empiricist and psychological approach was succeeded in turn by the philosophical views of Kant. The evolution of aesthetics can be tied to the evolution of a new kind of social subject, as Peter de Bolla has demonstrated.[3] Thus, by the end of the 18th century the most influential discussions of the sublime turned from a specific interest in literature to a more general aesthetics. That trend has continued to the present: in most studies *Peri hupsous* takes a back seat to explorations of the psychological, ethical and philosophical potential of the sublime in the work of Burke, Kant and others. The less focus on *Peri hupsous,* the less focus on the literary aspects of the sublime.

This is not the place to indulge in the more elaborated philosophical ideas of the sublime. My intention here is to demonstrate how the sublime was from the beginning dependent on literary representation. The sublime is usually associated with transport rather than rhetorical persuasion, with genius rather than skill, with elevation rather than style. All of this derives from *Peri hupsous,* the source of all discussion of the sublime, but the treatise still adheres to a rhetorical notion of literary representation which on the one hand strengthens elaborations on the notion of the sublime, on the other hand tends to be curiously overlooked. In fact, Longinus launches a particular figure of speech much more strongly than is ascertained by simply reading his explicit opinions. There is no trace of Aristotelian thought in *Peri huposous,* and mimesis is only used in the sense of finding inspiration in (rather than imitating[4]) great authors. The term is not used for mimesis-representation nor mimesis-composition, but, in spite of this, the level of mimesis-representation is essential in several respects, and at the end of the day terminology in itself will tie mimesis-representation to the philosophical and not least psychological workings of the sublime in the 18th century.

We have reached a general consensus about what was supposed to produce the sublime in 18th-century literature. As John Dennis put it: "Gods, Daemons, Hell, Spirits and Souls of Men, Miracles, Prodigies, Enchantments, Witchcraft, Volcanoes, Monsters, Serpents, Lions, Tigers, Fire, War, Pestilence, Famine, &c."[5] These elements are found in the landscape of the songs of Ossian or the Old Norse translations of Paul-Henri Mallet and Thomas Percy, not to mention the Gothic novels of the early 19th century and romanticism, where, of course, the sublime developed into a different philosophical and literary phenomenon. As Samuel H. Monk explained in his study of the sublime from 1935, *Peri hupsous* encouraged among its 17th- and 18th-century interpreters a wide range of beliefs often labeled "pre-romantic" and "romantic": a preference for flawed genius over flawless mediocrity; the idea that the sublime may be expressed in simple language and should not be understood as the *genus sublime* of rhetoric; the concept of the independence of individual judgement and the notion that language is a means of expressing that which is individual.[6] All of these ideas have certain consequences with regard to literary production, but they are not themselves literary techniques. The same is true of those motifs and landscapes most often associated with the sublime.

As R.S. Crane pointed out in his review of Monk's book, readers with a specific interest in rhetoric viewed *Peri hupsous* as a discussion of the literary means of conveying greatness. In contrast, readers with psychological, aesthetic and philosophical interests did not discuss "compositions and authors but 'the pleasures of the imagination.'"[7] Although the distinction between these two groups is not entirely easy to maintain,[8] the difference is important. The sublime as a philosophical issue has a great many influential sources besides *Peri hupsous* and only concerns itself briefly with literary technique. Being a rhetorical treatise, on the other hand, *Peri hupsous* promotes a literary technique even though it deviates from conventional rhetoric – which explains why its primary means of describing the sublime is to define it through insufficient rhetorical devices.

The problem of defining *Peri hupsous* was addressed by Theodore E. B. Wood, who criticized Monk for exaggerating the rhetorical aspect of the treatise and for simplifying the development of the ideas of the sublime from a rhetorical to a psychological focus.[9] Wood clarifies important differences in various definitions of the concept of the sublime and demonstrates that the development was much more complex, but it is important not to let the rhetorical and technical parts of *Peri hupsous* vanish from sight. Indeed, Longinus speaks of the sublime as something that exceeds craftsmanship – and psychological aspects are certainly at hand. However, regardless of the precise nature and degree of focus on psychology, the impact of *Peri hupsous* cannot be evaluated properly without taking into account what literary technique it propounds, explicitly and not least implicitly. In order to understand the role of psychology and imagination correctly, we must see the sublime as related to the rhetorical tradition.

* * *

What literary technique *Peri hupsous* conveys as the literary sublime is a complicated issue since a main feature of the work is its elusiveness. The author seems to practise a sort of sublime writing himself, far from the ordinary uses of language in a treatise of its kind.[10] That is why two such prominent scholars as Elder Olson and William K. Wimsatt came to view the treatise in completely different ways. Wimsatt considered Longinus to be incapable of creating a sufficient definition, while Olson made Longinus out to be a kind of Aristotle.[11] As might be expected, Wimsatt's "unsystematic" and sensitive interpretation was the one that won followers. For example, his observation that several of Longinus's figures lead to abnormal syntax and broken structures[12] underlies, in a sense, most later studies of the sublime. To Thomas Weiskel, "[t]he true function of the sublime is to legitimate the necessary discontinuities in the classical scheme of signification and to justify the specific affective experience which these discontinuities entailed."[13] Paul Fry stresses "that it is much the same, though never wholly the same, whether one speaks of nature or art, author or audience; or whether one speaks ... of unconsciously or consciously imposed form,"[14] while George B. Walsh discerns in *Peri hupsous* a method of "representation masquerading as expression," due to two different concepts of language.[15]

Common to most examinations of Longinus is thus the problem of the relationship between author, text and audience, and the violation of traditional rhetorical categories. In the following, I will attempt to understand one aspect of the treatise, not by systematizing it but by relating it to the systematization of the contemporary rhetorical tradition. The nucleus of the synthesis of rhetoric and the expressive sublime, I suggest, is inherent in the reorganization of traditional rhetorical devices in *Peri hupsous.* This does not explain the sublime, but it may to some extent explain the literary impact of the sublime according to *Peri hupsous.* Eventually, the technique of the sublime advanced in *Peri hupsous* may shed additional light on the general development of imagery in 18th-century literature, as well as on the interrelations between literary technique and the developing idea of imagination as the essence of poetry. I will first discuss the explicitly propounded techniques of the sublime, and then examine the implicit thrust of *Peri hupsous.*

The explicit argument

In chapter 8, Longinus begins his systematic discussion with these influential assertions:

> There are, one may say, some five most productive sources of the sublime in literature, the common groundwork, as it were, of all five being competence in speaking, without which nothing can be done.

> [1] The first and most powerful is the power of grand conceptions ... [2] the second is the inspiration of vehement emotion. These two constituents of the sublime are for the most part congenital. But the other three come partly from art, namely [3] the proper construction of figures – these being of course of two kinds, figures of thought and figures of speech – and, over and above these, [4] nobility of language, which again may be resolved into choice of words and the use of tropical and elaborated diction. [5] The fifth cause of grandeur, which gives form to all those already mentioned, is dignified and elevated word-arrangement.[16]

Features of the speaker's working process as commonly defined – invention (*inventio*), disposition (*dispositio*), adornment (*elocutio*), memory (*memoria*), performance (*actio*) – are easily recognizable here, but the manner in which the sources relate to common rhetorical theory is not clear. After this, the sources are more closely examined one by one, with the exception of the second source, emotion (*pathos*), which is said by Longinus to be treated elsewhere.[17]

The first and most important source is discussed in five main sections: the sublime as an echo of a noble mind (ch. 9); selection and organization of material (10); amplification (*auxesis*: 11–12); imitation (*mimesis*: 13–14); and visualization (*phantasia*: 15). Although the sections include comments on many different levels of literary discourse, the subject of the sections always corresponds to conventional *inventio* in one way or another: finding the suitable expression, aspect, element, image or repetition of the subject. Organization is presented as highly important to the creation of the effect of greatness, as is imitation, which, according to Longinus, is more or less a way of assuming part of the spirit and greatness of great authors, and is thus closely connected to the power of conceiving great thoughts.[18] The role of amplification is not as clear, but repetition and amplification should probably be understood as fundamental to the sublime, as Fry has shown.[19]

These topics are all related to the first source of the sublime, one that is not so much the result of artifice as an inherent quality in the author. Moreover, before considering the figures of artifice connected with the sublime in chapter 16, Longinus evidently felt it necessary to examine one essential aspect of this first source of the sublime in more detail – visualization:

> Weight, grandeur, and urgency in writing are very largely produced, dear young friend, by the use of "visualizations" [*phantasiai*]. This at least is what I call them; others call them "image productions [*eidôlopoiias*]." For the term *phantasia* is applied in general to an idea which enters the mind from any source and engenders speech, but the word has now come to be used predominantly of passages where, inspired by strong emotion, you seem to see what you describe and bring it vividly before the eyes [*hup' opsin*] of your audience. That *phantasia* means one thing in oratory and another in poetry you will yourself detect, and also that the object of the poetical form of it is to enthral, and that of the prose form to present things vividly, though both indeed aim at the emotional and the excited.[20]

In 15.8, Longinus further qualifies the distinction between the use of *phantasia* in poetry and rhetoric: "[T]hese examples from poetry show an exaggeration which belongs to fable and far exceeds the limits of credibility, whereas the most perfect effect of visualization in oratory is always one of reality and truth." Clearly, although discussing *phantasia* as an aspect of the congenital sources of the sublime, Longinus treats it as a rhetorical device. He discusses the use of the word *phantasia* and says that the phenomenon is called "image-production" (*eidolopoiia*) by others. This word, a relative of the word "poetry" (*poiêsis*), naturally stresses the aspects of "making" or "production." Obviously, *phantasia* is an alternative term to what we have previously met in the form of terms such as *enargeia, evidentia, representatio* and, the Latin equivalent in Mathias, *imaginatio*. Longinus even uses the key words "before the eyes," albeit as *hup' opsin* instead of *pro ommatôn*. The technical aspect of *phantasia* is further underscored by the distinction between poetical and rhetorical uses of the figure. The poetical use leads to astonishment or enthralment (*ekplêxis*), while the rhetorical use leads to vividness (*enargeia*).

We have seen the device of visualization lavishly mentioned in the poetological tradition from Aristotle, and it has also had its specific place in the very basic rhetorical system. Quintilian puts it this way:

> The person who will show the greatest power in the expression of emotions will be the person who has properly formed what the Greeks call *phantasiai* (let us call them "visions"), by which the images of absent things are presented to the mind in such a way that we seem actually to see them with our eyes and have them physically present to us.[21]

Quintilian explains that these images must be conjured forth in order to win a case, and continues:

> The result will be *enargeia,* what Cicero calls *illustratio* and *evidentia,* a quality which makes us seem not so much to be talking about something as exhibiting it. Emotions will ensue just as if we were present at the event itself.[22]

This most potent rhetorical device for exploiting the emotions of the audience is what Longinus presents among the congenital sources of the sublime in circumstances where discussion *of pathos* is missing. There is, of course, also a function of the term *phantasia* that is not rhetorical: Aristotle himself uses it to describe a faculty of the soul in *On the Soul.* Even in his *Rhetoric,* he uses the word not to designate a rhetorical figure, but in the sense of an ability to create mental images, a sense close to the modern connotations of the word "fantasy."[23] This double function may partly explain why a clearly rhetorical device is placed under the first source of the sublime instead of being discussed among other figures.[24] Still, according to Longinus, *phantasia* deals with expressing great thoughts rather than conceiving them.

The rhetorical effect that *phantasia* is supposed to have is *enargeia,* or *evidentia* in Latin. Other figures can also provoke *enargeia* – most importantly vivid present adverbs of time and space such as "here" and "now," and apostrophe.[25] As might be expected, these figures are described among other rhetorical figures in chapters 23–27 of *Peri hupsous.* Although it is possible that *phantasia* is treated separately because it is a figure of thought rather than a figure of speech[26] – a distinction that of course makes *phantasia* more suited to contexts that treat questions of invention – the author himself explicitly states that figures of thought are associated with the third, rather than the first, source of the sublime. Every instance of *phantasia* in *Peri hupsous* is to be understood in the sense of "image" or "visualization," in the same way as the verb *phantazein,* which Longinus uses in the sense "make visible."

As Wimsatt has remarked, metaphors are put at a surprising disadvantage in *Peri hupsous.* He discerns more or less an "inversion of values" in the fact that metaphor is treated under the fourth source of the sublime, while figures that effect abnormalities of syntax, like *asundeton, huperbaton, periphrasis* and the rhetorical question, are given much more attention.[27] Considering that *pathos* is the second source of the sublime, it seems strange that metaphor is placed in such a remote spot, since this device was commonly appreciated as an excellent way of persuading the intellect because of its impact on the senses and emotions. However, in *Peri hupsous* tropic imagery such as metaphor is ranked low, and instead an alternative kind of imagery, *phantasia,* is heavily advocated. *Phantasia* in itself has no tropic dimensions, but exclusively effectuates vividness. In that way it provides excellent support for metaphors and allegories, since they are more efficient if the sign is forceful, as Longinus's comment on allegory in Homer suggests (9.6–7). But *phantasia,* unlike metaphor and allegory, is not said by Longinus to be a useful figure – in fact, it is not even treated as a figure. Instead, it is made part of the first source of the sublime: the ability to conceive great thoughts. Could there be a more efficient way of promoting a specific rhetorical device? As I will try to demonstrate, this question can be answered in the affirmative.

The implicit argument

Chapter 16 and onwards in *Peri hupsous* consists mainly of a rather conventional presentation of figures and tropes. The first part of the treatise, through chapter 15, is what is usually regarded as the treatise on the sublime. Chapter 15, where *phantasia* is discussed, is thus the final point of the important and influential part of the treatise. Even so, chapter 9 is the first section to elaborate upon great thoughts as a prominent source of the sublime, the best-known part of *Peri hupsous* in the 18th century – in part because it contains a quotation from Genesis as an example of the sublime expressed in simple language.[28] Chapter 10, and probably chapter 8, where the "Longinian" theories are expanded and embellished with magnificent examples, can be considered as nearly as influential. Essential to the impact of *Peri hupsous* is that even though these central chapters do not explicitly mention *phantasia,* the figure *phantasia* is conspicuous in nearly every quotation used to exemplify the sublime.

No particular technique or figure is treated in chapter 9: the nine quotations in the chapter as it is preserved illustrate the sublime and its opposite in various ways. Strikingly, the examples are often accompanied by comments about how they constitute pictures "seen" by the audience (e.g. 9.5–6). The word *phantasmata* in the sense "imaginative pictures" is used for the battle of the gods (9.6), which is, of course, a highly visual episode. Vivid representation is also a striking feature in five of the other examples. The following comment is made about a simile from Homer:

> Far as a man can see with his eyes in the shadowy distance,
> Keeping his watch on a hilltop, agaze o'er the wine-dark ocean,
> So far leap at a bound the high-neighing horses of heaven. ...
>
> He uses a cosmic interval to measure their stride. So supreme is the grandeur of this, one might well say that if the horses of heaven take two consecutive strides there will then be no place found for them in the world. Marvellous too is the imaginative picture[s] [*phantasmata*].[29]

Vividness is also a striking aspect in two other examples: Homer's verses about how Poseidon moves at sea (9.8) and, to a somewhat lesser extent, his verses about Ares (9.11). The last example in the chapter demonstrates the manner in which Homer creates a striking situation in front of the audience by using adverbs of place:

> There then Ajax lies, great warrior; there lies Achilles;
> There, too, Patroclus lies, the peer of the gods in counsel;
> There, too, my own dear son.[30]

Homer's description of Strife (*Iliad* 4.442–4), mentioned but not quoted after the lacuna at 9.4, also appeals to sight:

> Small is the crest that she rears at the first, but behold her thereafter
> Planting her head in the skies, while she treads with her feet on the earth.[31]

Thus, out of the nine preserved quotations exemplifying the sublime in chapter 9, six are strongly visual, although the example interrupted by the lacuna (9.4) displays no vividness. The two remaining examples do not offer detailed or overwhelming pictures, but they are still closely connected to sight and image, since both are founded on the opposition between light and impenetrable darkness. The quotation from Genesis is one of them (9.9); the other is a prayer of Ajax:

> Zeus Father, rescue from out of the mist the sons of Achaia,
> Brighten the heaven with sunshine, grant us the sight of our eyes.
> Just so it be in daylight, destroy us.[32]

Thus, despite the fact that this extraordinarily influential chapter of *Peri hupsous* is not explicitly devoted to visualization or imagery, these are precisely the attributes that its examples demonstrate as vital to the sublime.

Chapter 10, which discusses the selection and organization of material, gives the same impression. No particular figure is treated here either, but two examples of what is not sublime are given, along with two examples of what is sublime, the second of which is taken once again from Homer:

> He fell on the host as a wave of the sea on a hurrying vessel,
> Rising up under the clouds, a boisterous son of the storm-wind.
> The good ship is lost in the shroud of the foam, and the breath of the tempest
> Terribly roars in the sails; and in their heart tremble the sailors,
> By the breadth of a hand swept out from under the jaws of destruction.[33]

Prior to this vivid and forceful description, Longinus provides a sensitive reading of Sappho's "Phainetai moi," which has been preserved for us only here:

> I think him God's peer that sits near you face to face,
> and listens to your sweet speech and lovely laughter.
> It's this that makes my heart flutter in my breast. If I
> see you but for a little, my voice comes no more and
> my tongue is broken.
> At once a delicate flame runs through my limbs; I see
> nothing with my eyes, and my ears thunder.
> The sweat pours down: shivers grip me all over. I am
> grown paler than grass, and seem to myself to be
> very near to death.
> But all must be endured, since ...
>
> Is it not wonderful how she summons at the same time, soul, body, hearing, tongue, sight, skin, all as though they had wandered off apart from herself? She feels contradictory sensations, freezes, burns, raves, reasons, so that she displays not a single emotion, but a whole congeries of emotions. Lovers show all such symptoms, but what gives supreme merit to her art is, as I said, the skill with which she takes up the most striking and combines them into a single whole.[34]

Although scholarly attention regarding this commentary on Sappho has generally focused upon meta-poetical qualities,[35] Longinus's words must also be understood as a highly appreciative response to Sappho's ability to render passion vividly, while also making herself visible within the emotions she represents. Here, the scene is not grand or frightening, but rather evokes a moment of poignant expression.

The figure of the sublime

The first part of *Peri hupsous,* dealing with the congenital sublime instead of artificial techniques, is thus marked throughout by one pervasive literary device: the figure *phantasia.* This emphasis appears to be on the foundation of the different kinds of ambivalence that have often been noticed in the treatise. Fry's argument about the lack of distinctions between nature and art, author and audience, as well as the interchangeability between spirit and letter, seems to be consistent with the repositioning of *phantasia* from art to nature that we have just examined. Even the "chtonic," earthbound aspect of the Longinian sublime that Fry advances seems partly connected to the pervasive concretion of the figure.[36] It is also questions of this kind that rule Walsh's examination of Longinus's two ways of using language: one corresponding to the nature of language and one corresponding to the nature of souls.[37]

One might trace the impact down another path – from Joseph Addison's discussions of the imagination in *The Spectator* in 1712 to the point when, around the turn of the 19th century, imagination came to be understood as the essence of poetry. The starting-point of this discussion was Aristotle's *phantasia,* which in his *On the Soul* and *Rhetoric* is described not as a literary technique but as a human faculty.[38] But what technical device could be more appreciated by the writers and readers of the eighteenth and nineteenth centuries than the one with the same name as the essence of poetry? The word *imagination* may have been the primary connection between mental faculty and stylistic device, but the connection was practically inevitable. Fancy, a Middle English adaptation of *phantasia* or *phantazein,* was later distinguished by Samuel Taylor Coleridge from imagination. He had predecessors, but in general "fancy" was used synonymously with "imagination." So, Addison uses both words "promiscuously" in his essays on the imagination.[39]

The stylistic device *phantasia* produces what is more commonly called *enargeia* or *evidentia* – and thus also what is labelled *representatio* by Averroës and Mathias. The term *phantasia* originally derives from a connection between imagination and visualizing discourse, but the stylistic device became more known under other names. To Longinus, it has nothing to do with mimesis, whereas in Averroës and Mathias *phantasia* is in fact synonymous with mimesis (translated and transformed). In the 18th century, it seems, Aristotle's speculations on the human faculty of imagination once again became associated with the stylistic device.[40] Since I first published my analysis of the argument in *Peri hupsous,* the importance of *phantasia* to the understanding of the sublime has been proposed also by Karl Axelsson, who provides examples of how the sublime was associated with the imagination in English 18th-century critics and how the interest in the sublime had precursors in 17th-century discussions on the imagination.[41] What should be further emphasized is that the reception of the theory of the sublime to a great degree is a matter of terminology.

The terminology of the sublime

Why did the interest in the sublime intensify after the middle of the 18th century? *Peri hupsous* contained several traits that suited the evolving aesthetics, and the idea of the sublime in itself, as Peter de Bolla has demonstrated, suited certain social and scientific discourses of the time. But *Peri hupsous* had been available at a much earlier date:[42] it was published by Robortello in 1554, and again by Paulus Manutius the next year, but it was the edition of Franciscus Portus in 1569 that would prove to be the most influential edition. While a Latin translation by Gabriele dalla Pietra was published in 1612, it was only with Nicolas Boileau-Despréaux's translation in 1674 that it became widely known, perhaps in great part due to the prestigious placing in the renowned critic's *Œvres diverses*.[43] *Traité du Sublime* thus became very influential, but the original had to a large extent been adapted to Boileau's own ideas and ideals. Substantial conclusions of the translation were Longinus's statement that elevation does not always require the highest level of style, and that flaws do not necessarily make a work worthless. Since *Le grand* and *le sublime* were tempered by Boileau's reason and taste, it is not strange that the French 17th-century Longinus exerted an entirely different influence than the Longinus of the 18th century. However, the changes were not only the result of Boileau's aesthetic ideals, but also caused by issues of terminology and translation. Boileau faithfully rendered *hupsos* with *sublime* and *megethos* with *grandeur*, but the essential technique of the sublime, *phantasia*, was translated into *image*. In the prominent chapter VIII (in *Traité* numbered VI), where Longinus lists the five sources of the sublime and describes the first one in a manner which makes the technique *phantasia* its essence, Boileau renders "[t]he first and most powerful is the power of grand conceptions" as "the first and most considerable is a certain elevation of spirit, which makes us think more successfully of things" (la premiere et la plus considerable est *une certaine Elevation d'esprit, qui nous fait penser heureusement les choses*).[44] The original's "powerful" (*kratiston*) becomes "considerable," "grand conceptions" (*noêsis adrepêbolon*) becomes "successful thinking of things" with a touch of elevation added. Boileau's translation of chapter XV (which in *Traité du Sublime* is numbered XIII) follows the original rather closely, but the terminology reduces the potential of grandeur. One could say that the original's "imagemakings," *eidolopoiias,* is amplified into "paintings or fictions," *Peintures,* ou *Fictions,* and since *phantasia* is translated as *image* there is no potential to directly associate it with the faculty of imagination in such a way as was to be the case in the 18th-century reception.[45] The change is altogether remarkable: the first source of the sublime is no longer the ability to exploit imagination fully, but to create successful ways of thinking about things. The spirit is to be elevated, but only as a means of successfully transferring ideas. Thus, the faculty of imagination is substantially removed from the field of associations in Boileau's translation. The reason for this may have been that psychology at the time was less developed and less connected with aesthetic thinking than it would be in the 18th century. *Traité du Sublime* can be said to present the foremost technique of the sublime as a method of demonstrating things pedagogically, practically eliminating its association with the faculty of imagination.

The sublime became really important in the British discussion, but the voice of Boileau is unmistakable in the English translation of Leonard Welsted in 1712.[46] The first source of the sublime is here said to be "a certain Force and Superiority of Genius, which prompts a Man to think Happily and Greatly." The chapter on *phantasia,* as in Boileau numbered XIII, commences as follows:

> There are other Images, my Illustrious young Friend, by some call'd Paintings, or Fictions, which are also of great use to give Discourse Pomp, Magnificence, and Weight. The Word Image, is taken in general for every Thought that is proper to produce an Expression, and that creates in the Mind a Picture of somewhat, be it in what manner it will. But it is yet received in a more particular and confined Sense, for those Discourses we make, when through any extraordinary trans-

port of Mind we seem to view the things we speak of, and when we place them in their full Light, before those who hear us.[47]

The chapter division and the expansion of *eidolopoiias* into "Paintings, or Fictions," as well as the translation "image," derive directly from Boileau. To be sure, this translation did not generate a great deal of interest in Longinus. The same year, Addison launched his discussion of imagination and its "greatness" in *The Spectator*, but the translation which was to set its mark was that of William Smith, first published in 1739 and then in several new editions. In this influential translation, Smith exploits the connection between image and imagination in a way fully compatible with the possibilities of the word *phantasia*. His rendering of the sources of the sublime in chapter VIII begins thus: "The First and most excellent of these is a Boldness and Grandeur in the Thoughts" – which is more succinct and loyal than Boileau and Welsted. Smith's rendering of chapter XV is as follows:

> VISIONS, which by some are called Images, contribute very much, my dearest Youth, to the Weight, Magnificence, and Force of Compositions. The Name of an Image is generally given to any Idea however represented in the Mind, which is communicable to others by Discourse, but a more particular Sense of it has now prevailed; "When the Imagination is so warm'd and affected, that you seem to behold yourself the very things you are describing, and to display them to the life before the Eyes of an Audience."[48]

Smith mostly speaks of "images," just as Boileau and Welsted did, but he adds one important feature: *imagination*. Longinus's words *hup' enthousiasmou kai pathous*, "through enthusiasm and passion," become "Imagination ... warm'd and affected." The translator's freedom is to recompense the ambiguity of *phantasia* by translating it as "image" and then inserting "imagination" by its side. This is not true to the wording of Longinus, but it sets the pace for any future reception. On the same page Smith then speaks of how "to move and strike the Imagination" and of the poet seeing "the Furies with the Eyes of his Imagination": in the former case "imagination" is a kind of interpretation of *pathêtikon* and *sunkekinêmenon*, "agitated," in the latter case it renders the verb *efantasthê*, which means that the poet has visualized that which he communicates to his audience. Smith's extrapolation of the faculty of imagination into the discussion of the literary technique of *phantasia* clearly mirrors the aesthetic discussion of his time – both as a reflection and as a stamp, making its imprint on generations to come.[49]

In Charles Carthy's translation of 1762, the first source of the sublime is reduced to "a *Richness of bold and happy Sentiments*," which certainly diverts attention from the imagination. On the other hand, in chapter XV he interpolates into "Visions or Images, as the Fictions of the Imagination are called by some," clearly marking the connection between literary technique and the faculty of imagination.[50]

Thus, the translations of Boileau and Welsted do not inspire an association between the literary technique and the mental faculty. It is with the translation of Smith that this is achieved: he is not able to render the homonymity between literary technique and mental faculty, *phantasia*, but he reconstructs it, firmly tying *image* to *imagination*.

Fantasy merges with fantasy

Much attention in *Peri hupsous* is focused on the soul of the speaker and things that can be regarded as psychological, even metaphysical. However, the word *phantasia* is used not of the imagination, but of a rhetorical figure. It was naturally connected to contemporary theories of the imagination, but Longinus keeps the discussion technical.[51] The sublime can in no way be reduced to a rhetorical figure, but one principal rhetorical figure can be attributed to the sublime: that of visualization. The explicit argument of *Peri hupsous* is based on a reorganization of the devices of diction: the figure *phantasia* is moved from the usual toolbox of *elocutio* to the discussion of the speaker's natural gifts. The implicit argument enforces the importance of the figure even more, as Longinus brings out and comments upon the figure lavishly even when it is not really the topic of discussion. This does not mean that Longinus does not hold *phantasia* to be a rhetorical device: it means that it is the essential rhetorical device. Neither does it mean that imagination is not important in the Longinian system: it is the mental faculty which makes the rhetorical figure so useful. Still, it is the literary technique, not the mental faculty *phantasia* which is Longinus's focus of attention. Longinus's method of approaching the sublime from his rhetorical standpoint opens the way for both continuity with regard to earlier rhetorical systems and deliverance from the traditional rules of rhetoric. Longinus does not define the sublime, but by connecting it to *phantasia* he delivers it from genre and topic.

The primary effect *of Peri hupsous* was the connection of the sublime to a particular set of motifs and scenes, often strongly passionate, but this effect was itself dependent upon the promotion of the rhetorical figure *phantasia*. During the 18th century, interpretations of *Peri hupsous* tied the sublime even more firmly to distinct motifs. As the sublime became more and more closely associated with the impact on the person experiencing it, a search began for objects that were apt to create the sublime state of mind. Thus, the sublime became even more loosely connected to language and text, and the objects or transmitters of the sublime could be anything magnificent or terrifying.[52] What is conveyed in the motifs and scenes of *Peri hupsous* is the literary technique of visualization. Longinus states that *phantasia* often involves the supernatural and the incredible, a use of the figure which is most easily connected to the forceful expressions of pre-romanticism. At the same time, the promotion *of phantasia* could exert an almost equal influence on neoclassicism. The distinction Longinus made between poetical and rhetorical *phantasia* was that the former leads to astonishment (*ekplêxis*), the latter to clarity (*enargeia*). The neoclassical emphasis on the dictum *ut pictura poesis* may thus be connected with the rhetorical rather than poetical use of *phantasia*. The lesson of visualization is technically quite the same in both uses; what differs is the ends.

Putting metaphor and other tropes in a rather remote place, the author of *Peri hupsous* propounded another aspect of figurative language as absolutely essential to the sublime. Of all rhetorical devices, *phantasia* could be described as the one that most efficiently manipulates the audience into following their (received) emotions instead of their intellect, and it must thus be considered from a rhetorical standpoint as one of the most pragmatic figures. Yet this same figure paradoxically became central to the development of the literary and theoretical tenets of pre-romanticism and romanticism.

The technical aspects *of Peri hupsous* are to some extent representative of the changes from classicism to pre-romanticism and romanticism. While allegory, metaphor and other tropes tend to be emphasized in most rhetorical systems, *Peri hupsous* gives the predominant place to *phantasia,* a figure that by definition lacks a tropic dimension even though it certainly may serve to make an allegory or other device effective. Visualization could be said to coincide with the general tendencies of pre-romanticism, as, for example, in the songs of Ossian or Gray's "Norse" poems. Soon, though, the images that corresponded to rhetorical *phantasia* began to convey more or less elaborate spheres of association. They became signs in a completely different way than metaphor and allegory. Although this well-known circumstance of course depended on a wide variety of developments in European literature, it may have had its direct theoretical counterpart in the influential speculations by both Burke and Kant about the sublime. In this way, the images of *phantasia* could obtain symbolic values, and, at that stage, the sublime changed identity and became part of romantic aesthetics. The development of romantic symbolism could lend authority from the blending of Aristotelian *phantasia* – the faculty of imagination – and Longinian *phantasia,* the rhetorical figure essential to the sublime. The two variants developed from the word for "appearing," becoming visible, but they did live rather separate lives until they were tied together in the 18th century.

In a sense, *phantasia* defines the nature of poetry and art in a manner closely connected with the term mimesis. Mimesis and *phantasia* both are – or effect – representations.[53] To a certain extent, the faculty of imagination can be equalled to mimesis-composition: it concerns *what* is thought of or evoked more than *how* this is presented. Even more, the rhetorical figure of *phantasia* corresponds to mimesis-representation: verbal representation is the means of suggestive discourse. Mimesis-representation in itself does not have to be overwhelming, but it should be effective, and as we have seen in Averroës and others, *representatio, evidentia,* or with Longinus's term *phantasia,* becomes the soul of poetry. His ideal of visualization comes rather close to that of Averroës and Mathias, but downplays metaphor. Longinus's *phantasia* belongs to mimesis-representation, but it expands into mimesis-composition as it is associated with the mental faculty – not restricted to "story" or "plot," but to a whole poetic universe.

CHAPTER NINE

The symbol and the categories of rhetoric

Even though the doctrine of imitation was increasingly questioned from the late 18th century onwards, the focus on mimesis-representation did not diminish but rather achieved a higher position than before, as language was appointed the foremost artistic medium. The new philosophical foundation of language in a sense strengthened the focus on the linguistic dimension of the soul of poetry. In the previous chapter, we saw how the practical literary thrust of sublime aesthetics was that of visualizing and "lively" discourse. It is therefore natural to raise the question of how the central phenomenon of romantic aesthetics, the symbol, can be understood in the light of mimesis-composition and mimesis-representation.[1] Addressing this question will clarify on the one hand how symbolic reference was principally handled within the rhetorical tradition, and on the other how romantic theoreticians developed the concepts and categories at hand to define the symbol.

We have seen how Tesauro broadened the issue of mimesis-representation into the universal, and how he included figures and things, not only words, among the metaphorical signs. In this respect he was anticipating the romantic theoreticians: his theoretical background was the tradition of exegetics where symbolic reference had been discussed and analyzed long before the symbol as an aesthetic device was launched by the romantics. In tandem with the exegetical system of referentiality being firmly established, it is surprising that so few attempts were made to incorporate the symbol among the techniques of rhetoric before romanticism. Even when the symbol had been established as fundamental, what we might call the romantic's soul of poetry, it seems to have been kept rather distinctly apart from the usual rhetorical techniques. Even if this can be partly explained by the growing rejection of rhetoric and of the notion that thought and expression (*logos-lexis, res-verba*) can be clearly separated, it displays an attitude which is very different from the present-day manner of discussing metaphor and symbol as more or less parallel means of poetic diction.

The early Church fathers defined allegory within hermeneutics differently than within rhetoric. Scripture was interpreted according to the system developed by Origen, Augustine and others, creating a hierarchy of meanings of the text. The first level, *sensus litteralis* (*historicus*), is the proper and manifest meaning of the words, with actual events being described. Then there are three levels of *sensus spiritualis*: *sensus allegoricus* is the level where events in the Old Testament prefigure events in the New Testament – often called the typological level; *sensus moralis* advises how man should behave and act: this is the practically didactic level; *sensus mysticus* (*anagogicus*) conveys insights of the highest matters and higher theology.[2]

The central difference between profane-rhetorical and sacred allegory is that while rhetorical allegory posits that words refer to things, sacred allegory posits that things (persons, events) refer to things. Thus Augustine is able to speak of *allegoria in factis,* as opposed to rhetoric's *allegoria in verbis.* Exegetical, typological allegory is not constituted by words used in a tropical way, but by things conveying an allegorical meaning – this is also the case with the symbol. Rhetorical allegory, as any other trope, has a sign which is substitutive: it is a word used in the "wrong" sense. It must be "translated" and thereafter substituted with the word which literally corresponds to the thing to which it refers (when we understand that the lion is a metaphor for Achilles, there is no actual lion left in the course of events).[3] In the sacred allegory and in the symbol, the sign is not substitutive but analogous: it remains on the level of content and simultaneously refers to something else. Augustine exemplifies the principle of sacred allegory with the two sons of Abraham: they keep their facticity in the story at the same time as they are signs for something else (they also keep their historical facticity, as opposed to the literary symbol which only needs to keep its facticity within the narrative). Thus rhetoric's point of departure is that it is the *signifier* of the sign that carries the reference, while in exegetics it is the *signified* of the sign that carries the reference. The sign of rhetoric is the word, the sign of exegetics is the thing which the word signifies. Augustine introduces this kind of allegory with a discussion of tropes, calling this analogous allegory *aenigma*.[4] Around the year 700, the venerable Bede brought in Augustine's definitions in his *De Schematibus et Tropis*, treating exegetic allegory among the tropes.[5] He does not discuss the word "symbol," only "allegory," but what he demonstrates is the analogous referentiality which is common to sacred allegory and symbolism. Augustine had prepared the ground for it, but in Bede it is presented in a very basic rhetorical survey, made in the same way as Donatus in his elementary *Ars maior*.

The curious thing is that Bede's manoeuvre of inserting exegetic allegory into the rhetorical toolbox did not become the dominating method of categorizing stylistic devices but remained an exception. It is especially remarkable that the demarcation beween profane and sacred, rhetoric and hermeneutics, could be withheld if one considers the many examinations of rhetorical figures in the Bible that were made during the Renaissance.[6] There are many examples of referentiality in literary practice that through the centuries have come close to appearing as symbolism: one of the more illustrious ones is Shakespeare's *Hamlet*, where four characters who have all lost their father reflect each other and thus the thematics of the drama in different ways. Even though allegory in facts instead of words, related to symbolism, was possible in literary practice, it does not seem to have been introduced into rhetorical theory more than only very occasionally. One important explanation, it will turn out, is the way in which the categories of composition and representation were conceived. In the following, I will try to demonstrate how a categorizing principle has deferred symbolism to the class of rhetorical argument rather than the class of elocution and how this determined the development of the romantic symbol.

Definitions of the symbol

The definitions of the symbol have been many and are not congruous even among the theoreticians of romanticism, but the essence can be summarized with J.W. von Goethe's polarization of allegory and symbol:

> The objects which are represented in this [the symbolic] manner seem to simply stand for themselves and yet they convey meaning in the deepest sense, because of the ideal which always brings with it the universal. If the symbolic points at anything more, outside the representation [*Darstellung*], it will always be in an indirect manner.
>
> …
>
> Now, there are also works of art which show off with sagacity, wit and gallantry. To these we count the allegorical ones: from them, one can at least expect the benefit that they also destroy interest in the representation as such, force the spirit back to itself and pull away from its eyes that which is really represented. The allegorical differs from the symbolic in that it refers directly, while the symbolic refers indirectly.[7]

In this quotation, the following aspects are especially worth noting:

- Since the rhetorical discussion of tropes and figures always originates in the pair *verbum-res,* it is practically impossible to use it for purposes of defining the symbol, since the sign of the symbol is factual and not to be eliminated from the content after its reference has been defined. Rhetoric presupposes a "proper" word for the thing, a *nomen proprium,* and a transferred word for it, a *nomen improprium.* (To say "lion" and mean a lion is proper usage, while saying "lion" and meaning Achilles is improper usage.) The use of tropes and especially metaphor resides to a large extent in the fact that the sign creates a semantic colouring of the thing referred to, but the sign is by definition substitutive and signals that it is to be translated and then removed from the content level of the text (we realize that there is no actual lion in the story). In contrast to this system, the symbol is not substitutive but analogous: the sign remains in the content and refers to something at the same time.
- Consequently, rhetoric posits a direct translatability which means that the thing referred to by the trope can be rationally and unambiguously defined, while the romantic symbol is vague and intuitive. Within rhetoric this is a pedagogical simplification and a normative demand for clarity – which certainly does not preclude fascination for

obscuritas.[8] (And it is not always the case that the referentiality of the symbol is described as untranslatable.)

- The trope refers *directly* – the reference being its point of departure – while the symbol refers *indirectly* – the phenomenon which constitutes the sign exists in itself (at least within the fiction), and in addition it refers to something else. This makes it difficult to define a symbolic sign, while (theoretically) it is always easy, not to say necessary, to define a trope.
- Additionally, Goethe and others elsewhere speak of allegory as rational and discursive, while symbol is described as intuitive and condensed.[9]

In spite of the fundamental differences between rhetoric's tropes – allegory being defined as a trope comprising not a word but a whole statement[10] – and the symbol, they can in some respects be discussed within the same parameters. The allegory and the symbol are both defined as a relation where the universal is represented through the particular: if the difference is said to consist in the allegory beginning in the universal and finding an image of it in the particular, with the symbol beginning in the particular and letting it mirror the universal (again with Goethe's words[11]), the difference must be sought in the authorial intention or in the genesis of the work. The above quotation from Goethe may seem clear, but the sentence preceding it implies that the difference is constituted by a certain *emotion*: the objects represented are determined "by a deep emotion, which – if it is pure and natural – coincides with the highest and best objects, at best making them symbolic."[12] Again, we lack clear distinctions in the pursuit of defining the symbol.

In practice, it may be difficult to separate allegory from symbol, not only because the reference of allegory may be impossible to define clearly, but also because whoever wishes to discuss a symbol actually needs to discuss its reference. Still, tropes such as the metaphor resemble the symbol more than the allegory does, since these signs consist in single words or objects, while the allegory consists in a longer sequence of words or objects.[13] In this respect the symbol (but not Augustine's *allegoria in factis*) comes closer to metaphor: they are both non-discursive).[14]

Augustine and Bede placed sacred allegory among the tropes; in practice, separating the symbol from the tropes in accordance with entirely clear criteria is not easy. Yet their way of placing symbolism in the category of *elocutio* did not catch on. Instead, symbolism appealed to another principle of categorizing within the rhetorical system.

Outside the system of tropes

In the *Poetria* of Master Mathias, as discussed in chapter three, persuasion was of the utmost importance. As was briefly mentioned, Mathias elaborates on *consideratio*, Averroës and his version of Aristotle's *opsis*, the meaning of which has changed from "spectacle" into a kind of persuasion:

> *Consideracio*, however, is nothing but the presentation of uncertain things – not, however, through rational arguments or persuasions (since this is not the poet's business) but through visualizations so certain and plausible that the matter does not seem to have been made up. This happens when things pertaining not at all or little to the theme are nevertheless inserted as signs [*res ... intersignia*] of an event. An example of this is the passage in St. John on the miracle of the five pieces of bread: "There was much grass in the place," etc.[15]

Mathias's example is the story from the gospel according to John of how Christ fed 5,000 people with two fish and five loaves of bread. This incredible story, Mathias explains, is made more credible by virtue of the fertile grass on the site. The grass is actually there on the level of content, but is simultaneously a sign of abundance, referring to the feeding of the assembled people. It strengthens the narrative not rationally, but semiotically – through its figurative (universal) sense of physical and spiritual abundance. Mathias does not specify the meaning of this concrete sign but obviously interprets it in the light of the following lines of the biblical quotation: "Then Jesus declared, 'I am the bread of life. He who comes to me will never go hungry, and he who believes in me will never be thirsty'" (John 6:35).

Mathias's focus on visual effect is the same as we saw in chapter three on how mimesis was transformed into visualization, but here it is another kind of poetic proof, strengthening the impact of the discourse, residing in content rather than form. The technique of strengthening the argument, as it were, is related to classical rhetorical argumentation with different kinds of proof – and in *Poetria*, this passage is followed by a discourse on classical *loci* (*who, what, where, by means of what, why, how* and *when*). Since Mathias discusses these issues in relation not to rhetoric but to poetics, this kind of proof is not rational but "imaginative." However, the foundation of the literary device Mathias here describes is clearly rhetorical proof. In his *Institutio oratoria*, Quintilian speaks of *signum* (*sêmeion, indicium, vestigium*) as a sensible sign which supports a proposition of the state of things, as when blood indicates that a murder has been committed.[16] It is a sign *that* something has happened rather than a sign *for* something, but the central issue is that it is a sign which supports a proposition. This is the kind of rationale that Mathias applies: his *res intersignia* correspond to *signum*. The sign is analogous: concrete and factual on the level of content. The reference is vague, but apparent, concerning the relation between physical and spiritual hunger and saturation. The grass is something in itself and also points beyond itself, without giving up its proper meaning. The sign is also said to be indirect, insofar as it is only partly relevant to the proposition. Had it been a metaphor, one would have had to interpret it and then substitute it with the referent. Mathias's description of how the sign works not rationally but visually-imaginatively also corresponds well with Goethe's criteria for the symbol.

Mathias's discussion of *res intersignis* is a highly illustrative attempt to expand the rhetorical repertoire with literary forms from the exegetical tradition. In doing so, Mathias does not try to group symbol among the tropes: instead, he connects it with argument and proof, and comes close to Quintilian's *signum* – the primary differences being the context in which it is discussed and the nature of the example. At the same time it should be recalled that Mathias regards *representatio*, visualization, as the soul of poetry, and his *res intersignis* is an example of what may be visualized. Here, it might be appropriate to bring to mind that an important aspect of the romantic symbol is that "liveliness" which is often mentioned, for instance by A.W. Schlegel and also Kant, who heavily emphasized *hupotuposis*, synonymous with the visualizing technique of *evidentia, representatio, enargeia*.[17] Still, when Mathias introduces *res intersignis*, very similar to the symbol, in the rhetorical system, he does not place it among the tropes or figures. Instead of categorizing it as *elocutio,* he refers it to *inventio*. Thus, the symbolic is treated not as a stylistic device but as an argumentative technique: not on the level of form, but on the level of content.

In contrast to the rhetorical system where word refers to thing (*verbum-res*), Augustine concluded that events and things in the Bible refer to things (*res-res, facta-res*): this is the well-known typological allegory. The sign is concrete and actual on the level of content – analogous with the referent. Both sign and referent are there simultaneously, while the sign, for example, of a metaphor is substitutive. His definition falls outside of the rhetorical system of tropes, but this kind of reference is the foundation of the romantic symbol. It was defined within hermeneutics but was not congruous with rhetoric's system of tropes and figures.

However, this does not mean that analogous referentiality was incongruous with rhetoric's categories on the whole. As we have seen, Mathias dealt with that kind of sign under the category of *inventio* instead of *elocutio*. This seems to be a natural way of reasoning within the rhetorical categories: in fact, analogous referentiality had already been established there. An essential kind of rhetorical argument is the *exemplum*. When the rhetorician advances a good or bad example in order to inspire, deter, or to point out a precedence, for instance, he for the most part uses a person from history or myth. Whether the person has actually existed or not is irrelevant in this context: the person is actual on the level of content and is posited as an image for illuminating a particular situation. If, for example, Alexander the Great is referred to as an example of the valour of a commander, he becomes a sign for that abstraction and simultaneously for the person discussed in the context. The *exemplum* is categorized as a kind of argument and is therefore discussed as part of *inventio,* not *elocutio,* although it offers an analogous referentiality. In literary texts it often functions as a kind of simple symbolism, for example in 17th- and 18th-century novels where new characters are introduced in the story as insertions which mirror the protagonist in a positive or negative manner.

This mechanism is apparent not only in Mathias, but also when the symbol is treated in romantic theory. When Friedrich Schelling described how the allegorical image *refers* but the symbolic image *is,* he used the following example:

> So the holy Magdalene not only *means* regret, but is living regret itself. So the image of the holy Cecilia, patron saint of music, is not an allegorical image but a symbolic one, while it exists independently of its meaning, without losing its meaning. So too the image of Christ, since it lucidly represents the whole identity between divine and human.[18]

With classical terminology Magdalene is a perfect *exemplum* when the issue is regret and penance. As a sign, she exists and refers simultaneously, which allows Schelling to define her as a symbol (but observe how unambiguously the reference of this symbol is defined!). Allegorical art, then, is that kind which shows allegorical figures that obviously only mean something else and are not in themselves factual. However, Schelling underscores that paintings with historical motifs are symbolic for the reason that history itself is a form of the symbolic.[19] History consists in concrete, actual signs for diverse universal truths and is thus symbolic. Also the representation of history's *exempla* becomes symbolic. In addition, rhetorical discussions seldom find a need to define the reference of *exempla* with precision: this vagueness also resembles that of the symbol. The symbol was not much discussed as part of rhetoric's *exemplum* either, but this was obviously the natural connection for a theoretician such as Schelling to make.

While the *exemplum* implies a narrative, there is also the kind of proof that is less discursive: the *signum, sêmeion, indicium* or *vestigium*, physical things which prove a fact, and which Mathias turned into a poetic technique and labelled *res intersignis*.[20] Both these kinds of referentiality belong to rhetorical argument and proof, clearly separated from *elocutio*. Thus, they are separated from artistic diction, but by definition they come to bear a close resemblance to the symbol.

The word symbol

The word *symbol* was used frequently even before it became a romantic-aesthetic phenomenon, but synonymously with words such as allegory, hieroglyph, number, emblem or mathematical symbols.[21] Etymologically, it means "forging together" and its primary meaning is a "tally, i.e. each of two halves or corresponding pieces" which prove the holder's identity or confirm a treaty, etc.[22] Aristotle, who uses the word in *On Interpretation* in the sense of "sign" without a figurative dimension, regarded a spoken word as a *symbolon* for the referent, with the written word a *symbolon* for the spoken word.[23] The word appears in the work of Renaissance humanists in hieroglyphics and emblematics: here it is commonly used for images that carry a particular reference. A *Dissertatio de Symbolis*, printed and defended in Uppsala in 1672, can be considered to present rather representative notions. It is here stated that the symbol is an *indicium*, a sign for something hidden, and so hieroglyphs, emblems, parables, *aenigmata* and *apologi* can be joined together under the rubric *symbolum*.[24] In the same vein, the symbol is defined as an obscure means of learning and ability to discern true from false, "a sign which symbolically suggests and figures."[25]

Words used synonymously with *symbolum* are *indicium* and *signum* – terms that were central in rhetorical discussions of argument and proof. It is not evident whether *symbolum* is defined as a concrete, analogous sign or as a substitutive one. The *Dissertatio* seems to admit both, since the subdivisions hieroglyph and emblem are images and thus concrete signs, while parable and *aenigma* can be understood as verbal discourses, that is, substitutive signs like the rhetorical allegory. Even if the definition is not entirely clear, the examples that are given demonstrate how the symbol was usually understood. By way of introduction, the symbol is ascribed the meaning of rings and coins used to seal treaties. Thereafter, the symbol is exemplified with Egyptian hieroglyphs and Scythian symbols in, for example, the form of animals which have been used in the place of letters (*pro literis*). Reference is here made to Olaus Magnus, who in his *History of the Nordic Peoples* asserted that the inhabitants of the North had "used images of animals in the place of letters."[26] The examples concern ideographic alphabets, corresponding to the letters, but ideographic alphabets employ a kind of natural signs that are considered to convey – or hide – further meanings.[27]

While no unequivocal definition is established, the examples bring forth signs that are things, not words. The most striking example is not intended as an example but demonstrates how closely symbolism is connected to the exegetic and hermeneutic sphere: in the last line of the preface, a prayer is directed to God, "You who have deigned to show Yourself to man in the symbol of a dove."[28] This example demonstrates that the function of the ideogram as a letter is secondary and the thing itself primary: the sign is veritably concrete and actual, referring without losing its own facticity.

On the whole, the dissertation treats the "symbol" as a thing, or a word or an image representing a thing, which is factual on the level of content and refers to something else. At the same time, Tesauro in his mannerist poetics, as seen earlier, spoke of metaphor in a very broad sense, but seems to have developed a similar view on the symbolic. He distinguishes between "Argutezza *Verbale, Lapidaria,* e *Simbolica,*" and since he has made not only *argutezza* but also metaphor into an overarching principle of poetry and art, he can then speak of "Metafora in *Oggetto* & in *Attione.*"[29] To Tesauro, metaphor is practically any artifact, but the symbolic sign is concrete and actual, and even includes dance.

Poetry, painting, symbolism and visuality

Every image is a language *in rebus,* while the text is a language *in verbis,* to borrow a distinction from emblematics.[30] In contrast to poetry, the art of painting cannot use substitutive signs. What is painted on the canvas is on the level of content and cannot be removed. Even an allegorical personification, for example of Fortune, cannot be substituted in the same way as a literary trope. The limits are not entirely clear: an element of a painting can more or less signal its own status as illusory, and the disparate elements in a literary allegory which sticks to the allegorical level cannot be removed. Yet it is impossible to accomplish a metaphor in a painting. Only language admits that kind of substitutive reference, and the foundation of the trope system presupposes that the trope is substitutive and signals that it should be substituted.

The lapdog which in paintings such as van Eyck's *Arnolfini's Wedding* represents fidelity is perhaps the closest one comes to a metaphor in painting. The dog appears in the painting by virtue of its reference, but it still cannot be substituted: it both *is* and *refers.* Because of the preconditions of language, this kind of analogous reference – a precondition of the medium – has no place in the trope system. If painting tries to emulate poetry's metaphor the result will be (more or less) a symbol. If poetry tries to emulate painting's symbol the result will be not a metaphor but a literary symbol: this seems to be what happens with the advent of romanticism, when poetry is discussed with less restrictions from rhetoric but under the influence of the other arts.

Still, the distinction between allegory and symbol is often vague: how does one decide whether the thing represented takes its point of departure in the particular or the universal? And if one can establish that the point of departure is the particular, how does one know that it is symbolic and not simply void of meaning? To Goethe, as to Kant and A.W. Schlegel, a crucial criterion seems to be liveliness, *Lebendigkeit*:

> It makes a great difference if the poet searches for the particular through the universal, or sees the universal in the particular. From the former arises allegory, where the particular is only valid as an example of the universal. The latter is really the nature of poetry: it formulates a particular without thinking of or referring to the universal. He who expresses this particular in a lively way attains the universal as well without thinking of it or noticing it at a late stage.[31]

And as we have seen, Kant insisted on *hupotuposis*, synonymous with *evidentia*, and A.W. Schlegel on *das lebendige*. Thus, it would seem, we are back in the familiar discussions of visualizing techniques. The ideals and aesthetic underpinnings vary considerably over time, but the theoretical considerations on visualization are a matter of relative constancy from Aristotle to the romantics. At this late stage, it seems reasonable to understand the will to visualization partly as a consequence of the influence from the art of painting. While the visualizing techniques can be said to reside in mimesis-representation, it is clear that the soul of poetry transgresses the dichotomy of *logos* and *lexis*. The symbol now seems to find its place in *inventio* and *dispositio*, mimesis-composition – as the soul of poetry did according to Aristotle, albeit on the basis of other definitions.

* * *

The symbolic did not find a natural place in the rhetorical system, but in different contexts it was categorized either as *elocutio*, that is, in the sphere of mimesis-representation, or as *inventio*, that is, closer to the sphere of mimesis-composition. Augustine and Bede treated it among the tropes although there was no real room for concrete, actual signs and analogous reference there. Mathias, in turn, treated it not among the tropes but among the arguments, and in so doing he chose the same way of categorizing as Schelling would do much later. This seems to have been the maneouvre most consistent with the rhetorical system, since it already contained the arguments and especially *exemplum* with its analoguous referentiality – not least as the symbol originally is a sign of identity or a treaty, etc., carrying with it from the very beginning the sense of "proof." Symbol and allegory are commonly compared and discussed together, but this does not mean that they can be categorized together. It seems to be this dynamic vacillation between categories that lies at the heart of the evolution of romanticism. The symbol becomes a poetic technique, but relates to content rather than form, and its reference will thus always be more vague than in a metaphor. This of course suits the romantic will to bridge oppositions and blend content and form. It also corresponds to the predilection for *obscuritas*, where it has been shown how obscurity and intuitive interpretation has been much easier to defend within Christian exegetics and modern aesthetics than within conventional rhetoric.[32]

CHAPTER TEN

Emotions and the system of genres

The texts which have been discussed in the preceding chapters all concern the issue of emotions in different ways. As we have seen, emotions became more and more important in the theories of poetry and especially when lyric became a dominating genre. However, one crucial aspect of the development of genre theory is the ambivalent attitude towards emotions. The history of the theories of emotions is indeed diversified, but at the heart of the matter, in the words *pathos* and *passio* themselves, resides an anxiety concerning the lack of control, the suffering and even sinfulness of being subjected to emotions, or, rather, passions.[1] Pleasure and emotion have been a sensitive topic throughout history, and our attention will in this chapter be directed to how the development of the system of genres and aesthetics can be understood in the light of emotions. It is a well-known fact that the rise of aesthetics in the 18th century comprised a new appraisal of sensual impression (*aisthêsis*) and sensuality. Simultaneously, lyric – closely associated with emotion – was appointed a major genre next to epic and drama. This appraisal of lyric and emotion could hardly have taken place earlier in history, since it depends partly on scientific progress, not least within psychology, and partly on an apparent change of moral values connected with emotions.

The development within the system of poetics can be described as a continuous negotiation of categories – not in the same way as the vacillation between mimesis-composition and mimesis-representation hitherto discussed, but in a related manner. Within Aristotelian discussions room is made to transfer the emotions from the role of instrument and effect to the role of object of poetry. At the same time, the shift from an instrumental function of emotions to a place as object of poetry seems to be the result of different attempts to categorize the arts as analogous to one another. In the Renaissance attempts were made to define painting through the categories of rhetoric, and aestheticism attempted to describe poetry not through the categories of rhetoric as before, but rather in the light of the other arts. The incongruity between word and image effected dislocations between content and form, with the discarding of rhetoric by aesthetics being the result. These dislocations appear to be most visible concerning the treatment of emotions.

The instrumental emotions

Although Aristotle appointed fable, character and thinking to be tragedy's objects, the first chapter of his *Poetics* made room for the emotions as an important object of poetry. He did so by comparing poetry with the art of dancers: "they too, through rhythms translated into movements, create mimesis of character, emotions [*pathê*], and actions" (1447a).[2] This does not necessarily imply an understanding of poetry as mimesis of character, emotion(s) and actions: the passage might be understood as concerning not poetry but only dance. However, the whole context serves as a foil for a comparison with poetry, and the correspondence with the ensuing description of poetry's objects makes it close at hand to believe that emotions can be an object of poetry even though they are not discussed as such there. *Pathê* is here placed in a central position, substituting poetry's thought as a main object – "actions" being considered equivalent to *muthos*, which is later said to be the mimesis of actions. This lays the ground for two assumptions: that in dance the counterpart of thought is *pathos* and that *pathos* must be an object of poetry although it is not further discussed in that way. Clearly, the important objects of poetry are *muthos*, character and thought.

The meaning of *pathê* and *pathos* is not self-evident. The comparison with dance makes "emotion" plausible, but elsewhere in the *Poetics*, *pathos* mainly means "suffering." This is evident in chapter 11, where Aristotle defines *pathos* as a component of the plot, on a par with reversal (*peripeteia*) and recognition (*anagnôrisis*): "suffering is a destructive or painful action, such as public deaths, physical agony, woundings, etc."[3] This meaning applies to other occurences as well, and in the same vein Aristotle can speak of a work as *pathêtikos* or *apathês*, meaning that it portrays or does not portray suffering.[4] On one occasion (1455a31), *pathos* is said to be conveyed by gestures and is exemplified as distress or anger: the word here seems to mean "emotion" rather than suffering, while *pathos* is not a part of *muthos*, not an object of tragedy, but rather an instrument. Thus, on the whole and especially considered as an object, *pathos* means "suffering" or "infliction" in the *Poetics*. It is clearly part of the content, that is, an object, and when *pathos* is mentioned as an object in the first chapter its meaning can be seen to refer to "suffering" rather than "emotions." Thus, the description of *pathos* as "a destructive or painful action" appears to imply that *pathos* is subsumed within *action*.

Aristotle certainly takes interest in the emotions of the audience, as an *effect* of poetry, but he does not use the word *pathos* in that connection. In the well-known discussion of *katharsis*, purifying of emotions, he uses the qualifier *pathêma*, related to, but apparently not the same as, *pathos*:

> Tragedy, then, is mimesis of an action which is elevated, complete, and of magnitude; in language embellished by distinct forms in its sections; employing the mode of enactment, not narrative; and through pity and fear accomplishing the catharsis of such emotions [*pathêmatôn katharsis*].[5]

Central to the definition of tragedy in the sixth chapter, then, are the emotions of *eleos* and *phobos*, pity and fear. This, it can be suggested, is part of Aristotle's focus on the didactic value of poetry: these emotions are a response to the sufferings portrayed, and, as Halliwell puts it, "[t]he combination of pity and fear ... represents tragedy as tapping a deep and quasi-universal sense of human vulnerability. ... Tragedy, on this view, contains patterns of suffering which explore the experience of limitations upon human control of life."[6] The meaning of *katharsis* is controversial, but it seems that Aristotle, in contrast to Plato's critique of the emotions effected by tragedy in the *Republic*, viewed *katharsis* in accordance with his overall positive opinion that emotions are connected to experience and learning.[7] Behind this opinion was Aristotle's way of defining emotion as supporting reason, in contrast to earlier theories that opposed emotion to reason.[8]

While Plato believed that the emotions aroused by tragedy made people more susceptible to such emotions in real life, Aristotle's *katharsis* could thus be understood as a "resistance *both* to the idea of emotions as dangerous *and* to the notion of increased susceptibility."[9] When speaking of emotions, it makes a great difference which kinds of emotions are dealt with: fear and pity are the least sensual and pleasurable emotions, and thus the emotions most readily legitimized. In other places, Plato severely criticized aspects of representation that concern poetry more connected with lyric than with drama and epic. Especially in *Gorgias* he describes rhetoric as *hêdonê*, implying exaggerated pleasure and lust, flattery, feigning, make-up and short-term delights. This expressly applies to poetry, although theatre is also mentioned, but any sensual delight in words is seen to be responsible for exaggerated pleasures and voluptuousness.[10] In the *Republic*, Plato is less harsh, but when the imitator poet is said to know nothing of reality, only appearance, it is not only his degree of knowledge but also his seductive instruments – words, phrases, colours, rhythm, metre, harmony, adornment, seeing things only through words – that are highligted.[11] These charges are not specifically levelled at drama, but at all seductive verbal representation. So, also in the *Republic*, Plato transfers linguistic desire to bodily desire:

> [I]n regard to the emotions of sex and anger, and all the appetites and pains and pleasures of the soul which we say accompany all our actions, the effect of poetic imitation is the same. For it waters and fosters these feelings when what we ought to do is to dry them up, and it establishes them as our rulers when they ought to be ruled.[12]

Plato levels invectives against poetry because it is seen to create illusions and distract audiences from following the right course of action, because mimesis is associated with malign and demeaning feigning, and since rhetoric indulges in sensuous voluptuousness not least through pleasing language, thus seducing audiences. Although seldom explicitly discussed, this "fear" of voluptuous language seems to have been more or less commonplace within the rhetorical tradition, and it created a need to distance oneself from association with such voluptuousness.[13] When Aristotle tries to establish poetry as something good, he naturally refrains from speaking of the pleasures of poetry or emotions related to pleasure.

Aristotle uses *hêdonê*, "pleasure," and *hêdus*, "pleasurable," several times in the *Poetics*, but he clearly makes it dependent on the legitimate emotions pity and fear, and on a general aspect of learning. Summarizing – and privileging – tragedy's advantages ahead of those of epic, he concludes that music and spectacle add pleasure to the tragedy, a statement, however, that comes at the very end of the treatise.[14] Already in chapter 4 he relates that images may give pleasure because of their colour, which actualizes Plato's overall critique of representation in words and painting.[15] However, the sentence is introduced by heavy stress on the real pleasure of mimesis: "understanding gives great pleasure not only to philosophers but likewise to others too."[16] The pleasure of poetry thus comes mainly from understanding, and from pity and fear which are means of understanding. In this way, Aristotle distances poetry considerably from the Platonic critique of linguistic voluptuousness and decadence. This should perhaps be understood as part of Aristotle's apologetic project, a cautious stance which may also explain why he dissociates poetry from the actors' histrionic activities and does not discuss lyric together with tragedy and epic: lyric was associated with voluptuousness and could thus incite Platonic critique. Defining the soul of poetry as *lexis*, mimesis-representation, would have been to subject it to Plato's critique of rhetoric and representation. The soul of poetry being *muthos*, content and structure, poetry becomes less reproachable.

It would be difficult to argue strongly for this being the reason for Aristotle's negligence of lyric, pleasure and emotions, but it appears to be part of the general background to his *Poetics* and might explain the absence of lyric in his discussion of genres. It is also apparent that the subsequent tradition as a whole displayed a great interest in placing emotions within poetics. Aristotle's early words on *pathos* as an object of art, replacing thought, were sometimes interpreted as "suffering," sometimes as "emotions" or "passions." So, for example, Robortello in 1548 translates it as "perturbationes," heavy emotions, while Castelvetro in 1570 retains "suffering" in the form of "tormenti."[17]

If we interpret Aristotle's *pathê* in the first chapter as "emotions," it is an object which is not further discussed. But if we interpret it as "suffering," it is an object that forms part of the plot as stated in chapter 11. More significant, however, are the emotions pity and fear: importantly, they are not objects of poetry, but effects. Thus, the important emotions in Aristotle's *Poetics* are neither part of *logos* nor *lexis*, rather they are instrumental: effects on the audience, means of influencing, manoeuvering, achieving reactions and insights. This is entirely in accordance with the rhetorical view of emotions. The instrumental value of emotions was accentuated in Averroës's interpretation of the *Poetics*, as discussed in chapter two: poetry's aim here, just as rhetoric's, is to persuade, but while rhetoric uses rational argument, poetry uses imaginative persuasion, which obviously caters to the emotions. The imagery which becomes the soul of poetry according to Averroës, as we have seen, is very much influenced by *On the Soul*.

The emotions turned into objects of poetry

After the sharpened instrumentalization in Averroistic theory – as it was received in learned Europe – the emotions gradually come to be considered not as instruments so much as a focus of human interest. In this chapter only a few examples will be used to draw an outline, with Minturno's *L'arte Poetica* from 1564, which was only briefly mentioned in the chapter on the Italian Renaissance, as one of the most illuminating examples. We have seen that Robortello in 1548 infinitely widened the range of poetic objects, but Minturno speaks of poetry on the whole as imitation of people – an imitation which is made in different ways. In accordance with Aristotle, Minturno initially speaks of *what* is imitated, with which *means*, and *how*, but then concludes: "The things we imitate are customs (*costumi*), emotions (*affetti*) and actions (*fatti*) of people."[18]

While Aristotle in his main discussion stated that fable, character and thought were poetry's objects, Minturno picks up the comparison with dance that Aristotle had made in passing before explaining the different parts of poetry. Minturno's "actions" and "customs" correspond with Aristotle's fable and character respectively, but Minturno simply swaps Aristotle's thought for "emotions." Actions, just like in Aristotle's first chapter, can be understood as the material of *muthos*, and accordingly Minturno later says that *favola* is the central issue.[19] The significant change is that Aristotle's words on dance have become the overarching definition of poetry, *pathê* being understood as emotions, not suffering. The emotions, which according to Minturno can be pleasant *affetti* as in the poems of Petrarch, or *passiones* which are fairly equivalent to sins, are important not least as means of portraying customs, *costumi* (not entirely equivalent to Aristotle's *êthê*).[20] In that respect, emotions are used instrumentally here, too, but in an indirect way. The emotions taken up by Minturno belong to content: they are defined as objects of poetry.

Another interesting trait in Minturno may be connected to his view on emotions as an object of poetry. His *L'arte Poetica* is a very early example of the tripartite genre theory which would have its breakthrough in the 18th century.[21] While Aristotle's system made drama and epic the main genres, tripartite genre theory added lyric. Although the tripartite genre theory is closely associated with the development of the fine arts (as treated in chapter 6), Minturno had already offered an example of it 200 years earlier. He elaborately discusses the lyric, or "melic" poetry, and evidently associates it with emotions, both positive ones and those which are sinful, the "pathetic" ones. However, he does not define lyric as a genre of emotions, at least not directly. Instead, he underscores that lyric comes from God and relates it to prayer and thanksgiving.[22] Thus, he can be said to tie lyric to emotions, but to such emotions that are guaranteed as being legitimate, deriving from love for God. At that point in time, it may not have been possible to emphasize emotions more unreservedly, not even after having divided them into good ones and bad ones.

Minturno, by associating lyric with emotions, but making them both – in the origin of lyric – derive from God and subordinating them under the intention to display customs, Aristotle's character, is able at once to introduce emotions as an object of poetry and to place lyric as a genre on a par with epic and drama. Although the role of emotions is not entirely clear, since they become a means for portraying customs, Minturno's need to legitimize them by connecting lyric's emotionality to godly love seems considerable.

While Minturno demonstrates an attempt to assign to lyric the status as the unquestioned third genre, it was during the 18th century, and as most elaborated in the work of Charles Batteux, that this attempt was realized. Batteux defined the common principle of the arts as *imitation* in the sense of representation, developing Aristotle's definitions, with the object becoming the distinctive criterion separating lyric from the other genres. While the primary object of epic and drama is actions, lyric resorts to emotions. Since this was the first comprehensive examination of the fine arts and the first comprehensive discussion of genre where lyric was defined as a distinct genre, *Les beaux arts réduits à un même principe* at the middle of the 18th century marks a crucial turn. Emotions had earlier been seen primarily as instruments for persuading and influencing, and as instruments they could not be defined in relation to the system of genres. At best, it seems that they could be subordinated by Minturno under the objects, but only as instruments used to portray customs and people. The definition of a lyric genre, it appears, could only take place by redefining emotions from instruments into objects, and this was possible when emotions were not associated so strongly with vice. Another precondition for lyric to become one of the main genres, within the theoretical system, appears to have been that poetry as a whole now came to be considered not from the viewpoint of rhetoric, but from the viewpoint of the other arts.

EMOTIONS AND MEDIA

The rhetorical system had before the 18th century dominated not only the view of literature, but also the view of the sister arts. That is, rhetoric was also used to define, primarily, painting. Batteux is hardly representative of the novelties of aestheticism, but he is highly representative of the theory of the fine arts and the tripartite genre theory. In order to structure the tripartite genre theory, he had to put forward emotions and lyric. Thus, it is possible to make a simplified historical line which charts how emotions were redefined from instruments to objects, a line, it is possible to conclude, that was fundamental for the development of the fine arts. But how did this redefinition take place? It was fulfilled at a stage when rhetoric was being discarded as an explanatory model – and yet it appears to have been a result of the (considered) value of rhetoric as an explanatory model.

By definition, rhetoric's theory of figures is based on the human body. This is quite natural, as rhetoric was from the beginning developed for oral situations. As rhetoric was adapted for a written culture, elements such as *memoria* and *actio* were weakened, but their techniques nevertheless lived on. The nucleus of the art of pleasant and effective formulation, *elocutio,* is the body. *Schêma,* the Greek word for the Latin *figura,* means "gesture": the rhetorical figure should thus be understood as a recreation of the speaker's gesture.[23] The rhetorical devices, collectively, should function in the same way as the speaker's corporeal expressions. Large parts of rhetoric – mainly the physical expressions and the verbal ones, the figures – deal with the possibility of exploiting the audience's emotions in order to win the case. Within the rhetorical concept, emotions are an essential instrument in argumentation. Quintilian's description is striking:

> [W]here force has to be brought to bear on the judges' feelings and their minds distracted from the truth, there the orator's true work begins. ... Of course, proofs may lead the judges to *think* our Cause the better one, but it is our emotional appeals that make them also *want* it to be so; and what they want, they also believe. For as soon as they begin to be angry or to feel favourably disposed, to hate or to pity, they fancy that it is now their own case that is being pleaded, and just as lovers cannot judge beauty because their feelings anticipate the perception of their eyes, so also a judge who is overcome by his emotions gives up any idea of inquiring into truth; he is swept along by the tide, as it were, and yields to the swift current.[24]

The power of the emotions being considered so great, the other side of the coin will be that what the rhetorician most fears is an adversary who exploits emotions more efficiently than himself. The emotions are instrumental, they are part of the physical performance and the verbal figures, *form*. The art of painting, seen from this perspective, also imitates the gestures and expressions of living bodies. However, it does so in a much more direct manner than literature: it represents the gestures and expressions of the speaking or acting body in a portrait. The rhetoric of the image will be to represent gestures which, in turn, represent emotions, and this means that the emotions turn into objects. Whoever interprets an image rhetorically will have to read gestures, facial expressions, etc., in content rather than in form. The mechanism at work here is that while poetry consists in verbal representation, form, painting consists in content. To rhetoric and poetry, viewed from a rhetorical point of view, emotions are instruments and form, in painting they become object and content.

Evidently, this is a generalization and there certainly are exceptions. Painting can, for instance, use colours, light and perspective to affect the audience's emotions. And the rhetorical view of poetry entails that one way of using emotions instrumentally is to represent them in content: exemplary visualizations of what happens to the choleric, greedy, etc. Still, the following proposition seems reasonable: how the inner is represented, i.e. how emotions are made into objects, was more a matter for painting than poetry. For literature – seen through rhetoric – the issue was rather how to use emotions as instruments. In the former case emotions are primarily objects, in the latter instruments. While these are tendencies, not all-encompassing truths, they are important, since the question of how emotions were defined – explicitly or implicitly, consciously or unconsciously – is vital to genre theory and thus to the development of the fine arts. This becomes clearer in the theory of painting proposed by Leon Battista Alberti.

RHETORIC APPLIED ONTO PAINTING

The analogy between poetry and painting is impossible to avoid, and during the Renaissance a number of attempts to define painting – and music – with the categories of rhetoric were made.[25] Rhetoric was simply the system closest at hand. In comparing poetry and painting it becomes natural to identify rhetoric's *inventio* and *dispositio* with the plan and outline of the painting, while *elocutio* corresponds to colour – entirely in accordance with the notion of *colores rhetorici,* the ornaments of language.[26] When Leon Battista Alberti wrote his *De Pictura* (1435), he modelled it on the structure of Quintilian's rhetorical treatise with remarkable consistency.[27] He speaks of the painting's *compositio,* corresponding to rhetoric's *dispositio,* and *historia,* corresponding – but not identical – to rhetoric's *inventio.*[28] In this passage, Alberti distinctly treats rhetoric's *inventio, dispositio* and *elocutio*:

> We divide painting into three parts, and this division we learn from Nature herself. As painting aims to represent things seen, let us note

> how in fact things are seen. In the first place, when we look at a thing, we see it as an object which occupies a space. The painter will draw around this space, and he will call this process of sketching the outline, appropriately, *circumscriptio*. Then, as we look, we discern how the several surfaces of the object seen are fitted together; the artist, when drawing these combinations of surfaces in their correct relationship, will properly call this *compositio*. Finally, in looking we observe more clearly the colours of surfaces; the representation in painting of this aspect, since it receives all its variations from light, will aptly here be termed *receptio luminum*.[29]

Circumscriptio structurally corresponds to *inventio, compositio* to *dispositio* and *receptio luminum,* the reception of light which comprises colour,[30] to *elocutio. Circumscriptio* concerns the lines drawn,[31] sketching what will then be ordered and clothed in colours. To these, Alberti adds *historia,* which can be broadly understood as the subject matter, the story to be related. In that respect *historia* resembles *inventio,* but Alberti links it to *compositio,* since it concerns the order of the whole.[32]

Alberti makes the usual comparison between *elocutio* and colour and then posits, somewhat vaguely, *circumscriptio* and *compositio* as the equivalents of *inventio/dispositio*. It may thus seem that literature and painting correspond rather well in terms of the distinction between content and form. However, one fundamental difference between the arts causes an important dislocation. The manipulation of emotions, *movere,* was considered highly important by many Renaissance theoreticians within rhetoric as well as painting, and it was as important to Alberti as it had been to Quintilian. But the emotions are treated in different ways. The above quotation of Quintilian can be compared to the following words by Alberti:

> A *historia* will move spectators when the men painted in the picture outwardly demonstrate their own feelings as clearly as possible. Nature provides – and there is nothing to be found more rapacious of her like than she – that we mourn with the mourners, laugh with those who laugh, and grieve with the grief-stricken. Yet these feelings are known from movements of the body. We see how the melancholy,

> pre-occupied with cares and beset by grief, lack all vitality of feeling and action, and remain sluggish, their limbs unsteady and drained of colour. In those who mourn, the brow is weighed down, the neck bent, and every part of their body droops as though weary and past care. But in those who are angry, their passions aflame with ire, face and eyes become swollen and red, and the movements of all their limbs are violent and agitated according to the fury of their wrath. Yet when we are happy and gay, our movements are free and pleasing in their inflexions.[33]

Quintilian would have consented to the instructions as to how the body expresses emotions. Brian Vickers and Jacqueline Lichteinstein have demonstrated how Alberti uses prescriptions from Quintilian and Cicero on the orator's delivery and applies them to the characters within the painting.[34] Heinrich Plett has shown how other Renaissance authors also adapted the categories of rhetoric so as to suit painting – in his examples, it is evident how rhetorical *actio* is defined as action and expression not in the painter but in the characters of the painting.[35] The central issue is that while Quintilian spoke of emotions in physical delivery, Alberti transfers them to a discussion of content, that which is portrayed: that is where, says Alberti, the emotions are located. Quintilian on the other hand was speaking of the presentation of the content, i.e. form, the physical performance primarily, secondarily the transmission into text, the figures, which are the emotional expressions of the text. Manipulating emotions is central to Quintilian, but to him emotions have practically no place as an object, only as instruments. Alberti is certainly interested in affecting the audience's emotions and his objectified emotions obviously serve instrumental functions, but when he transfers rhetoric's discussion of emotions he has to dislocate them from *actio* and – not to forget – *elocutio* to *inventio*, and perhaps to some extent *dispositio*. The impact of this dislocation from, roughly speaking, form into content seems to have been considerable.

From instrument to object – to soul

Classical rhetoric transferred the expressions of the body to the word and adopted the word for "gesture," *schêma*, for rhetorical figure. The function of the figures was not least to cause effect by moving emotions – with figures being part of form or *lexis*. In his analysis of poetry, Aristotle, who was part of this tradition, focused a great deal of attention on emotions and their effect on the audience – while making limited room for the emotions as objects of poetry. While *pathos* in the sense of "suffering" and "affliction" is a central object, the emotions are mainly interesting as instruments for purposes of achieving the intended effect on the audience. The instrumental view on emotions lived on, but gradually the emotions gained status as the objects of poetry. Minturno exemplifies an early attempt to introduce emotions as the object of lyric, but it was fulfilled by Batteux, in his attempt to find the common denominator of poetry and the other arts.

The transfer of emotions from instruments to objects can thus be seen within the tradition of Aristotelian genre theory. More or less simultaneously, different types of categorizing the arts took place: first the attempts to define painting through the rhetorical system and then the attempt to define poetry in the light of the other arts.

Alberti had rhetoric as his natural model when he tried to structure the art of painting in the 15th century. However, the discrepancy between word and image is particularly lucid when it comes to emotions. While Quintilian speaks of the orator's use of emotions as an instrument in his performance, Alberti transfers these emotions and their expressions to content, making them objects instead, a mechanism that appears to be vital to the development of genre theory. Several other factors would later support this development, and by the first half of the 18th century genre theory had advanced so far that lyric could be defined as an exact parallel to epic and drama – with the difference that it represents emotions instead of actions.

One of the conditions for making emotions an object of poetry thus seems to have been the early attempts to define painting by using the categories of rhetoric. It was theoreticians such as Alberti who assigned emotions to content, making them into objects, and without that dislocation of categories it would perhaps not have been possible for lyric to have been defined as a genre. What happens in the 18th century is that poetry, instead of applying rhetoric's definitions to painting and music, to a greater extent is interpreted in the light of painting and music; Batteux, significantly, deliberated upon the fine arts as a whole. Within painting emotions were already, and easily, defined as objects rather than instruments, since they were on the level of content. Music is commonly described as the art most clearly devoted to feelings, and by definition it is a kind of hybrid: it cannot represent physical objects or persons, but has to be seen as representing emotions. In this respect, emotions function as objects, but at the same time they are represented by being effected. That is, music's object is emotions, but these can only be represented by being used instrumentally.[36] These two ways of viewing the development of genre theory – within Aristotelian theory and when comparing the sister arts to each other – need to be supplemented with several other factors, especially the changing appreciation of emotions – from destructive affect to creative and positive emotion.

The shift from instrumental emotions on the level of form to emotions as an object of poetry – as well as painting, music or dance – is a further shift from mimesis-representation towards the pole of mimesis-composition. To be sure, the transfer of the emotions into objects neither meant that their effect became less interesting, nor that they were in any sense confined to the place of objects. Jean-Jacques Rousseau, representative in his radicality, certainly also took a keen interest in the use of emotions, only not in the instrumental way of rhetoric. And by the turn of the 18th century, the development had reached a point where emotions could simply be proclaimed the soul of poetry.

The Swedish author Thomas Thorild, heavily influenced by German *Sturm und Drang*, launched forceful emotion as a new principle of poetry towards the end of the 18th century. What is more, after having been exiled from Sweden and settling in Greifswald, he even wrote a dissertation on the topic: *The Power of Poetry, that is, Passion* (*Vis Poëtica, seu Pathos*, 1801). Here, directly renouncing the mendacious fiction of Aristotle, Thorild announces that true and original poetry is not *muthos*, but *pathos*.[37] Although with different practical results, this way of defining the soul of poetry as emotion can be seen as the base of one of the cornerstones of European romanticism: William Wordsworth and Samuel Taylor Coleridge's *Lyrical Ballads*. The first edition was published in 1798, and in the preface to the second edition in 1800, Wordsworth submitted his well-known definition of poetry as "the spontaneous overflow of powerful feelings."[38] Emotions now not only occupied a central position as objects, but seemed to abound and incarnate any aspect of poetry. They were not instrumental in the traditional sense but seemed to have become a kind of medium of poetry.

Wordsworth can thus be said to mark an end to the development of the role of emotions in poetry as discussed in this chapter. At the same time, he is illustrative of the development treated in the two preceding chapters. The Longinian ideal of the image as a means of employing human imagination on the one hand, the aesthetic discussions of the symbol in terms of universal reference on the other hand, and in addition the unconditional recognition not only of emotions but even of pleasure: all of these Wordsworth collects and condenses with direct reference to Aristotle:

> Aristotle, I have been told, has said, that Poetry is the most philosophic of all writing: it is so: its object is truth, not individual and local, but general, and operative; not standing upon external testimony, but carried alive into the heart by passion; truth which is its own testimony, which gives competence and confidence to the tribunal to which it appeals, and receives them from the same tribunal. Poetry is the image of man and nature. The obstacles which stand in the way of the fidelity of the Biographer and Historian, and of their consequent utility, are incalculably greater than those which are to be encountered by the Poet who comprehends the dignity of his art. The Poet writes under one restriction only, namely, the necessity of giving immediate pleasure to a human Being possessed of that information which may be expected from him, not as a lawyer, a physician, a mariner, an astronomer or a natural philosopher, but as a Man. Except this one restriction, there is no object standing between the Poet and the image of things; between this, and the Biographer and Historian, there are a thousand.[39]

Conclusion

For obvious reasons, a study of the soul of poetry cannot and should not attempt to be exhaustive: there will always be other examples confirming the tendencies outlined here or suggesting alternative ones. Tracing the development of poetological or aesthetic ideas involves a number of uncertainties, to such an extent that ambiguity may be said to be the topic of examination. The definition of "poetry" is elusive: Aristotle speaks primarily of tragedy, with his definition of the soul of poetry thus originating from that genre, as well as epic. Subsequent theoreticians often focus on lyric, thus redefining poetry at the same time as redefining its soul. When Aristotle describes *muthos*, the composition of actions, as the soul of tragedy – representative of poetry – "soul" should be understood as more or less synonymous with "starting-point," "principle," "goal" or "essence" (*arkhê*, *telos*, even *ousia*). In the tradition of poetics, these terms are used differently in different languages, connected to different theoretical frameworks.

The term "mimesis" embodies a wide range of meanings, and its vagueness is already apparent in Aristotle. Even his fundamental dictum that the poet is a "poet by virtue of mimesis, and his mimesis is of actions" is ambiguous: should mimesis of actions be understood as the composition of actions into *muthos* or the verbal representation of *muthos*? Thus, the ground is laid for radically different interpretations of the soul of poetry. In addition, Aristotle's renowned praise of metaphor was very influential, but metaphor has to be understood not as mimesis-composition, but as part of mimesis-representation. That is, metaphor is praised not only as a cognitive device but also as a more refined instance of mimesis: it is the discerning of similarities. Still, it cannot be regarded as being connected with Aristotle's understanding of the soul of poetry, which, in turn, was to be the case in several reinterpretations of his *Poetics*.

Aristotle himself pointed to *muthos* as the soul of poetry, but at the same time he left to posterity a great deal of uncertainty in this respect. In the tradition of poetics, mimesis is reinterpreted in various ways, but it mainly hovers between the two instances which have here been named mimesis-representation and mimesis-composition. In Aristotle, mimesis is usually contextually defined: when he compares poetry to the other arts, the common denominator of these mimetic acts is their media, with poetry's mimesis thus being verbal representation, *lexis*, mimesis-representation. When he compares poetry to history, the common denominator is content and thus poetry's mimesis resorts to *muthos*, mimesis-composition. In the same way, when Aristotle discusses the different parts of tragedy, his focus is on *muthos*. Since his definition of poetry emerges from tragedy, it is natural that the focus is on actions and story. Contrariwise, the emphasis is on verbal representation when followers develop Aristotle's poetics with a definition of poetry emerging from lyric. The definition obviously hinges on genre: mimesis-composition is temporal and sequential, mimesis-representation is not. As soon as poetry is approached from a predominantly rhetorical and instrumental point of view, the soul of poetry also slants at mimesis-representation. The possibility of variation between these two instances is practically inexhaustible, and even though there is also a range of other instances of mimesis, it is these two that have been at the focus of this study.

The varying definitions and terms have subsequently generated much confusion, but also new interpretations and adaptations of Aristotelian poetics. Even different sets of associations attached to the terms in different languages have spurred conflicts, which in turn would further confuse the definition of the soul of poetry. The ambiguity of terms also concerns the discussions of verisimilitude, which are often appended to poetological discourses. Latin *verisimilitudo*, as the English *verisimilitude*, is so comprehensive that it embraces and thus obscures very different meanings. Thus, in renderings of Aristotle, who foremost spoke of probability in the sequence of events, verisimilitude could be transformed into the question of how convincingly words can represent a given physical object. In French classicism, verisimilitude was widened even further into the creation of elaborate "necessity."

* * *

Having commenced with a discussion of Aristotle's *Poetics*, the analysis in this study has focused on how Aristotle's treatise may be understood from a rhetorical point of view, partly because the categories developed within rhetoric were the resource available to Aristotle when defining his poetics, partly because the reception of the *Poetics* has to a very great extent been governed by a rhetorical apprehension of literature. In this way, the basic definitions of mimesis are made and the relation between mimesis-composition, resulting in *muthos* or fable, and mimesis-representation, resulting in *lexis* or verbal representation, is clarified.

While Aristotle proclaimed the soul of poetry to be *muthos*, his most immediate interpreter, Averroës, shifted the essence of poetry from mimesis-composition to mimesis-representation. In the Arabic tradition, Aristotle's *Poetics* was supplemented with his *Rhetoric* and *On the Soul* to the effect that the soul of poetry was overwhelmingly understood as imagery: both visualization and metaphor. *Muthos* more or less disappeared from the scene, but with Averroës's follower Mathias Lincopensis the relocation of categories was even more radical: Mathias melts down fiction into metaphor, proclaiming that this is as much lie as poetry is allowed to indulge in. The cleric Mathias is most renowned as the father confessor of Saint Bridget of Sweden, having launched her career and helped present her influential visions. As Bridget's visions became appreciated very much because of their vivid and "realistic" discourse, the question of the connection between Aristotle and this politically influential saint has to be addressed. There is no trace of *muthos* in Averroës's and Mathias's reinterpretations of Aristotle, but the soul of poetry according to them, visualization, appears to have been exercised from the first moment in her visions.

In the Italian Renaissance it was the Arabic Aristotle who first became influential and only gradually did the original Greek text make its way into the debate. This created a double view on the soul of poetry, most visible in Francesco Robortello, who on the one side presents Aristotle's view on the soul of poetry in a fairly loyal way, on the other side introduces Aristotle's *Poetics* prefaced by his own view on poetry, which is closely aligned to the Averroistic view. Lodovico Castelvetro defends Aristotle's view and even elaborates an interpretation of the *Poetics* into rhetorical categories, thereby in a sense returning to Aristotle's basic premises. This results in a division between "poetry in words" and "poetry in things," a division which would be developed in Charles Batteux's discussion of the fine arts and remain influential long after rhetoric had been dethroned in romantic theory. Others were more influenced by Averroës's extolling of visualization and metaphor, and the most spectacular result is to be found in Tesauro's famous baroque poetics. Tesauro's accentuation of conceit, wit and metaphor calls for being interpreted as a spectacular variation of Averroistic poetics, and Tesauro, in redefining imitation, rests on a mistranslation of Aristotle: while Aristotle in his *Rhetoric* stated that words are imitations (in that they represent things), Tesauro has the quotation changed into "metaphorical words are imitations." Imitation thus reaches a considerably higher degree of artifice. Furthermore, Tesauro expands the comparison between the arts by widening the concept of metaphor: making it comprise also physical artifacts, such as sculpture, he redefines referentiality on the whole. Claiming authority by referring to exegetics, he is able to introduce a system where not only words, but also things, may constitute the sign.

After a long period of adaptations which shifted the soul of poetry from mimesis-composition to mimesis-representation, Aristotle's categories were rather faithfully rendered by Pierre Corneille and Jean Racine. Still, even if the categories were not substantially relocated, they were certainly developed in specific ways, not least regarding the moral use of poetry. One effect of their need for elaborating verisimilitude was the use of "double motivation," aiming at supporting verisimilitude with the assistance of necessity. This provided a key to understanding an important aspect of the French classicist drama.

Reaching the 18th century and the arrival of the theory of the fine arts, the distinctions of mimesis prove useful in clarifying the debate between Charles Batteux and his translator/opponent/competitor J. A. Schlegel. The quarrel between the two largely emanated from terminological issues. Batteux regarded imitation to be the governing principle of the arts, that is, mimesis-representation. In criticizing Batteux, Schlegel instead viewed Batteux's imitation as other kinds of mimesis, above all histrionic feigning, and although constantly criticizing Batteux's concept of the soul of poetry he in effect ended up adopting a similar view. Batteux launched lyric as a main genre by carefully, although not faithfully, developing Aristotle's categories and letting lyric be the representation of emotions in a way corresponding to tragedy's and epic's representation of actions. When Schlegel, and others after him, instead interpreted Batteux's description of the essence of poetry as the poet feigning – and not representing – emotions, one reason for the misunderstandings appears to have been that the word "imitation" was rendered as *Nachahmung* in German, a concept more negatively loaded with values of unoriginal mimicking. Even though the principle of imitation was questioned in later aesthetic discussions, I argue, this was in a sense primarily a shift of words. The essence of poetry according to Batteux was its ability to represent through (artistic) language, with the centrality of language as a medium being upgraded rather than questioned in romantic theory. To be sure, several of Batteux's derivative opinions on poetry were discarded, but not his basic definition of the soul of poetry. Without disregarding all the considerable differences between these kinds of aesthetics, it may be concluded that, just as was seen in the previous chapters, the development of aesthetics and notions of the soul of poetry is constantly and creatively subjected to the inherent imprecision of vocabulary.

The study then leaves the theoretical discussions directly based on Aristotle's *Poetics* and instead tests what ground for general conclusions has been laid through the distinction between mimesis-representation and mimesis-composition. Three concluding chapters focus on the sublime, the symbol and the role of emotions in genre theory and aesthetics. All of these have in various ways laid claim to the position of the soul of poetry, although not connecting directly to Aristotle's *Poetics*.

The primary source of the sublime, (Pseudo-)Longinus's *On the Sublime*, was devised as a rhetorical treatise in the first centuries AD. The sublime should not be reduced to rhetoric, but its rhetorical aspect is vital for understanding the stylistic effect of the sublime. As the sublime was developed into psychological, philosophical and aesthetic theories during the 18th and 19th century, the rhetorical aspect obviously became less apparent, but in order to understand this development the basic literary device needed to be clarified. The analysis showed that one specific device – *phantasia* – was particularly emphasized in *On the Sublime*. The figure *phantasia*, more commonly discussed in terms of *enargeia, hupotuposis, evidentia* or *representatio*, was moved from the context of the other rhetorical figures and received preferential treatment, adjacent to the introductory discussion of that version of sublime which was held to emanate from a great spirit and that could not be learned as a skill. Not only is this specific device of visualization stressed in the explicit theoretical discussion, it is also heavily, albeit implicitly, reinforced in the important introductory chapters which present the sublime style and thought. Practically every example is characterized by its visualizing techniques, and thus *phantasia* takes the place of the central trait of the sublime by explicit as well as implicit argument. Indeed, throughout *On the Sublime,* Longinus almost seems to be following his own advice: figures are natural allies of sublimity, but must be cleverly concealed in order to have efficacy (17.1–2).

Phantasia comes close to mimesis, especially in the sense of mimesis-representation, which was brought to the fore in the discussions on the Averroistic reinterpretation of Aristotle's *Poetics*. That it became so influential at the same time as the mental faculty of the imagination began to receive pronounced attention in the 18th century is hardly surprising: here, the stylistic device *phantasia* merged with the mental faculty *phantasia* and became fundamental to the developing aesthetics.

The symbol, being a primary aesthetic trait of romanticism, is nowadays often discussed in connection with metaphor and allegory, but historically it has rarely been included among the rhetorical devices. Through a discussion of theories and practices concerning referentiality within exegetical, rhetorical and other traditions, the symbol, despite its similarities with the tropes, has lent itself to being categorized not primarily within the poetic diction of *elocutio*, but rather within the argumentative structuring of *inventio*. The referential system of the symbol was so different from the tropes that it appears to have been more readily understood in analogy with rhetoric's proof and *exemplum*. One essential aspect of proof, discussed already by Aristotle but forcefully introduced into poetics by his interpreters, is the power of visualization. In this way the rhetorical tradition appears to merge with romantic aesthetics: the theoretical demands for vividness and lively visualization are remarkably constant from Averroës to the romantics.

Having been treated with considerable suspicion, the emotions during the 18th century finally made their way into the sanctum of poetics. As Batteux definitively established lyric as a main genre, emotions were made the object of this genre in a way consistent with Aristotle's system but presupposing a more lenient view on emotions than was prevalent in Aristotle's context. The redefinition of Aristotle's generic categories can be traced as a continuous negotiation of the character of emotions: not only concerning the question whether passions should be regarded as vices, but foremost concerning the question whether emotions are instruments or objects of poetry. By following the various functions of emotions in different theories, not only regarding poetry but also painting, it appears that attempts were made in the Renaissance to define painting through the categories of rhetoric, clarifying an incompatibility between poetry and painting, which in turn led to the fact that emotions were defined not only as instruments, but also as objects. Conversely, painting's potential of treating emotions as objects seems to have influenced the definition of poetry when the fine arts were launched in the 18th century, enabling lyric to be firmly established among the literary genres.

The questions of visualization, symbol and emotion obviously cannot be distinctly separated from each other. As a final example, I show how they merge in William Wordsworth's preface to *Lyrical Ballads* from 1800 and 1802, often considered the starting-point of English romanticism. While this study has been concerned with demarcating and clarifying various redefinitions of the soul of poetry, different theoretical directions and different ways of categorizing language and art, Wordsworth eloquently demonstrates how firmly they belong together at the end of the day.

Notes

INTRODUCTION

1 "ἀρχὴ μὲν οὖν καὶ οἷον ψυχὴ ὁ μῦθος τῆς τραγῳδίας" (*Poetics* 1450a38–39). Quotations and translations are from *Aristotle. Poetics,* edited and translated by Stephen Halliwell, Loeb Classical Library XXIII (Cambridge, MA, 1999).

2 "τὸν ποιητὴν μᾶλλον τῶν μύθων εἶναι δεῖ ποιητὴν ἢ τῶν μέτρων, ὅσῳ ποιητὴς κατὰ τὴν μίμησίν ἐστιν, μιμεῖται δὲ τὰς πράξεις" (*Poetics* 1451b27–29).

3 Aristotle, *Poetics* 1450a38–39 (see note 1). In *On the Soul,* Aristotle explains that the soul is *arkhê* and *telos* as well as "essence," *ousia*: "But the soul is the cause and first principle of the living body. The words cause (*aitia*) and first principle (*arkhê*) are used in several separate senses. But the soul is equally the cause in each of the three senses to which I have referred; for it is the cause in the sense of being that form from which motion (*kinêsis*) is derived in the sense of the purpose or final cause, and as being the substance (*ousia*) of all the bodies that have souls" (*On the Soul* 415b9–12). It should be noted that to Aristotle essence is form (*Metaphysics* 1035b34–39; cf. 983a28), and thus the soul of poetry is form. Cf., more generally, Wilfrid Sellars, "Substance and Form in Aristotle," in *Aristotle: Substance, Form and Matter,* edited with introductions by Terence Irwin, 140–151; Richard McKeon, "Aristotle's Conception of Language and the Arts of Language," in *Critics and Criticism: Ancient and Modern,* ed. R.S. Crane (Chicago, 1952), 176–231.

4 M.H. Abrams, *The Mirror and the Lamp: Romantic Theory and the Critical Tradition* (New York, 1953).

5 The potential of the concept shows itself also in modern studies, ranging from Erich Auerbach's *Mimesis. Dargestellte Wirklichkeit in der abendländischen Literatur* (Berne, 1946) over Paul Ricoeur's *Temps et récit* I–III (Paris, 1983–87) to Kendall Walton's *Mimesis as Make-Believe: On the Foundations of the Representational Arts* (Cambridge, MA, 1990), to mention only a few. Cf. Terence Cave, "The Afterlife of the *Poetics,*" in *Making Sense of Aristotle: Essays in Poetics,* ed. Øivind Andersen and Jon Haarberg (London, 2001), 197–214.

6 On different interpretations of the concept, see among others D.W. Lucas, *Aristotle. Poetics.* Introduction, commentary and appendices by D.W. Lucas (Oxford, 1968), 258–272, and Stephen Halliwell, *Aristotle's Poetics* (London, 1986), 109–137.

7 Richard McKeon, "Literary Criticism and the Concept of Imitation in Antiquity," in *Critics and Criticism: Ancient and Modern,* ed. R.S. Crane (Chicago, 1952), 147–175, 160. Paul Ricoeur, *Time and Narrative* I (Chicago, 1984), 33. From this, Ricoeur himself defines three stages of mimesis, the first concerning the preconception of the surrounding world from which the poem develops, the second being the creative construction of a plot, and the third being the meeting of the poem('s world) with the receiver('s world) (46–51). Ricoeur sees these stages in Aristotle but elaborates them himself (33).

8 Gerald F. Else, *Plato and Aristotle on Poetry,* edited with an introduction by Peter Burian (Chapel Hill, 1986), 74–88, 75.

9 Such problems are outlined in Stephen Halliwell, *The Aesthetics of Mimesis: Ancient Texts and Modern Problems* (Princeton and Oxford, 2002), 244–381.

10 Halliwell, *Aristotle's Poetics,* 121. Criticism of McKeon: Halliwell, *The Aesthetics of Mimesis,* 152. See also Hermann Koller, *Die Mimesis in der Antike. Nachahmung, Darstellung, Ausdruck* (Berne, 1954); Göran Sörbom, *Mimesis and Art: Studies in the Origin and Early Development of an Aesthetic Vocabulary* (Uppsala, 1966); and Maria Kardaun, *Der Mimesisbegriff in der griechischen*

Antike. Neubetrachtung eines umstrittenen Begriffes als Ansats zu einer neuen Interpretation der platonischen Kunstauffassung (Amsterdam, New York, Oxford and Toronto, 1993).

11 Halliwell, *Aristotle's Poetics*, 137; see also 134–135.

12 Halliwell, *The Aesthetics of Mimesis*, 152. "Reduced to a schematic but nonetheless instructive dichotomy, these varieties of mimetic theory and attitude can be described as encapsulating a difference between a 'world-reflecting' model (for which the 'mirror' has been a common though far from straightforward metaphorical emblem), and, on the other side, a 'world-simulating' or 'world-creating' conception of artistic representation" (Halliwell, *The Aesthetics of Mimesis*, 23).

13 Halliwell, *The Aesthetics of Mimesis*, 174.

14 Halliwell, *The Aesthetics of Mimesis*, 5.

15 As the sliding meaning of terms and concepts is crucial to the study, many of the quotations I adduce must be seen in the original. For the sake of convenience I translate quotations, but also give the original. When available, I have used existing translations, but when required they have been slightly modified.

CHAPTER ONE
ARISTOTLE

1 "ὥστε τὰ πράγματα καὶ ὁ μῦθος τέλος τῆς τραγῳδίας, τὸ δὲ τέλος μέγιστον ἁπάντων" (*Poetics* 1450a22–23).

2 "ἀρχὴ μὲν οὖν καὶ οἷον ψυχὴ ὁ μῦθος τῆς τραγῳδίας, δεύτερον δὲ τὰ ἤθη" (*Poetics* 1450a38–39). In the first quotation, Aristotle mentions events, *pragmata*, together with plot, just as he in 1450a32 says that tragedy "has a plot and structure of events." This seems to indicate that *muthos* only concerns personal action, *praxis*, but the distinction is not clear: in 1450a4 he appears to regard them as the same thing: "the plot is the mimesis of the action [*mimêsis praxeôs*]—for I use 'plot' to denote the construction of events [*sunthesin tôn pragmatôn*]."

3 "ἐποποιία δὴ καὶ ἡ τῆς τραγῳδίας ποίησις ἔτι δὲ κωμῳδία καὶ ἡ διθυραμβοποιητικὴ καὶ τῆς αὐλητικῆς ἡ πλείστη καὶ κιθαριστικῆς πᾶσαι τυγχάνουσιν οὖσαι μιμήσεις τὸ σύνολον· διαφέρουσι δὲ ἀλλήλων τρισίν, ἢ γὰρ τῷ ἐν ἑτέροις μιμεῖσθαι ἢ τῷ ἕτερα ἢ τῷ ἑτέρως καὶ μὴ τὸν αὐτὸν τρόπον. ὥσπερ γὰρ καὶ χρώμασι καὶ σχήμασι πολλὰ μιμοῦνταί τινες ἀπεικάζοντες (οἱ μὲν διὰ τέχνης οἱ δὲ διὰ συνηθείας), ἕτεροι δὲ διὰ της φωνῆς, οὕτω κἀν ταῖς εἰρημέναις τέχναις ἅπασαι μὲν ποιοῦνται τὴν μίμησιν ἐν ῥυθμῷ καὶ λόγῳ καὶ ἁρμονίᾳ, τούτοις δ' ἢ χωρὶς ἢ μεμιγμένοις" (*Poetics* 1447a13–23).

4 Cf. Halliwell, *Aristotle's Poetics*, 123–124.

5 "Ὅμηρος δὲ ἄλλα τε πολλὰ ἄξιος ἐπαινεῖσθαι καὶ δὴ καὶ ὅτι μόνος τῶν ποιητῶν οὐκ ἀγνοεῖ ὃ δεῖ ποιεῖν αὐτόν. αὐτὸν γὰρ δεῖ τὸν ποιητὴν ἐλάχιστα λέγειν· οὐ γάρ ἐστι κατὰ ταῦτα μιμητής. οἱ μὲν οὖν ἄλλοι αὐτοὶ μὲν δι' ὅλου ἀγωνίζονται, μιμοῦνται δὲ ὀλίγα καὶ ὀλιγάκις" (*Poetics* 1460a5–9).

6 "ἐπεὶ δὲ πράξεώς ἐστι μίμησις, πράττεται δὲ ὑπὸ τινῶν πραττόντων οὓς ἀνάγκη ποιούς τινας εἶναι κατά τε τὸ ἦθος καὶ τὴν διάνοιαν (διὰ γὰρ τούτων καὶ τὰς πράξεις εἶναί φαμεν ποιάς τινας, καὶ κατὰ ταύτας καὶ τυγχάνουσι καὶ ἀποτυγχάνουσι πάντες), ἔστιν δὲ τῆς μὲν πράξεως ὁ μῦθος ἡ μίμησις, λέγω γὰρ μῦθον τοῦτον τὴν σύνθεσιν τῶν πραγμάτων, τὰ δὲ ἤθη, καθ' ὃ ποιούς τινας εἶναί φαμεν τοὺς πράττοντας, διάνοιαν δέ, ἐν ὅσοις λέγοντες ἀποδεικνύασίν τι ἢ καὶ ἀποφαίνονται γνώμην. ἀνάγκη οὖν πάσης τῆς τραγῳδίας μέρη εἶναι ἕξ, καθ' ὃ ποιά τις ἐστὶν ἡ τραγῳδία· ταῦτα δ' ἐστὶ μῦθος καὶ ἤθη καὶ λέξις καὶ διάνοια καὶ ὄψις καὶ μελοποιία. οἷς μὲν γὰρ μιμοῦνται, δύο μέρη ἐστίν, ὡς δὲ μιμοῦνται, ἕν, ἃ δὲ μιμοῦνται, τρία, καὶ παρὰ ταῦτα οὐδέν" (*Poetics* 1449b35–1450a12).

7 Since Aristotle is more interested in form than in matter here, I prefer the word "composition" to "construction."

8 "ἐν τούτοις γὰρ ποιοῦνται τὴν μίμησιν" (*Poetics* 1449b33). Halliwell translates this as "lyric poetry and diction, for these are the media in which they render the mimesis." Translating *toutois*, "through these," with "the media in which" is an excellent expansion, but by translating *poiountai* with "render," the translation eliminates an important aspect of the original's ambiguity. They (the actors) *make mimesis* when they deliver that *mimesis* which is the linguistic representation of that *mimesis* which is *muthos*, the construction of plot. They thus do render,

but it is not one limited instance of mimesis which is then rendered in ways delimited from mimesis. Mimesis is the *muthos* as well as the rendering of *muthos* in words. It is also acting – an aspect, however, that will not be examined here.

9 In the *Poetics*, chapter 6, Aristotle uses *logos* in an entirely different sense, referring to the spoken sections – as opposed to the sung ones – of tragedy (1450b12).

10 In the same vein, Aristotle regards the voice as mimesis: "The poets, as was natural, were the first to give an impulse to style; for words are imitations, and the voice also, which of all our parts is best adapted for imitation, was ready at hand; thus the arts of the rhapsodists, actors, and others, were fashioned" (Ἤρξαντο μὲν οὖν κινῆσαι τὸ πρῶτον, ὥσπερ πέφυκεν, οἱ ποιηταί· τὰ γὰρ ὀνόματα μιμήματα ἐστίν, ὑπῆρξε δὲ καὶ ἡ φωνὴ πάντων μιμητικώτατον τῶν μορίων ἡμῖν· διὸ καὶ αἱ τέχναι συνέστησαν, ἥ τε ῥαψῳδία καὶ ἡ ὑποκριτικὴ καὶ ἄλλαι γε). Aristotle, *Rhetoric*, with an English translation by John Henry Freese (London and New York, 1926), 1404a8.

11 However, the comparison with painting does include a correspondence also with *muthos*. When Aristotle in chapter 6 claims that *muthos* is the soul of poetry while character is secondary, he adds: "A similar principle also holds in painting: if one were to cover a surface randomly with the finest colours, one would provide less pleasure than by an outline of a picture [*leukograhêsas eikona*]" (*Poetics* 1450a39–1450b3). One could thus surmise that character is here paralleled with colours while *muthos* is paralleled with the plan, structure, contours, but we are probably meant to grasp colour as words and outline, structure, as *muthos*.

12 Halliwell, *Aristotle's Poetics*, 17, cf. 344–349.

13 Cf. Halliwell, *Aristotle's Poetics*, 345.

14 Halliwell, *Aristotle's Poetics*, 348–349.

15 *Plato. Cratylus, Parmenides, Greater Hippias, Lesser Hippias*, with an English translation by H.N. Fowler (London and Cambridge, MA, 1953), 423D–424A; 430E–431A.

16 See Halliwell, *Aristotle's Poetics*, 344.

17 For a discussion of Aristotle's insertion of order into mimesis from another point of view, see Arne Melberg, *Theories of Mimesis* (Cambridge, 1995), 43–50.

18 Plato, *Critias* 107B and *Cratylus* 423D–424A; 430E–431A. See further Halliwell, *The Aesthetics of Mimesis*, 37–71.

19 As Halliwell proposes, *logos* also implies "meaning, or the common factor in all language" (Halliwell, *Aristotle's Poetics*, 344).

20 "χρὴ δὲ καὶ ἐν τοῖς ἤθεσιν ὁμοίως ὥσπερ καὶ ἐν τῇ τῶν πραγμάτων συστάσει ἀεὶ ζητεῖν ἢ τὸ ἀναγκαῖον ἢ τὸ εἰκός, ὥστε τὸν τοιοῦτον τὰ τοιαῦτα λέγειν ἢ πράττειν ἢ ἀναγκαῖον ἢ εἰκὸς καὶ τοῦτο μετὰ τοῦτο γίνεσθαι ἢ ἀναγκαῖον ἢ εἰκός" (*Poetics* 1454a33–36).

21 Halliwell, *Aristotle's Poetics*, 101–106. For an investigation of the concepts throughout Aristotle's works, see Dorothea Frede, "Necessity, Chance, and 'What Happens for the Most Part' in Aristotle's *Poetics*," in *Essays on Aristotle's "Poetics,"* ed. Amélie Oksenberg Rorty (Princeton and London, 1992), 197–219.

22 "τὸ μὲν γὰρ εἰκός ἐστιν ὡς ἐπὶ τὸ πολὺ γινόμενον" (*Rhetoric* 1357a15). Halliwell, *Aristotle's Poetics*, 101.

23 "δεῖ χρῆσθαι ὅταν ἢ ἐλεεινὰ ἢ δεινὰ ἢ μεγάλα ἢ εἰκότα δέῃ παρασκευάζειν· πλὴν τοσοῦτον διαφέρει, ὅτι τὰ μὲν δεῖ φαίνεσθαι ἄνευ διδασκαλίας, τὰ δὲ ἐν τῷ λόγῳ ὑπὸ τοῦ λέγοντος παρασκευάζεσθαι καὶ παρὰ τὸν λόγον γίγνεσθαι" (*Poetics* 1456b3–7).

24 Especially prominent in *Rhetoric* chapter III.x–xi (1410b–1413a).

25 "Δεῖ δὲ τοὺς μύθους συνιστάναι καὶ τῇ λέξει συναπεργάζεσθαι ὅτι μάλιστα πρὸ ὀμμάτων τιθέμενον· οὕτω γὰρ ἂν ἐναργέστατα ὁρῶν ὥσπερ παρ' αὐτοῖς γιγνόμενος τοῖς πραττομένοις εὑρίσκοι τὸ πρέπον καὶ ἥκιστα ἂν λανθάνοι τὰ ὑπεναντία" (*Poetics* 1455a22–26).

26 "ἐπεὶ γάρ ἐστι μιμητὴς ὁ ποιητὴς ὡσπερανεὶ ζωγράφος ἤ τις ἄλλος εἰκονοποιός, ἀνάγκη μιμεῖσθαι τριῶν ὄντων τὸν ἀριθμὸν ἕν τι ἀεί, ἢ γὰρ οἷα ἦν ἢ ἔστιν, ἢ οἷά φασιν καὶ δοκεῖ, ἢ οἷα εἶναι δεῖ" (*Poetics* 1460b8–11).

27 In Aristotle, the overarching sense of "convincing" is contained in the term *pithanos*. On a few occasions he speaks of the "plausible" (*pithanos*), once in chapter 9, when he concludes that that which has actually happened is undeniably possible (*dynaton*), and thus plausible (*pithanon*:

Poetics 1451b15–18). Another occurence is when he speaks of the false in chapter 24, and there returns to issues concerning *muthos*: "Things probable though impossible should be preferred to the possible but implausible [*apithana*]" (*Poetics* 1460a26). *Pithanos* thus has an overarching sense of "convincing," covering any kind of plausibility.

28 See e.g. Karsten Friis-Jensen, "Horace and the Early Writers of Arts of Poetry," in *Sprachtheorien in Spätantike und Mittelalter*, ed. Sten Ebbesen (Tübingen, 1993), 360–401.

29 See e.g. McKeon, "Aristotle's Conception of Language," 170–171. Cf. Päivi Mehtonen, "A Medieval and Modern Battle of Arts," in *The Rhetoric of Cicero in its Medieval and Early Renaissance Commentary Tradition*, ed. Virginia Cox and John O. Ward (Leiden and Boston, 2006), 289–312, 303–304.

CHAPTER TWO
AVERROËS'S ADAPTATION

1 See Halliwell, *Aristotle's Poetics*, 288–293. Halliwell offers a concise outline of the afterlife of the *Poetics* in "*Nachleben* of the *Poetics*," 286–323. Cf. E.N. Tigerstedt, "Observations on the Reception of the Aristotelian *Poetics* in the Latin West," *Studies in the Renaissance* 15 (1968), 7–24.

2 See O.B. Hardison, *The Enduring Monument: A Study of the Idea of Praise in Renaissance Literary Theory and Practice* (Chapel Hill, 1962) and "The Place of Averroës' Commentary on the *Poetics* in the History of Medieval Criticism," in *Medieval and Renaissance Studies* (Durham, NC, 1970), 57–81, 57–58; Ismail M. Dahiyat, *Avicenna's Commentary on the "Poetics" of Aristotle: A Critical Study with an Annotated Translation of the Text* (Leiden, 1974).

3 See mainly *Classical and Medieval Literary Criticism: Translations and Interpretations*, ed. Alex Preminger, O.B. Hardison Jr. and Kevin Kerrane (New York, 1974), 341–348, but also the presentations of the Arabic Aristotle in H.A. Kelly, "Aristotle-Averroës-Alemannus on Tragedy," *Viator: Medieval and Renaissance Studies* 10 (1979), 161–210, esp. 161–172, and *Medieval Literary Theory and Criticism c. 1100–c. 1375: The Commentary-Tradition*, ed. A.J. Minnis and A.B. Scott (Oxford, 1988).

4 See e.g. H.A. Kelly, "Aristotle-Averroës-Alemannus on Tragedy"; Richard Walzer, *Greek into Arabic: Essays on Islamic Philosophy* (Oxford, 1962); Wolfhart Heinrichs, *Arabische Dichtung und griechische Poetik. Hazim al-Qartagannis Grundlegung der Poetik mit Hilfe aristotelischer Begriffe* (Beirut, 1969); Salim Kemal, *The Philosophical Poetics of Alfarabi, Avicenna and Averroës: The Aristotelian Reception* (London and New York, 2003); Deborah Black, *Logic and Aristotle's "Rhetoric" and "Poetics" in Medieval Arabic Philosophy* (Leiden, New York, Copenhagen and Cologne, 1990).

5 Minnis and Scott, eds., *Medieval Literary Theory and Criticism*, 279–281.

6 Dahiyat, *Avicenna's Commentary on the "Poetics" of Aristotle*, 15.

7 Minnis and Scott, eds., *Medieval Literary Theory and Criticism*, 282–284.

8 Preminger, Hardison Jr. and Kevin Kerrane, *Classical and Medieval Literary Criticism*, 342.

9 Hardison, *The Enduring Monument*.

10 Bernard Weinberg, *A History of Literary Criticism in the Italian Renaissance* I–II (Chicago, 1961), 356; Hardison, *The Enduring Monument*, 203. Daniel Javitch has criticized Weinberg for over-emphasizing the rhetorical perspective of the reception and thus not seeing the innovations that were made (Daniel Javitch, "The Assimilation of Aristotle's *Poetics* in Sixteenth-Century Italy," in *The Cambridge History of Literary Criticism* III, ed. Glyn P. Norton (Cambridge, 1999), 53–66).

11 Minnis and Scott, eds., *Medieval Literary Theory and Criticism*, 282.

12 *Aristoteles Latinus* XXXIII. *Editio altera. De arte poetica. Translatio Guillelmi de Moerbeka....*, ed. L. Minio-Paluello, *Accedunt Expositio media Averrois sive "Poetria" Hermanno Alemanno interprete et Specimina Translationis Petri Leonii* (Brussels and Paris, 1968), 61.

13 *Aristoteles Latinus* XXXIII, 52.

14 "Et sermones poetici sermones sunt imaginativi. Modi autem imaginationis et assimilationis tres sunt: duo simplices et tertius compositus ex illis. Unus duorum simplicium est assimilatio rei ad rem et exemplatio eius ad ipsam. Et hoc fit in qualibet lingua aut per dictiones proprias illi lingue, ut est hec dictio 'quasi' vel 'sicut', et que istis similantur, que nominantur sinkathegoreumata similitudinis; aut per sumptionem ipsius similis cum suo assimilabili vel loco sui assimilabilis. Et istud nominatur in hac arte 'concambium' et ..." (42/289). Text from *Aristoteles Latinus* XXXIII, translation from Minnis and Scott, eds., *Medieval Literary Theory and Criticism*. Translations not available in the latter are either my own or from Preminger, *Classical and Medieval Literary Criticism*. In such cases, page numbers are 349 and above. I occasionally add the original terms.

15 So Aristotle in *Rhetoric* III.x.3 (1410b), where metaphor is thus stated to be superior to simile because it is shorter and more effective, as it does not explicate the element of comparison.

16 "Et sciendum est tibi quod in hanc divisionem intrant species poematum que moderni nostri temporis nominant transumptionem et translationem, ut cum dicitur 'pratum ridet', 'litus aratur'" (42/290).

17 "Et imaginatio et representatio in sermonibus poeticis fit ex parte trium rerum: scilicet ex parte soni convenientis, et ex parte ponderis, et ex parte ipsiusmet assimilationis. ... et [est] representatio seu imitatio in dictione, scilicet in sermonibus representativis seu imaginativis prolatis absque metro seu pondere" (42/290).

18 "Et assimilatio et representatio laudationibus pertinet rerum que sunt in summo virtutis et bonitatis. Quemadmodum ergo pictor peritus depingit rem prout ipsa est in sua existentia, ita quod iracundum et ridentem et pigrum representat pingendo, licet ipsorum accidentia hec potius sint ex parte anime, sic oportet ut poeta in sua representatione pingat et formet rem quamlibet prout in ipsa est, et prout ei competit, ita quod imitetur quod exprimat mores et habitudines anime" (58/365).

19 Hardison (*The Enduring Monument*, 203–204) states that "Averroës defined poetic imitation as the use of metaphor because to speak of an object with the right and proper word is not imitation but representation," but it is not possible to see Averroës maintaining such a distinction. Besides the quotations above, the following excerpts also contradict that conclusion: "Et causa in hoc est quoniam homo inter cetera animalia delectatur in assimilatione rerum quas iam in sensu percepit et in earum representatione seu imitatione (45). Et dico per circulationem imitationem contrarii eius quod intenditur ad laudandum. ... Directio autem est imitatio rei tantum" (53).

20 *Rhetoric*, III.x–xi (1410b–1413a). Although closely related, actuality/visuality, *energeia*, is kept distinct from metaphor: see Dirk M. Schenkeveld, "*Ta asteia* in Aristotle's *Rhetoric*: The Disappearance of a Category," in *Peripatetic Rhetoric after Aristotle*, ed. William W. Fortenbaugh and David C. Mirhady (New Brunswick, NJ, 1994), 1–14, 7, cf. Lawrence D. Green, "Aristotelian Lexis and Renaissance Elocutio," in *Rereading Aristotle's Rhetoric*, ed. Alan G. Gross and Arthur E. Walzer (Carbondale and Edwardsville, IL, 2000), 149–165, 160.

21 Kemal, *The Philosophical Poetics of Alfarabi*, 40–51; cf. Päivi Mehtonen, "Essential Art: Matthew of Linköping's Fourtheenth-Century Poetics," *Rhetorica* XXV (2007), 125–139, 131. On the relation between poetry, rhetoric and psychology in Aristotle's thinking, see Kathy Eden, *Poetic and Legal Fiction in the Aristotelian Tradition* (Princeton and Guildford, 1986), 62–111.

22 Kemal, *The Philosophical Poetics of Alfarabi*, 2–3, 53, 100–101.

23 Kemal, *The Philosophical Poetics of Alfarabi*, 244–245.

24 Kemal, *The Philosophical Poetics of Alfarabi*, 269.

25 See Kemal, *The Philosophical Poetics of Alfarabi*, 267–270.

26 Eden, *Poetic and Legal Fiction*, 63.

27 *On the Soul*, e.g. 427b27–428a4.

28 *Rhetoric* III.x.3–4 (1410b).

29 Especially eloquent examples are: "Et propter hanc causam utimur in docendo exemplis, ut facilius intelligatur quod dicitur, propter hoc quod in eis est de motivo ymaginative; recipit ergo anima perfectius proposita secundum delectationem sui quam habet in exemplis" (45); "'Representatio' inquam, que generat in animabus passiones quasdam temperativas ipsarum ad miserendum aut timendum aut ad ceteras consimiles passiones quas inducit et promovet per hoc quod ymaginari facit in virtuosis de honestate et munditia. Representatio quippe non est nisi propter dispositiones que consequuntur virtuosos, non propter habitus, utpote sapientiales et consimiles, cum illorum fieri non possit ymaginativa representatio. Et ista representatio per sermonem completur quando coniungitur ei tonus et metrum; et in recitatoribus carminum reperiuntur dispositiones alie preter eas que sunt in metro et in oratione, que faciunt orationem magis representativam, scilicet gestus mutales et inmutationes vultuum, prout iam dictun est in libro Rethorice (47); Est autem operatio toni in poemate, quoniam preparat animam ad recipiendum ymagines rei cuius intenditur ymaginatio; est ergo tonus hoc quod acquirere facit animam aptitudinem per quam recipiat assimilationem et representationem rei cuius intenditur assimilatio, et facit quidem acquirere animam hanc habitudinem in unaquaque specierum poematis tonus conveniens illi speciei per eius simphoniam et compositionem ipsi (47); Quando ergo fuerint actiones possibiles et quasi reales amplius incidit per eas sufficientia persuasiva scilicet credulitas poetica motiva anime ad assequendum aliquid aut refutandum ipsum" (52).

30 "Et terminus substantialis, sive intelligere faciens substantiam artis laudandi, est quoniam ipsa est assimilatio et representatio operationis voluntarie virtuose complete que habet potentiam universalem in rebus virtuosis, non potentiam particularem in unaquaque rerum virtuosarum. 'Representatio' inquam, que generat in animabus passiones quasdam temperativas ipsarum ad miserendum aut timendum aut ad ceteras consimiles passiones quas inducit et promovet per hoc quod ymaginari facit in virtuosis" (47/285).

31 "Et hoc quod se habet ex hiis partibus tamquam principium et fundamentum est sermo fabularis representativus. Et pars secunda sunt consuetudines, et est illud in quo primitus usitata est representatio, scilicet est illud quod representatur (et est quidem representatio seu imitatio sustentamentum et fundamentum in hac arte; propterea quod non fit delectatio ex rememoratione rei cuius intenditur rememoratio absque sui representatione). Sed fit delectatio quidem et receptio ipsius quando representata fuerit" (48/295).

32 "Et bonitas narrationis poetice et perventio in ipsa ad finem complementi est quidem quando poeta in relationibus et narrationibus suis sic certitudinaliter narrat, ut rem narratam quasi presentem sub sensu et aspectu auditorum ponat, ita ut non solum rem narratam comprehendant, sed etiam quo intellectus contrariorum ipsius eos non perterreat" (62/369).

33 "Omne itaque poema et omnis oratio poetica aut est vituperatio aut est laudatio. Et hoc patet per inductionem poematum, et proprie poematum ipsorum, que fiunt de rebus voluntariis, scilicet honestis et turpibus. Et hoc modo se habet in artibus representativis" (41/349).

34 "tragedie ... sex partes sint: scilicet sermones fabulares representativi, et consuetudines, et metrum seu pondus, et credulitates, et consideratio, et tonus. Et signum huius est quoniam omnis sermo poeticus dividitur in assimilationem et in id per quod fit assimilatio. Et ea per que fit assimilatio tria sunt: representatio, et metrum, et tonus; et ea que assimilantur in laudando etiam tria sunt: consuetudines, credulitates, et consideratio (id est probatio recte credulitatis)" (48/294).

35 See Bernard Weinberg, *Aristotle's "Poetics" and English Literature: A Collection of Critical Essays*, edited and with an introduction by Elder Olson (Chicago and London, 1965), 360; Hardison, "The Place of Averroës' Commentary," 70; Minnis and Scott, eds., *Medieval Literary Theory and Criticism*, 286–287.

36 See Halliwell, *Aristotle's Poetics*, 299.

37 "tres maneries per quas fit representatio, scilicet per sermonem ymaginativum et metrum et tonum" (48).

38 "Et pars sexta est consideratio, scilicet argumentatio seu probatio rectitudinis credulitatis aut operationis non per sermonem persuasivam (hoc enim non pertinet huic arti neque est conveniens ei), sed per sermonem representativum; ars nempe poetrie non est consistens in argumentationibus neque in speculatione considerativa et proprie tragedia" (49).

39 "Et pars tertia tragedie est credulitas; et hec est potentia representandi rem sic esse aut sic non esse. Et hoc est simile ei quod conatur

rethorica in declaratione quod res existat aut non existat, nisi quod rethorica conatur ad hoc per sermonem persuasivum, et poetria per sermonem representativum" (49/296).

40 "Sunt fabule que referuntur per assimilationem et representationem seu imitationem, et dico 'fabulam' compositionem rerum quarum intenditur representatio aut secundum hoc quod sunt in semetipsis, aut secundum quod assuetum est in poeticis fingere eas, quamvis sit fictio mendosa. Et propter hoc dictum est quoniam sermones poetici fabule sunt. Recitatores ergo et renunciatores, ut in summa dicatur, sunt illi qui potentiam habent representandi consuetudines et credulitates hominum" (48), my translation.

41 Averroës also develops some issues on the structure and unity of story ("oportet ut ars in hoc imitetur naturam, videlicet ut, omnia que agit, agat secundum unum propositum et ad unum finem" (51).

42 "Et consuetudines comprehendunt actiones et mores" (48/294).

43 "Et oportet ut sit fabularis adinventio pavorosa dolorosa inventio quasi ante oculos constituta, que quasi ex visu fidem habeat. Quando enim fabularis narratio ambigua fuerit et adinventa adinventione dubitabili, non aget actionem que per ipsam intenta fuerat. Quod enim non crediderit quis non movebit eum neque ad timendum neque ad miserendum" (56/305–6).

44 "Iam ergo patet ex hiis que dicta sunt quot sunt maneries representationis et ex quibus artibus componuntur representationes per sermonem ita quod perveniat actio ad complementum" (43).

45 "representationes que fiunt per figmenta mendosa adinventitia non sunt de opere poete" (51/299).

46 "patet quoniam poeta non est poeta nisi per operationem fabularum et metrorum seu ponderum secundum quantitatem per quam potens sit ad operandum assimilationes et imitativas representationes. Et ipse quidem non operatur assimilationem nisi ad res voluntarias existentes in natura. Et non est de conditione sua ut imitetur seu representet res illas tantum que existentes sunt, sed et eas de quibus putatur quod possibilis sit earum consistentia. … nichil enim prohibet ut sumat res illas tamquam eas que nunc existunt. Non indigetur itaque in commotione ymaginativa poetica huius fabulis figmentalibus" (52/301).

47 Lausberg also shows that *evidentia* and *imaginatio* can be connected to one another (Heinrich Lausberg, *Handbuch der literarischen Rhetorik. Eine Grundlegung der Literaturwissenschaft.* 3.e Auflage (Stuttgart, 1990), § 810–812).

CHAPTER THREE
MATHIAS LINCOPENSIS

1 See Carl-Gustaf Undhagen, "Special Introduction," in *Sancta Birgitta. Revelaciones* I, ed. Carl-Gustaf Undhagen, Samlingar utgivna av Svenska fornskriftsällskapet 2:VII:1 (Uppsala, 1978), 38–226, 38.

2 "Sane stupendior est hec apparicio illa, qua se per carnem monstrauit. Illa carnis superficiem carnalibus oculis ingessit, hec Deum et hominem spiritualibus oculis ingerit" (*Sancta Birgitta. Revelaciones* I, 234–235).

3 Hjalmar Sundén, *Den heliga Birgitta. Ormungens moder som blev Kristi brud* (Stockholm, 1973), 11–17. See also Undhagen, "Special Introduction," 45 n52.

4 Following the translation of *The New English Bible. New Testament* (Oxford, 1961).

5 *De trinitate* XV.viii.40–44 (*Sancti Aurelii Augustini de Trinitate Libri XV [Libri XIII–XV]*, Cura et Studio W. J. Mountain, Corpus Christianorum L, A (Turnholti, 1968).

6 *De trinitate* XXV.ii.24–28.

7 "Quis enim non uidet cogitationem suam? Et quis uidet cogitationem suam (non oculis carnalibus dico sed ipso interiore conspectu)? Quis non eam uidet, et quis eam uidet? Quandoquidem cogitatio uisio est animi quaedam siue adsint ea quae oculis quoque corporalibus uideantur uel ceteris sentiantur sensibus, siue non adsint et eorum similitudines cogitatione cernantur; siue nihil eorum sed ea cogitentur quae nec corporalia sunt nec corporalium similitudines sicut uirtutes et uitia, sicut ipsa denique cogitatio cogitatur" (*De trinitate* XV.ix.54–62. Translation from *Writings*

of Saint Augustine 18. The Trinity, trans. Stephen McKenna (Washington, 1963)).

8 See *De trinitate* XV.viii.1–3.

9 *Rev.* IV.18: *Sancta Birgitta. Revelaciones* IV, ed. Birger Bergh, Samlingar utgivna av Svenska fornskriftsällskapet 2:VII:6 (Stockholm, 1991), 87–88. See e.g. Mereth Lindgren, "Birgitta och bilderna," in *Heliga Birgitta – budskapet och förebilden*, ed. Alf Härdelin and Mereth Lindgren (Stockholm, 1993), 231–251.

10 Anders Piltz, "Inspiration, vision, profetia. Birgitta och teorierna om uppenbarelsen," in *Heliga Birgitta – budskapet och förebilden*, ed. Alf Härdelin and Mereth Lindgren (Stockholm, 1993), 67–88, 78–84.

11 The version of Averroës that Mathias met may have been a revised one (Mehtonen, "Essential Art," 130). H.A.Kelly, in his presentation of Mathias's *Poetria* and its background, focuses on the discussion of dramatic genre and moral value of poet, "Aristotle–Averroës–Alemannus on Tragedy." See Birger Bergh, "Introduction," in *Magister Mathias Lincopensis. Testa Nucis and Poetria*, ed. and trans. Birger Bergh, Samlingar utgivna av Svenska fornskriftsällskapet 2:IX:2 (Stockholm, 1996), 7–13.

12 "Omnes plerumque sermocinales facultates circa sermones intellectuales arbitrantes insistere poetriam solam circa sermones imaginatiuos asserimus conuersari. Vnde merito similitudinem habet poeta cum pictore. Sicut enim pictor peritus rem, que in se delectabilis non esset aspicere, propter conuenienciam in disposicione parcium picture et colorum delectabiliter inuenitur representare, sic poeta perfectus delectat animam in faciendo rem secundum suas proprietates imaginari" (*Magister Mathias Lincopensis. Testa Nucis and Poetria*, ed. and trans. Birger Bergh, Samlingar utgivna av Svenska fornskriftsällskapet 2:IX:2 (Stockholm, 1996), § 5–6. The translation of *Poetria* is that of Bergh, but I here render *imaginatiuos* with "imaginative" instead of Bergh's "imitative" and occasionally insert the original terms. Bergh correctly translates *representacio* with "visualization," but I keep the original for clarity's sake).

13 "Completur autem imaginacio per tria, scilicet per *representacionem, tonum* et *metrum*, et sola quidem representacio est de esse poetrie" (§ 7).

14 Päivi Mehtonen effectively illuminates Mathias's idea of *essencialia* and *accidentalia* in poetry by placing him in between the Aristotelian and the Horatian tradition respectively (Mehtonen, "Essential Art").

15 "ostensio rei per sermonem, tanquam iam ante oculos fieri videatur" (§ 8, et passim).

16 "Aut enim representatur res per suas proprietates, secundum quas intelligibiliter representari potest … et hec representacio nominari potest *descripcio*" (§ 9).

17 "Consideracio uero non est nisi ostensio dubiorum et hoc non per raciones aut persuasiones (quoniam hoc non spectat ad poetam) sed per representaciones tam certe et veraciter factas, ut non credatur res ficta esse" (§ 66).

18 "Omnes itaque representaciones poetice sunt aut laudatiue aut vituperatiue."

19 "Vnde adinuenire fabulas et interponere in metris non spectat ad poetam, quoniam huiusmodi inuenciones non faciunt credulitatem, quam requirit sermo laudantis" (§ 32).

20 "Admittuntur tamen quandoque, si conuenienter fingantur et verisimiliter, maxime propter delectandum, nonnumquam eciam propter occultacionem alicuius veri per ipsas fabulas intellecti. Et tunc forte non eueniunt fabule sed aut methafore aut permutaciones huiusmodi, de quibus iam dudum diximus" (§ 33).

21 Mehtonen instead claims that "Although Matthew did focus on persuasive presentation, he also provided more latitude for fictional *representatio poetica* than did either the Horatian-Ciceronian or the Arabic-Aristotelian tradition alone." Mehtonen's strongest argument is that Mathias in *Testa nucis* (§ 20–22) describes *fabula* as a kind of *exemplum*, used by poets as a means of persuasion, and that one may borrow such *fabularia exempla* already invented by poets (Mehtonen, "Essential Art," 135–137). To the extent that Mathias's *Poetria* can be supplemented by his *Testa nucis*, it seems to me that he there speaks of poetry which already exists, not of how poetry should be devised. In any case, compared to Averroës, the *Poetria* speaks for itself.

22 Thus Deborah Black criticizes O.B.Hardison for exaggerating the idea of poetics as an "empty" discipline (Black, *Logic and Aristotle's "Rhetoric,"* 5–6).

23 "Ponitur autem res ante oculos, quando inducitur tanquam presencialiter operans, sicut in *Testa nucis* plenius ab Aristotile assumpsimus" (§ 11).

24 Aristotle, *Rhetoric* III.x.7–xi.4 (1411a–1412a); *Aristoteles Latinus* XXXI *1–2. Rhetorica. Translatio Anonyma sive Vetus et Translatio Guillelmi de Moerbeka*, ed. Bernhardus Schneider (Leiden, 1978).

25 "sicut poëtica non capiuntur a ratione humana propter defectum veritatis qui est in eis, ita etiam ratio humana perfecte capere non potest divina propter excedentem ipsorum veritatem. Et ideo utrobique opus est repræsentatione per sensibiles figuras" (*Summa theologiæ*, ed. Thomas Gilby (New York, 1964–81), 1a2æ. 101, 2. Cf. 1a. 1, 9).

26 See Bengt Strömberg, *Magister Mathias och fransk mendikantpredikan* (Stockholm, 1944).

27 See e.g. Anders Piltz, "Uppenbarelserna och uppenbarelsen. Birgittas förhållande till bibeln," in *Birgitta. Hendes værk og hendes klostre i Norden*, ed. Tore Nyberg (Odense, 1991), 447–469; Piltz, "Inspiration, vision, profetia. Birgitta och teorierna om uppenbarelsen"; Lindgren, "Birgitta och bilderna"; and Eva Odelman, "Uppenbarelsernas retorik," in *Heliga Birgitta – budskapet och förebilden*, ed. Alf Härdelin and Mereth Lindgren (Stockholm, 1993), 15–21, 19.

28 See e.g. Knut B. Westman, *Birgitta-studier* (Uppsala, 1911), 4; Birgit Klockars, *Birgitta och böckerna* (Stockholm, 1973), 29–30; Birger Bergh, "Birgittas djävulsskildringar," *Credo* 54 (1973), 108–115, 108–109; Kjerstin Norén, "The Soul Is Far Better by Nature than the Body," in *The History of Nordic Women's Literature* (http://nordicwomensliterature.net/article/soul-far-better-nature-body) (Själen är av långt bättre natur än kroppen. Om Birgitta av Vadstena," in *Nordisk kvinnolitteraturhistoria* I, ed. Elisabeth Møller Jensen, Eva Hættner Aurelius and Anne-Marie Mai (Höganäs, 1993), 120–134).

29 Birger Bergh, "Matts Övidsson, 'Nötskalet' och den heliga Birgitta," in *Vetenskap och retorik. En gammal konst i modern belysning*, ed. Kurt Johannesson (Stockholm, 2001), 88–95; Eva Odelman, "Lärd och folklig retorik hos Birgitta," in *Vetenskap och retorik. En gammal konst i modern belysning*, ed. Kurt Johannesson (Stockholm, 2001), 96–105.

30 "vel illa verba diuinitus ei data scribebat in lingua sua materna manu sua propria, quando erat sana, et faciebat illa translatari in lingua latina fidelissime a nobis confessoribus suis et postea ascultabat illa cum scriptura sua, quam illa scripserat, ne vnum verbum ibi plus adderetur uel deficeret, nisi que ipsa in visione diuinitus audierat et viderat. Si vero erat infirma, vocabat confessorem et scriptorem suum secretarium ad hoc specialiter deputatum, et tunc ipsa cum magna deuocione et timore Dei et aliquando cum lacrimis referebat ei verba illa in vulgari suo cum quadam attenta eleuacione mentali, quasi si legeret in libro, et tunc confessor dicebat illa verba in lingua latina illi scriptori, et ille scribebat illa ibidem in sua presencia, et postea cum erant verba conscripta, ipsa volebat illa ascultare et ascultabat valde diligenter et attente" (*Acta et processus canonizacionis beate Birgitte*, ed. Isak Collijn, Samlingar utgivna av Svenska fornskriftsällskapet 2:1 (Uppsala, 1924–31), 84). Cf. Odelman, "Uppenbarelsernas retorik"; Hans Aili, "St. Birgitta and the Text of the *Revelationes*: A Survey of Some Influences Traceable to Translators and Editors," in *The Editing of Theological and Philosophical Texts from the Middle Ages*, ed. Monika Asztalos (Stockholm, 1986), 75–91.

31 See Carl Gustaf Undhagen, "General Introduction," in *Sancta Birgitta. Revelaciones* I, ed. Carl-Gustaf Undhagen, Samlingar utgivna av Svenska fornskriftsällskapet 2:VII:1 (Uppsala, 1978), 1–37, 9–10; Klockars, *Birgitta och böckerna*, 17, 222; Jan Liedgren, "Magister Matthias' svenska kungörelse om Birgittas första stora uppenbarelse. Ett förbisett dokument i riksarkivet," 101–116.

32 See Lindgren, "Birgitta och bilderna," 231.

33 "Mater autem predicta mortua videbatur quasi serpere de tenebroso lacu et luto. Cuius cor abstractum erat et labia precisa, mentum quoque tremebat, dentes vero eius nitentes albi et longi collidebantur. Nares erant corrose et oculi eruti, dependentes ad genas duobus neruis. Frons videbatur immersa et loco frontis immane baratrum et tenebrosum. In capite vero deerat craneum, et cerebrum quasi plumbum ebuliebat

et quasi pix effluebat. Collum quoque eius circumuoluebatur sicut lignum, quod tornatur in torno seu in runcina, cui ferrum acutissimum oppositum erat, abradens sine consolacione. Pectus vero apertum erat plenum vermibus longis et paruis, quorum quilibet huc et illuc voluebatur super alium. ... Vnus quoque serpens longus et magnus traxit se per inferiora stomachi ad superiora, qui coniungens caput et caudam quasi arcus circuibat viscera continue quasi rota. Crura vero et tibie videbantur quasi duo baculi spinosi acutissimis aculeis pleni, pedes vero eius erant quasi buffonum" (*Sancta Birgitta. Revelaciones* VI, ed. B. Bergh, Samlingar utgivna av Svenska fornskriftsällskapet 2:VII:6 (Stockholm, 1991), 183–184).

34 Lindgren, "Birgitta och bilderna."

35 "penitencia est sicut bona lotrix macularum ... contritio vero est bona candidatrix" (Odelman, "Uppenbarelsernas retorik," 19).

36 "que vides me, non vides me nisi per similitudines corporales. Si enim videres me in ea forma, in qua sum, moreris ex timore, quia omnia membra mea sunt demones. Ideo vera est Scriptura, que dicit, quod, sicut iusti sunt membra Dei, ita peccatores sunt membra dyaboli. Sic ego nunc experior, quod demones affixi sunt anime mee, quia voluntas cordis mei disposuit me ad tantam deformitatem" (VI:52, 185).

37 "Tibi videtur, quod pedes mei sunt quasi buffonis. Hoc ideo est, quia stabiliter steti in peccato; propterea nunc demones stabiliter stant in me, et mordentes me numquam saciantur. Tibie vero et crura mea sunt quasi baculi spinosi, quia voluntatem meam habui secundum carnalem delectationem et voluptatem meam. ... Quod vero serpens vnus traxerat se per inferiora stomachi ad superiora et stans quasi arcus circuit quasi rota, hoc ideo est, quia voluptas et delectacio mea inordinata fuit et voluntas mea volebat omnia possidere et mulitipliciter expendere et indiscrete. Ideo nunc serpens circuit interiora mea, inconsolabiliter et immisericorditer me mordendo. Quod vero pectus meum apertum est et corrosum a vermibus, hoc veram Dei demonstrat iusticiam. Dilexi quippe putrida plus quam Deum, et ad transitoria erat amor cordis mei" (VI:52, 185–186).

38 It has been noted that the revelations where Bridget *sees* Christ, Mary and others are less common than the revelations where she *hears* them speak to her (Klockars, *Birgitta och böckerna*, 64). The means of visualization should thus be limited in these. Yet, it has also been noted that visualizing devices such as similes and images abound even in those auditive revelations (Lindgren, "Birgitta och bilderna," 231–232). Consequently, the techniques of visualization seem to be very much the same whether Bridget records her visual experiences or utterances she has heard.

39 Foremost Klockars, *Birgitta och böckerna*, and Lindgren, "Birgitta och bilderna."

40 "Audi que loquor et vade ad magistrum Mathiam, confessorem tuum, qui expertus est duorum spirituum secundum discrecionem, dic ei ex parte mea, que dico tibi, quia tu eris sponsa mea et canale meum et audies et videbis spiritualia, et spiritus meus permanebit tecum vsque ad mortem" (*Acta et processus canonizacionis beate Birgitte*, ed. Isak Collijn, Samlingar utgivna av Svenska fornskriftsällskapet 2:1 (Uppsala, 1924–31), 81). Cf.: "Reuelaciones quoque, quas habuerat in patria Swecie, semper eas reuelauerat magistro Mathie et isti testi loquenti cum humilitate, et obediebat super hoc, quicquid determinabatur a dicto magistro Mathia" (*Acta et processus canonizacionis beate Birgitte*, 489).

41 Jan Liedgren, "Magister Matthias' svenska kungörelse om Birgittas första stora uppenbarelse. Ett förbisett dokument i riksarkivet," in *Meddelanden från svenska riksarkivet för år 1958* (Stockholm, 1961), 101–116.

42 "vel illa verba diuinitus ei data scribebat in lingua sua materna manu sua propria, quando erat sana, et faciebat illa translatari in lingua latina fidelissime a nobis confessoribus suis et postea ascultabat illa cum scriptura sua, quam illa scripserat, ne vnum verbum ibi plus adderetur uel deficeret, nisi que ipsa in visione diuinitus audierat et viderat. Si vero erat infirma, vocabat confessorem et scriptorem suum secretarium ad hoc specialiter deputatum, et tunc ipsa cum magna deuocione et timore Dei et aliquando cum lacrimis referebat ei verba illa in vulgari suo cum quadam attenta eleuacione mentali, quasi si legeret in libro, et tunc confessor dicebat illa verba in lingua latina illi scriptori, et ille scribebat illa ibidem in sua presencia, et postea cum erant verba conscripta, ipsa volebat illa ascultare et ascultabat valde diligenter et attente" (*Acta et processus canonizacionis beate Birgitte*, ed. Isak Collijn, Samlingar utgivna av Svenska fornskrift-sällskapet 2:1 (Uppsala, 1924–31), 84).

43 "Reuelaciones quoque, quas habuerat in patria Swecie, semper eas reuelauerat magistro Mathie et isti testi loquenti cum humilitate, et obediebat super hoc, quicquid determinabatur a dicto magistro Mathia" (*Acta et processus canonizacionis beate Birgitte*, 489).

44 Regarding this tradition, see Friis-Jensen, "Horace and the Early Writers."

CHAPTER FOUR
THE ITALIAN RENAISSANCE

1 See Lane Cooper and Alfred Gudeman, *A Bibliography of the Poetics of Aristotle*, Cornell Studies in English XI (New Haven and London, 1928), 1–6, 19–25. I am grateful to Ulla Åkerström for valuable discussions of the Italian sources in this chapter.

2 "OMnis porro tragœdiæ quate*n*us aliqua i*n*signis est qualitate tragœdia partes sex esse necesse est. su*n*tq*ue* fabula & mores & dictio & a*nim*i sente*n*tia: & conspectus & melopoeia, q*ui*bus na*m*q*ue* imita*ntur* binæ su*n*t partes ut uero imita*ntur* una sicut quas imitantur tres" (*Aristotelis De Poetica interprete Georgio Valla Placentino* (Venice, 1498), r iii r).

3 "Pri*n*cipiu*m* igitu*r* & uelut a*n*i*m*a tragœdiæ e*st* fabula secu*n*do loco mores" (ibid.). Also the words in the first chapter, suggesting that emotions may, at least to dancers, be objects on the same level as actions, is faithfully rendered: "Veru*m* numero ipso imitant*ur* absq*ue* harmonia saltita*n*tes: hi siq*ui*de*m* numeroru*m* effigie mores: & affectus & actio*n*es imita*ntur*" (r i r).

4 Weinberg, *A History of Literary Criticism*, and "From Aristotle to Pseudo-Aristotle," in *Aristotle's "Poetics" and English Literature: A Collection of Critical Essays*, edited with an introduction by Elder Olson (Chicago and London, 1965), 192–200.

5 At times, Weinberg uses the terms "imitation-invention" and "imitation-elocution" in a way which roughly corresponds to mimesis-composition and mimesis-representation (however, mimesis-composition includes not only invention but also disposition and structure), but he simultaneously speaks of a "slipping" "from imitation to invention," see Weinberg, *A History of Literary Criticism*, 421.

6 Weinberg, *A History of Literary Criticism*, 60–63. As Weinberg here notes, the Platonic association of fable with lie is also important.

7 See Halliwell, *Aristotle's Poetics*, 317, 292n.

8 Weinberg, "From Aristotle to Pseudo-Aristotle," 196.

9 Weinberg, "From Aristotle to Pseudo-Aristotle," 197–199, and *A History of Literary Criticism*, 361–511.

10 Weinberg, "From Aristotle to Pseudo-Aristotle," 60.

11 "due esser le sorti della Imitatione poetica. Vna, laguale consiste nell'esprimere eccellentemente le nature et i costumi di quelle persone, che ci proponiamo d'imitare. Et questo è il fine della poesia ... Ma di queste sorti di imitationi lasciando la cura ad Aristotele, solamente tratteremo dell'altra, laquale consiste nelle parole, et ne modi di dire" (Bernardino Parthenio, *Della imitatione poetica* (1560), 92–94. Quoted from Weinberg, *A History of Literary Criticism*, 60).

12 Weinberg, *A History of Literary Criticism*, 389.

13 An interesting example of precise insight into Aristotle's categories is Francesco Patrizi's *Della poetica*, 1586 (treated by Baxter Hathaway, *The Age of Criticism: The Late Renaissance in Italy* (Ithaca, NY, 1962), 9–22, and Weinberg, *A History of Literary Criticism*, 64–65). Patrizi demonstrates that the word mimesis occurs in six different meanings in Aristotle's *Poetics* and *Rhetoric*. Among these meanings are both mimesis-composition and mimesis-representation. In poetics so dominated by rhetorical thinking, the dichotomy is obvious since it corresponds to that of *res-verba*.

14 As a rule, *imitatione* is also used of direct speech, as opposed to *narrazione*. This, however, will not be taken into account in the following.

15 Francesco Robortello, *In Librum Aristotelis de Arte Poetica Explicationes. Paraphrasis in*

Librum Horatii, Qui Vulgo de Arte Poetica ad Pisones Inscribitur (1548), Poetiken des Cinquecento 8 (Munich, 1968).

16 See Bernard Weinberg, "Robortello on the *Poetics*," in *Critics and Criticism: Ancient and Modern* (Chicago, 1952), 319–348.

17 See Weinberg, "Robortello on the *Poetics*," in *A History of Literary Criticism*, 66–68, 388–399.

18 "Quapropter actiones, & fabula, Tragoediae finis esse dicuntur" (*Explicationes*, 89).

19 *Explicationes*, 57 (Robortello describes *fabvla, mores, sententia* and *dictio* as those parts which are "essentiales"). Cf. Weinberg, "Robortello on the *Poetics*," 335–336; *A History of Literary Criticism*, 394.

20 "Qualis sit poëtica facultas, & quam habeat uim; Quem finum propositum; Quam materiem subiectam, ex qua opus suum conficiat" (1).

21 "Nunc illud consequi videtur, quod antea fuerat à me propositum, vt de fine facultatis huius aliquid dicamus" (2).

22 "Quem igitur alium finem poetices facultatis esse dicemus, quam oblectare per repræsentationem, descriptionem, & imitationem omnium actionum humanarum; omnium motionum; omnium rerum tum animatarum, tum inanimatarum?" (2).

23 "Et quoniam imitatio, & representatio hec per orationem fit; dicimus in poetice finem esse, sermonem imitantem, sicut in rhetorice sermonem persuadentem" (2).

24 Ulrike Zeuch, "Aporien in der Literaturtheorie der Frühen Neuzeit. Francesco Robortellos *In Librum Aristotelis De arte poetica explicationes* und die Folgen," in *Mimesis – Repräsentation – Imagination. Literaturtheoretische Positionen von Aristoteles bis zum Ende des 18. Jahrhunderts*, ed. Jörg Schönert and Ulrike Zeuch (Berlin and New York, 2004), 181–214.

25 See chapter 8.

26 Lodovico Castelvetro, *Poetica D'Aristotile vulgarizzata, et sposta (1570)*, Poetiken des Cinquecento 1 (Munich, 1967).

27 Bernard Weinberg, "Castelvetro's Theory of Poetics," in *Critics and Criticism: Ancient and Modern* (Chicago, 1952), 349–371, 362. Even if unity of action was the most original of the unities, Castelvetro's view on drama is really a consequence of the restrictions imposed by the two other unities (366).

28 "la dirittura della poetica consiste in rassomigliare con parole harmonizzate vna attione humana" (Weinberg, "Castelvetro's Theory of Poetics," 358).

29 See Weinberg, "Castelvetro's Theory of Poetics," 349.

30 "la mutatione & la riconoscenza, che sono due cose molto piu attrattiue" (75).

31 Klaus R. Scherpe points out that Castelvetro made the dichotomy (*Gattungspoetik im 18. Jahrhundert. Historische Entwicklung von Gottsched bis Herder*. Studien zur allgemeinen und vergleichenden Literaturwissenschaft (Stuttgart, 1968), 71fn). The Castelvetro quotation was treated by Hugo Bieber, *Johann Adolf Schlegels poetische Theorie* (Berlin, 1912), 180.

32 "Poesia è similitudine, o rassomiglianza d'historia. Et si come historia si diuide in due parti principali, cio è in materia & in parole, cosi poesia si diuide in due parti principali, che sono similmente materia, & parole, ma in queste due parti sono differenti tra se historia & poesia che historia non ha la materia, ce le sia apprestata dallo'ngegno dell'historico, ma le è apprestata dal corso delle mondane cose, o dal volere manifesto, o oculto di dio, & ha le parole apprestate dall'historico si, ma tali, quali s'vsano ragionando. Et poesia ha sua materia trouata & imaginata dallo'ngegno del poeta, & ha le parole non tali, quali s'vsano ragionando[.] Percio che non s'vsa tra gli huomini di ragionare in versi, ma le ha composte in misurati versi per l'opera dello'ngegno del poeta" (16).

33 Cf. Weinberg, "Castelvetro's Theory of Poetics," 368.

34 Weinberg, *A History of Literary Criticism*, 68. See also August Buck, "Einleitung," in Julius Caesar Scaliger, *Poetices libri septem*. Faksimile-Neudruck der Ausgabe Leipzig von Lyon 1561 mit einer Einleitung von August Buck (Stuttgart–Bad Cannstatt, 1987), v–xx, xvi.

35 Zeuch points out that Scaliger puts Robortello's theory that anything can be the object of poetry into system (Zeuch, "Aporien in der Literaturtheorie," 205), but this is an evident consequence of the focus on mimesis-representation.

36 Julius Caesar Scaliger, *Poetices libri septem*. Faksimile-Neudruck der Ausgabe Leipzig von Lyon 1561 mit einer Einleitung von August Buck (Stuttgart, 1987), esp. I.1. Cf. Buck's introduction and Zeuch, "Aporien in der Literaturtheorie," 203.

37 August Buck, "Einleitung," in Emanuele Tesauro, *Il Cannocchiale Aristotelico*, herausgegeben und eingeleitet von August Buck, Bad Homburg v.d.H. (Berlin and Zurich, 1968), XII–XIII.

38 Green, "Aristotelian Lexis and Renaissance Elocutio," 161. Cf. Green's "The Reception of Aristotle's *Rhetoric* in the Renaissance," in *Peripatetic Rhetoric after Aristotle*, ed. William W. Fortenbaugh and David C. Mirhady (New Brunswick, NJ, 1994), 320–348.

39 "questa evidenza, o energia nel rappresentare, è quella immitazione di cui tanto si disputa, propia del poeta e commune ad ogni individuo di poesia" (Sforza Pallavicino, *Da "Del Bene", Trattatisti e narratori del Seicento*, a cura di Ezio Raimondi (Naples, 1960), 218–262, 253).

40 "Or, se la poesia procura d'assomigliar l'istoria, come traccia essa le minutezze dall'istoria fuggite? Ma è possibile che un tal uomo non vedesse che, quantunque il finto sia immitazione del vero, tuttavia l'espressione del finto non è immitazione dell'espressione del vero, e che però non fa mestieri, per esempio, che'l pittore d'invenzione sappia l'arte di far bene i ritratti, dovendo quest'arte esprimer le cose quali sono, o belle o non belle che sieno, e dovendo per lo contrario il pittor d'invenzione formar le sue figure in maniera ch'elle assomiglino non già nel tutto, ma nelle parti separatamente considerate, qual si sia delle cose che sono o che furono, purché gustose a mirarsi, e così convenendo loro osservar diversi precetti? L'istoria vuole insegnar que' successi ch'è spediente altrui d'imparare. Né si cura gran fatto di fargli vivamente apprendere per non allungarsi con leggiero profitto dal fine suo. Però lascia le minutezze e poco usa le metafore, e meno le simiglianze e gli epiteti non necessari. La poesia vuol far apprendere ciò che ad apprender è dilettevole, e perché il diletto dell'apprensione nasce dalla vivacità di quella de dallo splendor de' colori ond'ella è dipinta, però la poesia non è inventrice di que' successi che, se fosser veri, gioverebbono a sapersi, ma finge quelli i quali, avvenga che falsi, riescon gustosi ad immaginarsi, e si studia di porli davanti agli occhi, disegnandoli al vivo colle circostanze minute e colorandogli con oltramarine tinture di metafore, di similitudini, di prosopopeie, d'aggiunti e d'altre figure ben espressive e pompose" (Pallavicino, *Del Bene*, 253).

41 "Ma la poesia non cerca la simiglianza del vero se non per far apprendera più vivamente il finto" (254).

42 *Il Cannocchiale Aristotelico*, 2–3. See Ernest B. Gilman, *The Curious Perspective: Literary and Pictorial Wit in the Seventeenth Century* (New Haven and London, 1978), 80.

43 Buck, "Einleitung," in Emanuele Tesauro (*Il Cannocchiale Aristotelico*), XV.

44 See, e.g., Eugenio Donato, "Tesauro's Poetics: Through the Looking Glass," *Modern Language Notes* 78 (1963), 15–30, 16.

45 Foremost Joseph Anthony Mazzeo, "Metaphysical Poetry and the Poetic of Correspondence," *Journal of the History of Ideas* 14 (1953), 221–234; Donato, "Tesauro's Poetics"; Mario Zanardi, "La metafora e la sua dinamica di significazione nel 'Cannocchiale Aristotelico' di Emanuele Tesauro," in *Giornale storico della letteratura italiana* CLVII (Torino, 1980), 321–368; Robert E. Proctor, "Emanuele Tesauro: A Theory of the Conceit," *Modern Language Notes* 88, no. 1 (1973), 68–94; J.W. van Hook, "'Concupiscence of Wit': The Metaphysical Conceit in Baroque Poetics," *Modern Philology* 84, no. 1 (1986), 24–38.

46 "gran Madre di tutte le Argutezze" (82).

47 "Talche l'Imitatione si può chiamar *Maestra de' Maestri*. Questa dunque (come saggiamente discorre il nostro Autore) fù la primiera insegnatrice della Poesia; la cui anima consiste nell'imitare" (115).

48 "Chiamo io dunque IMITATIONE, vna sagacità, con cui propostoti vna Metafora, ò altro fiore dell' humano ingegno" (116).

49 "Et questa è la *Metafora*, Madre delle Poesie, de' Simboli, & delle Imprese" (82).

50 On the Renaissance understanding of *lexis* as artistic discourse, see Green, "Aristotelian Lexis and Renaissance Elocutio."

51 "Tutta la forza di ciascun Vocabolo significante (come dicemmo) consiste nel rappresentare alla mente humana la cosa significata.

Ma questa Rappresentation si può fare, ò col Vocabulo nudo e propio, ilqual non richieda niun' oprea dell' ingegno: ò con alcuna significatione ingegnosa, che insieme rappresenti & diletti. Onde nascono due generali differenze della Oratione: l'vna Propia & Grammaticale: l'altra Retorica & Arguta" (235).

52 "Ἤρξαντο μὲν οὖν κινῆσαι τὸ πρῶτον, ὥσπερ πέφυκεν, οἱ ποιηταί· τὰ γὰρ ὀνόματα μιμήματα ἐστίν, ὑπῆρξε δὲ καὶ ἡ φωνή" (*Rhetoric* 1404a20–22).

53 "Arist. 3. Rhet. c. 1. Cæperunt autem, sicut natura postulat, id primò Poetæ mouere. Metaphorica enim nomina imitationes sunt" (115).

54 Buck, "Einleitung," in Emanuele Tesauro, *Il Cannocchiale Aristotelico*, XV. Buck refers to Hugo Friedrich, *Epochen der italienischen Lyrik* (Frankfurt am Main, 1964), 624n. Neither William of Moerbeke's nor the anonymous translation of Aristotle's *Rhetoric* has this addition, they simply read "nomina enim imitationes sunt" (*Aristoteles Latinus* XXXI 1–2, 123, 282).

55 O. B. Hardison says that *Il Cannocchiale Aristotelico* "is based on a peculiar theory of imitation that may have roots as far back as Averroës' commentary on the *Poetics*" (Hardison, *The Enduring Monument*, 18), and this seems to be true although it is difficult to agree with Hardison's description of Averroës in this place.

56 "Ὅτι μὲν οὖν τὰ ἀστεῖα ἐκ μεταφορᾶς τε τῆς ἀνάλογον λέγεται καὶ τῷ πρὸ ὀμμάτων ποιεῖν, εἴρηται. λεκτέον δὲ τί λέγομεν πρὸ ὀμμάτων, καὶ τί ποιοῦσι γίγνεται τοῦτο" (1411b1).

57 See pp. 396–427 and 286–288, where he initially refers to Aristotle's chapters III.10 and 11. Buck places the importance of vividness in the context of contemporary theory (XII–XIV).

58 "Percioche se tu dì, *Prata* AMOENA SVNT: altro non mi rappresenti che il *Verdeggiar* de' Prati. Ma se tu dirai, *Prata* RIDENT: tu mi farai (come dissi) veder la Terra essere vn' *Huomo animato*: il prato esser la *Faccia*: l'Amenità il *Riso lieto*. Talche in vna paroletta transpaiono tutte queste Notioni di Generi differenti, *Terra, Prato, Amenità, Huomo, Anima, Riso, Letitia*. Et reciprocamente, con veloce tragitto osseruo nella *faccia humana* le Notioni de' *prati*: e tutte le proportioni che passano fra queste & quelle, da me altra volta non osseruate. Et questo è quel veloce & facile insegnamento da cui ci nasce il diletto: parendo alla mente di chi ode, vedere in vn Vocabulo solo, vn pien teatro di merauiglie" (267). The translation is partly from Hook, "'Concupiscence of Wit'," 32.

59 *Aristoteles Latinus* XXXIII, 42.

60 See the discussion on p. 267.

61 "il più *ingegnoso* & *acuto*: il più *pellegrino* e *mirabile*: il più *giouiale* & *gioueuole*: il più *facondo* & *fecondo* parto dell' humano intelletto" (266; cf. 5).

62 "Da vna Specie ad altra farà (secondo il suo fauorito esempio) se tu chiami lo *Scudo*, TAZZA DI MARTE. Ouero la *Tazza*, SCVDO DI BACCO. Peroche la *Tazza* & lo *Scudo*, son due *Specie* similmente collocate sotto al medesimo *Genere* di COSA RITONDA: come due Sorelle procedenti dal medesimo Padre in questo modo" (281). Aristotle, *Rhetoric* 1407a, and *Poetics* 1457b.

63 Donato, "Tesauro's Poetics," 21–22. As the context imposed is arbitrary, Donato considers the poet's subjective angle to be greatly enhanced.

64 "*Significare vna Cosa per mezzo di vn' altra;* & non per gli propri Termini" (636).

65 "gli Angeli stessi, la Natura, il grande Iddio, nel ragionar con gli Huomini, hanno espresso con Argutezze, ò Verbali ò Simboliche, gli lor più astrusi & importanti secreti" (1–2; Buck: "Einleitung," in Emanuele Tesauro, *Il Cannocchiale Aristotelico*, XVII).

66 "Ma le cose più alte & peregrine ci vengono copertamente scoperte, & adumbratamente dipinte à chiaro oscuro, con tre maniere di *Simboli Figurati*; che da' Sacri Suolgitori de' Diuini arcani, grecamente chiamar si sogliono Senso TROPOLOGICO, ALLEGORICO, & ANAGOGICO; mà tutti son METAFORICI" (60).

67 See the discussion in chapter 9.

68 See Mazzeo, "Metaphysical Poetry," 227–228.

69 See also pp. 611 and 615–616.

70 "METAFORA: laquale altro non è, che *Poetica imitatione*, ti si può rappresentare, ò con *Parole*, ò con *Oggetti*, ò con *Attioni animate*" (611).

71 "PITTVRA E SCVLTVRA, son *Metafore rappresentanti vn'oggetto, per mezzo della Imitation de' colori in tauole, ò delle fattezze in rilieuo*" (732).

72 "Ar. 3. de Anima cap. 2. Idem accidit in intellectu quod in pictorum tabulis, in quibus

nihil pictum est, sed omnia pingi possunt" (15). Donato comments on the importance of visuality and the parallel between visualization and conceptualization (Donato, "Tesauro's Poetics," 23–24), but to assert Tesauro's independence from tradition overlooks the influence of Aristotle's *On the Soul* and the Averroistic tradition.

73 Translation from Ernest B. Gilman, *The Curious Perspective*, 80; "portò la vista humana per vna forata canna, la doue vccello non giunge. Con essi tragitta il mar senza vele: ti fà veder di presso le Naui, le Selue, & le Città, che fuggono l'arbitrio della pupilla: anzi volando al Cielo in vn lampo; osserua le macchie nel Sole: scopre le Corna di Vulcano in fronte à Venere: misura i Monti e i Mari nel globo della Luna: numera i pargoletti di Gioue: & ciò che Iddio ci nascose, vn piccol vetro ti riuela" (89–90).

74 "Talche possiam chiamar le sue Rettoriche Vn limpidissimo CANNOCCHIALE; per esaminar tutte le perfettioni, & le imperfettioni della Eloquenza" (2–3).

75 Gilman, *The Curious Perspective*, 80–81; cf. Donato, "Tesauro's Poetics," 24.

76 Dionigi Atanagi, *Ragionamento de la eccelentia et perfettione de la historia* (1559), see Weinberg, *A History of Literary Criticism*, 40–42.

77 "Poëta enim (vt idem testatur Arist.) quatenus fingit, rerum est poëta, non metrorum. Inuentio igitur insignis, & fabule constitutio, in qua ratio morum diligens habeatur, magis capit spectatores, quàm versus inopes rerum & magno cum pondere missi in scenam" (*Horatii Flacci liber De arte poetica Iacobi Grifoli Lucinianensis interpretatione explicatus (1550)*, Poetiken des Cinquecento 3 (Munich, 1967), 98). As Weinberg points out, Grifolo like Robortello defines diction as an object of poetry (Weinberg, *A History of Literary Criticism*, 418–420). Grifolo's reason for defining diction as an object seems to be his focus on scenic performance where the actor really has words as his objects (while Aristotle leaves the actor's imitation aside).

78 "nella forma che è l'eloquenza, nella materia, che è la cosa proposta, et nel fine, che è l'uditore, consiste ogni oratione & parlamento."

79 "actiones humanas imitando, suaui sermone animum excultum reddere." Translations and quotations of Lionardi and Maggi are from Weinberg, *A History of Literary Criticism*, 48, who discusses them as exponents of a scholastic method. Weinberg, *Aristotle's "Poetics,"* 380.

80 Antonio Sebastiano Minturno, *L'arte poetica (1564)*, Poetiken des Cinquecento 6 (Munich, 1976).

CHAPTER FIVE
FRENCH CLASSICISM AND THE NECESSITY OF PROBABILITY

1 See Weinberg, "Castelvetro's Theory of Poetics," 354–365. I am grateful to Anders Melkersson for valuable discussions of the French sources in this chapter.

2 On Corneille's and Racine's relation to Aristotle, see Halliwell, *Aristotle's Poetics*, 305–308.

3 Jean Chapelain, *Opuscules critiques*, with an introduction by Alfred C. Hunter (Paris, 1936), 153–197.

4 "le sujet, les moeurs, les sentiments, la diction, la musique, et la décoration du théâtre" (Pierre Corneille, *Œuvres complètes* III. Textes établis, présentés et annotés par George Couton (Paris, 1987), 123).

5 "Il faut observer l'unité d'action, de lieu, et de jour, personne n'en doute; mais ce n'est pas une petite difficulté de savoir ce que c'est que cette unité d'action, et jusques où peut s'étendre cette unité de jour, et de lieu. Il faut que le poète traite son sujet selon le vraisemblable et le nécessaire; Aristote le dit, et tous ses interprètes répètent les mêmes mots, qui leur semblent si clairs et si intelligibles, qu'aucun d'eux n'a daigné nous dire, non plus que lui, ce que c'est que ce vraisemblable et ce nécessaire. Beaucoup même ont si peu considéré ce dernier, qui accompagne toujours l'autre chez ce philosophe, hormis une seule fois, où il parle de la comédie, qu'on en est venu jusqu'à établir une maxime très fausse, *qu'il faut que le sujet d'une tragédie soit vraisemblable*; appliquant ainsi aux conditions du sujet la moitié de ce qu'il a dit de la manière de le traiter" (Corneille, *Œuvres complètes* III, 117–118).

6 "Ainsi, quoique l'utile n'y entre que sous

la forme du délectable, il ne laisse pas d'y être nécessaire" (Corneille, *Œuvres complètes* III, 119).

7 "Cela m'a fait considérer que les mœurs ne sont pas seulement le principe des actions, mais aussi du raisonnement. Un homme de bien agit et raisonne en homme de bien, un méchant agit et raisonne en méchant, et l'un et l'autre étale de diverses maximes de morale suivant cette diverse habitude. C'est donc de ces maximes, que cette habitude produit, que la tragédie peut se passer, et non pas de l'habitude même, puisqu'elle est le principe des actions, et que les actions sont l'âme de la tragédie, où l'on ne doit parler qu'en agissant et pour agir. Ainsi pour expliquer ce passage d'Aristote par l'autre, nous pouvons dire, que quand il parle d'une tragédie sans mœurs, il entend une tragédie où les acteurs énoncent simplement leurs sentiments, ou ne les appuient que sur des raisonnements tirés du fait" (Corneille, *Œuvres complètes* III, 133).

8 "C'est un privilège qu'il nous donne, et non pas une servitude qu'il nous impose. Cela est clair par ses paroles mêmes. Si nous pouvons traiter les choses selon le vraisemblable, ou selon le nécessaire, nous pouvons quitter le vraisemblable pour suivre le nécessaire, et cette alternative met en notre choix de nous servir de celui des deux que nous jugerons le plus à propos" (Corneille, *Œuvres complètes* III, 161–162).

9 "Pour éclaircir cette préférence mutuelle du vraisemblable au nécessaire, et du nécessaire au vraisemblable, il faut distinguer deux choses dans les actions qui composent la tragédie. La première consiste en ces actions mêmes, accompagnées des inséparables circonstances du temps et du lieu, et l'autre en la liaison qu'elles ont ensemble, qui les fait naître l'une et l'autre. En la première, le vraisemblable est à préférer au nécessaire, et le nécessaire au vraisemblable dans la seconde" (Corneille, *Œuvres complètes* III, 163).

10 On Aristotle, see Halliwell, *Aristotle's Poetics*, 101–106.

11 "Il faut placer les actions où il est plus facile et mieux séant qu'elles arrivent, et les faire arriver dans un loisir raisonnable, sans les presser extraordinairement, si la nécessité de les renfermer dans un lieu et dans un jour ne nous y oblige. J'ai déjà fait voir en l'autre Discours que pour conserver l'unité de lieu, nous faisons parler souvent des personnes dans une place publique, qui vraisemblablement s'entretiendraient dans une chambre; et je m'assure que si on racontait dans un roman ce que je fais arriver dans *Le Cid*, dans *Polyeucte*, dans *Pompée*, ou dans *Le Menteur*, on lui donnerait un peu plus d'un jour pour l'étendue de sa durée. L'obéissance que nous devons aux règles de l'unité de jour et de lieu nous dispense alors du vraisemblable, bien qu'elle ne nous permette pas l'impossible" (Corneille, *Œuvres complètes* III, 163).

12 "Nous sommes gênés au théâtre par le lieu, par le temps, et par les incommodités de la représentation, qui nous empêchent d'exposer à la vue beaucoup de personnages tout à la fois, de peur que les uns ne demeurent sans action, ou troublent celle des autres" (Corneille, *Œuvres complètes* III, 163).

13 Aristotle discusses *desis* and *lusis* in the 18th chapter of the *Poetics*.

14 Pietro Vettori, *Commentarii in primum librum Aristotelis de arte poetarum (1560)*, Poetiken des Cinquecento 9 (Munich, 1967). Also the edition of Heinsius has been preserved with Racine's notes (Halliwell, *Aristotle's Poetics*, 306).

15 "La fable est l'âme de la tragédie" (Jean Racine, *Principes de la Tragédie en Marge de la Poétique d'Aristote*, Texte établi et commenté par Eugène Vinaver (Paris, 1951), 15).

16 "Car ce sont les mœurs et l'inclination, *i. la disposition de l'esprit*, qui rendent les actions telles ou telles. Et par conséquent les mœurs et le sentiment, *ou la disposition de l'esprit*, sont les deux principes des actions" (Racine, *Principes de la Tragédie*, 13).

17 "Or il faut tousjours chercher dans les mœurs, aussi bien que dans la constitution de la fable, ou le nécessaire, ou le vraysemblable, c'est-à-dire qu'il faut que celui qui parle ou qui agit, fasse et dise tout nécessairement ou vraysemblablement; qu'une chose n'arrive point après l'autre que par nécessité, ou parce qu'il est vraysemblable qu'elle arrive ainsi" (Racine, *Principes de la Tragédie*, 29). Aristotle, *Poetics*, ch. 15, 1454a33–38.

18 "Il est donc manifeste que le desnoüement de la fable doit estre tiré de la fable mesme" (Racine, *Principes de la Tragédie*, 29).

19 Jean Racine, *Phèdre*, mise en scène et commentaires de Jean-Louis Barrault (Paris, 1946), 7.

20 "It is tempting to argue that for Racine as for Aristotle the concept of destiny is no more than a mythical premise whose effect can be allowed vaguely to hang around the drama, but which must not interfere with the probable dynamics of human action and passion" (Halliwell, *Aristotle's Poetics*, 307).

CHAPTER SIX
THE PRINCIPLE AND POLEMICS OF THE FINE ARTS

1 Charles Batteux, *Les beaux arts réduits à un même principe par l'abbé C. Batteux* (Paris, 1746), 5–6; cf. Göran Sörbom, "The Theory of Imitation Is Not a Theory of Art: Some Stages in a Conceptual Tradition," in *Understanding the Arts: Contemporary Scandinavian Aesthetics*, ed. Jeanette Emt and Göran Hermerén, Studies in Aesthetics 3 (Lund, 1992), 227. I am grateful to Britt-Marie Karlsson for valuable discussions of the French sources in this chapter.

2 On the reception, see foremost Manfred Schenker, *Charles Batteux und seine Nachahmungstheorie in Deutschland* (Leipzig, 1909) and Irmela von der Lühe, *Natur und Nachahmung. Untersuchungen zur Batteux-Rezeption in Deutschland* (Bonn, 1979).

3 Next to Schenker and Lühe, the polemics in itself has been treated foremost by Bieber, *Johann Adolf Schlegels poetische Theorie*; Lars Gustafsson, *Le poëte masqué et démasqué. Étude sur la mise en valeur du poète sincère dans la poétique du classicisme et du préromantisme* (Uppsala, 1968); and Anna Cullhed, *The Language of Passion: The Order of Poetics and the Construction of a Lyric Genre 1746–1806* (Uppsala, 2002).

4 See Scherpe, *Gattungspoetik im 18. Jahrhundert*, 26–57, 169–259; Lühe, *Natur und Nachahmung*, 24–25.

5 Lars Gustafsson first pointed it out, while Irmela von der Lühe described the controversy as an opposition devised for national and political reasons, and Cullhed has portrayed the same issues as an examination in discourse. Lars Gustafsson, "'Imitation' och 'äkthet'. En linje i 1700-talets diskussion om mimesisprincipen," *Samlaren. Tidskrift för svensk litteraturvetenskaplig forskning* (1959), 39–59, 55; Lühe, *Natur und Nachahmung*, e.g. 10, 154; Cullhed, *The Language of Passion*, 249–251.

6 Schenker, *Charles Batteux*, 35–36.

7 Bieber, *Johann Adolf Schlegels poetische Theorie*, 14, 48–49.

8 Gustafsson, *Le poëte masqué et démasqué*, 17–23, 34–35, 45, 70–76.

9 Scherpe, *Gattungspoetik im 18. Jahrhundert*, 71.

10 Tzvetan Todorov, *Theories of the Symbol*, trans. Catherine Porter (Oxford, 1982 [1977]), 115.

11 Lühe, *Natur und Nachahmung*, 106–107.

12 Cullhed, *The Language of Passion*, 244–251.

13 "Quelle est donc la fonction des Arts? C'est de transporter les traits qui sont dans la Nature, & de les présenter dans des objets à qui ils ne sont point naturels" (Batteux, *Les beaux arts*, 13).

14 "Imiter, c'est copier un modéle. Ce terme contient deux idées. 1°. le Prototype qui porte les traits qu'on veut imiter. 2°. la Copie qui les réprésente. La Nature, c'est-à-dire tout ce qui est, ou que nous concevons aisément comme possible, voilà le prototype ou le modèle des Arts" (Batteux, *Les beaux arts*, 12).

15 "Dans la premiere [partie], on examine quelle peut être la nature des Arts, quelles en sont les parties & les différences essentielles; & on montre par la qualité même de l'esprit humain, que l'imitation de la Nature doit être leur objet commun; & qu'ils ne différent entr'eux que par le moyen qu'ils employent, pour exécuter cette imitation. Les moyens de la Peinture, de la Musique, de la Danse sont les couleurs, les sons, les gestes; celui de la Poësie est le discours" (Batteux, *Les beaux arts*, ix–x).

16 See Scherpe, *Gattungspoetik im 18. Jahrhundert*, esp. 58–64, and Cullhed, *The Language of Passion*.

17 "De même donc que dans la Poësie épique & dramatique on imite les actions & les mœurs, dans le lyrique on chante les sentimens ou les passions imitées" (Batteux, *Les beaux arts*, 246).

18 In another context, Batteux speaks of first defining the genres according to the imitation itself, and then the object of this imitation. Thus invoking Aristotle's distinction between direct and indirect speech, he implicitly distinguishes drama from epic, and thereafter distinguishes lyric from them both (Batteux, *Les beaux arts*, 146–147).

19 As Klaus Scherpe has shown, this *analogon actionis* was new in the German theories and was soon developed as a way to constitute lyric as morally instructive (Klaus R. Scherpe, "Analogon Actionis und lyrisches System. Aspecte normativer Lyriktheorie in der deutschen Poetik des 18. Jahrhunderts," *Poetica. Zeitschrift für Sprach- und Literaturwissenschaft* 4 (1971), 32–59; Scherpe, *Gattungspoetik im 18. Jahrhundert*, 75).

20 "les Danseurs expriment les mœurs, les passions, les actions" (Charles Batteux, *Les quatre poëtiques: d'Aristote, d'Horace, de Vida, de Despréaux*, Avec les Traductions & des Remarques, Par M. l'Abbé Batteux.... I–II (Paris, 1771)).

21 "Si par *fiction*, ils entendent la même chose que *feindre*, ou *fingere* chez les Latins; le mot de *fiction* ne doit signifier que l'imitation artificielle des caractères, des mœurs, des actions, des discours, &c. Tellement que *feindre* sera la même chose que *representer*, ou plutôt *contrefaire*: alors cette opinion rentre dans celle que nous avons établie" (Batteux, *Les beaux arts*, 135).

22 "De tout ce que nous venons de dire, il résulte, que la Poësie ne subsiste que par l'imitation. Il en est de même de la Peinture, de la Danse, de la Musique: rien n'est réel dans leurs Ouvrages: tout y est imaginé, feint, copié, artificiel. C'est ce qui fait leur caractere essentiel par opposition à la nature" (Batteux, *Les beaux arts*, 22).

23 Bieber has offered the best explanation of Batteux's view on art and form (*Johann Adolf Schlegels poetische Theorie*, 60–62), but criticizes Batteux for inconsistency since he does not uphold the definitions of content and form. However, I do not think that this was Batteux's intention. To him, it was enough to define representation as the main principle of art.

24 "les Arts, dans ce qui est proprement Art, ne sont que des imitations, des ressemblances qui ne sont point la Nature, mais qui paroissent l'être; & qu'ainsi la matière des beaux Arts n'est point le vrai, mais seulement le vrai-semblable" (Batteux, *Les beaux arts*, 14). See Gustafsson, *Le poëte masqué et démasqué*, 16–17. Cf. Batteux, *Les beaux arts*, 56: "Le vrai est l'objet des Sciences. Celui des Arts est le bon et le beau. Deux termes qui rentrent presque dans la même signification, quand on les examine de près."

25 The notion of imitation as not just representation but specifically artistic representation is, as we have seen, more or less standard. The attempts to define it in words can be traced back at least to Italian 16th-century art. Vincenzo Danti, for example, distinguished between *imitare* (represent artistically) and *ritrarre* ("copy" from visible objects) (Martin Olin, *Views on Portraiture from Vasari to Jonathan Richardson*, Studies in Italian, French and English Art Theory (Lund, 1996), 18–19).

26 "Quelle est donc la fonction des Arts? C'est de transporter les traits qui sont dans la Nature, & de les présenter dans des objets à qui ils ne sont point naturels. C'est ainsi que le ciseau du Statuaire montre un héros dans un bloc de marbre. Le Peintre par ses couleurs, fait sortir de la toile tous les objets visibles. Le Musicien par des sons artificiels fait gronder l'orage, tandis que tout est calme; & le Poëte enfin par son invention & par l'harmonie de ses vers, remplit notre esprit d'images feintes & notre cœur de sentimens factices, souvent plus charmans que s'ils étoient vrais & naturels" (Batteux, *Les beaux arts*, 13–14).

27 "La Poësie, qu'on appelle du style, par opposition à celle des choses, qui consiste dans la création & la disposition des objets, contient quatre parties: 1°. les pensées. 2°. les mots. 3°. les tours. 4°. l'harmonie" (Batteux, *Les beaux arts*, 166).

28 "C'est sur ce plan qu'on doit dresser ce qu'on appelle la Fable, ou, si je l'ose dire, *la charpente* de l'Epopée" (Batteux, *Les beaux arts*, 200).

29 "Herr Batteux behauptet, daß die Nachahmung der schönen Natur der allgemeine und oberste Grundsatz der Poesie sey; ich behaupte, daß sie es nicht sey, sondern daß sie den Grundsatz der ausgebesserten Natur zur Seite habe, und deswegen einen höhern fodere, der beide unter sich fasse. Herr Batteux behauptet, daß die lyrische Poesie ihr Wesen, daß ihr anfangs bey ihrem Ursprunge eigen gewesen, abgeleget, und ein andres an sich genommen habe. Ich behaupte, daß einer Kunst ihr ursprüngliches Wesen allezeit bleiben müsse, ob es wohl erweitert werden könne; und das zwar darum, weil sonst damit zugleich die Existenz dieser Kunst aufhören würde, um der Existenz einer andern neuen Kunst Platz zu machen, die bloß und lediglich den Namen von jener erborgte. Herr Batteux behauptet, daß das Wahre, wenn es in Gedichten eine Stelle finden wolle, nicht anders, als unter der Maske der Nachahmung, erscheinen dürfe. Ich gebe zu, daß es diese Maske tragen könne, wie, um nur ein Exempel anzuführen, alsdann geschieht, wenn ein Poet unter einer der erdichteten oder nachgeahmten Personen seines Gedichts sich selber schildert, ihr seine eigne Denkungsart leiht; ihr seine eignen Empfindungen in den Mund legt. Aber ich behaupte zugleich, daß das Wahre nicht überall verbunden sey, diese Maske vorzunehmen, oft es nicht thue, ja oft es nicht thun solle; und daß es absonderlich vielen Oden nicht nur nichts nützen, sondern sogar schaden würde, wenn sie vom Leser für Nachahmung angesehen, und als solche beurtheilet würden. Nun entscheide man, ob wir bloß über Worte streiten. Was könnte weiter auseinander stehen, als beide Meynungen? – Ich glaube ja wohl, und finde es hier und da, daß Herr Batteux in der Anwendung anders empfindet, und urtheilet, als er nach seinen Grundsätzen lehret" (*Herrn Abt Batteux, königlichen Professors, Mitglieds der französischen Akademie, auch der Akademie der J[n]schriften und schönen Wissenschaften, Einschränkung der schönen Künste auf einen einzigen Grundsatz; aus dem Französischen übersetzt, und mit verschiednen eignen damit verwandten Abhandlungen begleitet von Johann Adolf Schlegeln* I–II (Leipzig, 1770), I, 371–372).

30 *Einleitung in die Schönen Wissenschaften; nach d. Französischen, mit Zusätzen vermehret von C.W. Ramler* (Leipzig, 1756–58) and several later editions.

31 "er kann daraus für seinen Hauptbeweis, *daß alle Poesie, auch die Ode, sich auf die Nachahmung einschränken müsse*" (363). I render Schlegel's use of larger characters with italics.

32 Gustafsson, "'Imitation' och 'äkthet'," 54. *Einschränkung* 1770, I, 371–372.

33 On Batteux's systematizing the issue of selection, see Ludwig Tavernier, "L'imitation de la belle nature. Zum Verständnis des Künstlers in der Nachahmungstheorie von Charles Batteux," in *Empfindung und Reflexion. Ein Problem des 18. Jahrhunderts*, ed. Hans Körner, Constanze Peres, Reinhard Steiner and Ludwig Tavernier (Hildesheim, Zurich and New York, 1986), 49–98.

34 "Que fit Zeuxis quand il voulut peindre une beauté parfaite ? Fit-il le portrait de quelque beauté particuliere, dont sa peinture fût l'histoire? Non: il rassembla les traits séparés de plusieurs beautés existantes" (Batteux, *Les beaux arts*, 24).

35 "Oder soll es die Ausbesserung der Natur seyn? Aber die will ja Herr Batteux selbst von der Nachahmung genau unterschieden wissen" (*Einschränkung* 1770, I, 376).

36 "Die lyrischen Gedichte sind ohne Zweifel Poesie, denn sie sind der Ursprung derselben, die erste Gattung von Gedichten. Im Anfange herrschte gar keine Nachahmung in der Ode, und auch nach ihrer vollkommnern und mannigfaltigern Ausbildung findet man viele, die keine Spur der Nachahmung an sich haben; also ist die Nachahmung nicht der oberste und allgemeine Grundsatz der Poesie" (*Einschränkung der schönen Künste auf einen einzigen Grundsatz. Aus dem Französischen übersetzt, und mit einem Anhange einiger eignen Abhandlungen versehen* (Leipzig, 1759), 193, cf. 175; *Einschränkung* 1770, I, 361).

37 "L'objection la plus apparente contre le principe universel de l'imitation est tirée de l'origine de la poësie, qui dans le commencement, dit-on, ne fut que l'expression du cœur & par conséquent de la vérité. La réponse est I°. Que la poësie depuis qu'elle est réduite en art est si différente de ce qu'elle étoit dans le commencement, que son origine ne peut faire une preuve suffisante, pour établir ce qu'elle doit être aujourd-hui. Les élémens de la poësie, sont les idées, les images, les sentimens, tout cela fut créé avec les hommes; mais tout cela ne fait pas la poësie, 'comme les tons ne font pas la musique, & les couleurs la peinture'. C'est M. Sch[le]gel qui le dit lui-même" (Charles Batteux, *Principes de la litterature. Nouvelle édition* I (Paris, 1764), 302).

38 "D'ailleurs, pourquoi les Cantiques sacrés nous paroissent-ils, à nous, si beaux? N'est-ce

point parce que nous y trouvons parfaitement exprimés les sentimens qu'il nous semble que nous aurions éprouvés dans la même situation où étoient les Prophetes? & si ces sentimens n'étoient que vrais, & non pas vraisemblables, nous devrions les respecter; mais ils ne pourroient nous faire l'impression du plaisir. De sorte que, pour plaire aux hommes, il faut, lors même qu'on n'imite point, faire comme si l'on imitoit, & donner à la vérité les traits de la vraisemblance" (Batteux, *Les beaux arts*, 239).

39 Cf. Scherpe, "Analogon Actionis und lyrisches System," 38–39.

40 "Oder sollte etwan der Nachahmer der Psalmen in den Empfindungen, die er ausdrücket, demjenigen Dichter ähnlich seyn, welcher die Empfindungen eines Helden *vorgiebt*, itzt als Brutus, itzt als Cato, itzt als Cäsar redet? Sollte er dem Schauspieler ähnlich seyn, welcher durch Hülfe seiner Kunst sich in Feuer setzet, und diese Empfindungen *an sich nimmt, bloss um sie glücklicher ausdrücken zu können*, nicht um sie ernstlich, als seine eigne, fühlen zu wollen; welcher diese Empfindungen in den Zuschauern *erregt, daß ihre Herzen dadurch auf einige Zeit zu ihrer Ergetzung getäuschet werden*, nicht daß sie darinnen haften sollen? Dann wird er zwar noch immer ein Dichter seyn; aber ein Dichter, der seinem Herzen desto weniger Ehre macht, ie mehr er von der Seite des poetischen Ruhmes gewinnt; einem freygeisterischen Voltäre nicht unähnlich, der, wenn er will, auch christliche Tragödien schreiben kann" (*Einschränkung* 1770, I, 365).

41 "Les monologues de Polieucte, de Camille, de Chimene, sont des morceaux lyriques: & si cela est; pourquoi le sentiment qui est sujet à l'imitation dans un Drame, n'y seroit-il pas sujet dans une Ode? Pourquoi imiteroit-on la passion dans une Scéne, & qu'on ne pourroit pas l'imiter dans un Chant?" (Batteux, *Les beaux arts*, 243).

42 So Gustafsson, *Le poëte masqué et démasqué*, 16–18; Cullhed, *The Language of Passion*, 245–246.

43 "Alors l'imitation Poëtique se réduit aux pensées, aux expressions, à l'harmonie, qui doivent être conformes au fonds des choses. Si les sentimens ne sont pas vrais et réels, c'est-à-dire, si le Poëte n'est pas réellement dans la situation qui produit les sentimens dont il a besoin; il doit en exciter en lui, qui soient semblables aux vrais, en feindre qui répondent à la qualité de l'objet. Et quand il sera arrivé au juste dégré de chaleur qui lui convient; qu'il chante: il est inspiré" (Batteux, *Les beaux arts*, 244–245).

44 "De même donc que dans la poësie épique et dramatique on imite les actions et les moeurs, dans le lyrique on chante les sentimens ou les passions imitées. S'il y a du réel, il se mêle avec ce qui est feint, pour faire un tout de même nature : la fiction embellit la vérité, et la vérité donne du crédit à la fiction" (Batteux, *Les beaux arts*, 246).

45 "Je n'avois à y prouver que deux choses: la premiere, que les sentimens peuvent être feints & imités comme les actions; je crois que M. Schlegel conviendra que cela est vrai. La seconde, que tous les sentimens exprimés dans le lyrique, feints ou vrais, devoient être soumis aux régles de l'imitation poëtique, c'est-à-dire, qu'ils devoient être vraisemblables, choisis, soutenus, aussi parfaits qu'ils peuvent l'être en leur genre, & enfin rendus avec toutes les graces & toute la force de l'expression poëtique. C'est le sens du principe de l'imitation, c'en est l'esprit."

46 "les régles du goût ne sont que des conséquences du principe de l'imitation" (Batteux, *Les beaux arts*, xii). Likewise, for example, Batteux states that imitation must be made according to good taste, p. 23.

47 "Toutes les Régles sont des branches qui tiennent à une même tige" (Batteux, *Les beaux arts*, ij).

48 See Joyce S. Rutledge, *Johann Adolph Schlegel* (Berne and Frankfurt am Main, 1974), 218.

49 "Die Poesie wird also der sinnlichste und angenehmste Ausdruck des Schönen, oder des Guten, oder des Schönen und Guten zugleich, durch die Sprache, seyn" (*Einschränkung* 1759, 367).

50 Batteux, *Les beaux arts*, x; *Einschränkung* 1770, I, 8.

51 See Gustafsson, "'Imitation' och 'äkthet'," 54; Lühe, *Natur und Nachahmung*, 154; Cullhed, *The Language of Passion*, 249.

52 The fact that Batteux thinks that the poet can leave his mark on his poem might be seen as contrary to a notion of the poet "as the imitator, who slips in and out of roles, without any attempt to reveal an authentic character" (Cullhed, *The Language of Passion*, 293), but as is evident, Batteux's view on poetry as imitation does not exclude the poet leaving his mark on the poem, nor that authentic emotions may be at hand.

53 Todorov, *Theories of the Symbol*, 112, 113.

54 Johann Christoph Gottsched, *Versuch einer Critischen Dichtkunst vor die Deutschen* (Leipzig, 1730), 94. It is thus difficult to agree with Scherpe that "Bei Aristoteles konnte die Fabel nicht als gesonderte Nachahmungsart in Erscheinung treten, da Fabelprinzip und Nachahmungsprinzip identisch waren und er keine Dichtung anerkannte, in der diese Identität nicht nachweisbar war" (Scherpe, *Gattungspoetik im 18. Jahrhundert*, 32–33).

CHAPTER SEVEN
THE *NACHLEBEN* OF IMITATION

1 See Halliwell's discussion of authors such as A.W. Schlegel, Schelling, Schopenhauer and Coleridge (Halliwell, *The Aesthetics of Mimesis*, 358–369). A study that extends into new ways of understanding romantic literature and the concept of mimesis is Mattias Pirholt, *Metamimesis: Ideology and Representation in the Novels of Early German Romanticism* (forthc.).

2 Cullhed, *The Language of Passion*, 251–307, esp. 303. For a treatment of the development in a wider perspective, see Renate Schlüter, *Zeuxis und Prometheus. Die Überwindung des Nachahmungskonzeptes in der Ästhetik der Frühromantik*, Bonner romanische Arbeiten (Frankfurt am Main, 1995).

3 "Denn entweder ahmt man die Natur nach, wie man sie vorfindet, so wird es vielleicht nicht schön ausfallen; oder man bildet sie schön, so ist es keine Nachahmung mehr. Warum sagen sie nicht gleich: die Kunst soll das Schöne darstellen; und lassen die Natur ganz aus dem Spiele, so wäre man der Quälerey los, daß die Kunsterscheinungen zur Natur in diesem Sinne umgedeutet werden müssen, was nicht ohne die äußerste Gewalttätigkeit möglich ist" (A.W. Schlegel, "Über das Verhältniß der Kunst zur Natur, über Täuschung und Wahrscheinlichkeit, über Styl und Manier," in *Vorlesungen über Ästhetik I [1798–1803]*, ed. Ernst Behler, *Kritische Ausgabe seiner Vorlesungen* 1, Kritische Ausgabe der Vorlesungen 1, ed. Ernst Behler and Frank Jolles (Paderborn, Munich, Vienna and Zurich, 1989), 253. Cullhed, *The Language of Passion*, 254.

4 Cullhed, *The Language of Passion*, 253–254.

5 "Die Sprache ist entweder aus Tönen der Empfindung ganz allein, oder aus Nachahmungen der Gegenstände ganz allein, oder aus beiden zusammen entstanden ... Da es der beste Beweis ist, etwas sey gut nachgemacht, wenn man die vorgestellte Sache für die wirkliche halten kann, so fließt aus dem grob verstandenen Grundsatze der Nachahmung natürlich her, daß man sich in der Kunst die *Täuschung* zum Ziel setzen müsse, und daß alles, was die Täuschung stört, fehlerhaft sey" ("Über das Verhältniß der Kunst zur Natur," 253).

6 "die Kunst soll die Natur nachahmen." See Halliwell, *The Aesthetics of Mimesis*, 361.

7 A.W. Schlegel, *Briefe über Poesie, Silbenmaß und Sprache, Sämmtliche Werke*, ed. Eduard Böcking (Leipzig, 1846), 7, 112. See Ernst Behler, *German Romantic Literary Theory* (Cambridge, 1993), 265–270.

8 See Ralph W. Ewton Jr, *The Literary Theories of August Wilhelm Schlegel* (The Hague and Paris, 1972), 22–25. The following discussion heavily relies on Ewton's structuring of various sources in A.W. Schlegel's writings.

9 "Die Sprache, die wunderbarste Schöpfung des menschlichen Dichtungsvermögens, gleichsam das große, nie vollendete Gedicht, worin die menschliche Natur sich selbst darstellt" (A.W. Schlegel, *Briefe über Poesie*, 104; Ewton, *The Literary Theories*, 40). Cf. "Poesie [ist] die umfassendste und vielseitigste von allen Künsten; die übrigen sind mehr oder weniger durch ihre besonderen Mittel der Darstellung auf gewisse Gegenstände beschränkt: der Poesie allein ist es gegeben, das gesamte Gemüth des Menschen auszusprechen, sein ganzes äußeres und inneres Dasein abzuschildern" (A.W. Schlegel, "Vorerinnerung," in *Geschichte der klassischen Literatur, Kritische Schriften und Briefe* III, ed. Edgar Lohner (Stuttgart, 1964), 14).

10 "Wird nun Natur in dieser würdigsten

Bedeutung genommen, nicht als eine Masse von Produkten, sondern als das Produzierende selbst, und der Ausdruck Nachahmung ebenfalls in dem edleren Sinne, wo es nicht heißt, die Äußerlichkeiten eines Menschen nachäffen, sondern sich die Maximen seines Handelns zu eigen machen, so ist nichts mehr gegen den Grundsatz einzuwenden, noch zu ihm hinzuzufügen: die Kunst soll die Natur nachahmen" (A.W. Schlegel, *Kants Kritik der ästhetischen Urteilskraft, Die Kunstlehre. Kritische Schriften und Briefe* II, ed. Edgar Lohner (Stuttgart, 1963), 91).

11 See Ewton, *The Literary Theories*, 55–56.

12 "Denn jedes Ding stellt zuvörderst sich selber dar, d.h. es offenbart sein Inneres durch sein Äußeres, sein Wesen durch die Erscheinung (es ist also Symbol für sich selbst); demnächst das, womit es in näheren Verhältnissen steht und Einwirkungen davon erfährt; endlich ist es ein Spiegel des Universums. In jenen schrankenlosen Übertragungen des poetischen Stils liegt also, der Ahnung und Anforderung nach, die große Wahrheit, daß eins alles und alles eins ist" (A.W. Schlegel, *Kants Kritik der ästhetischen Urteilskraft*, 83).

13 "Die gegenseitige Verkettung aller Dinge durch ein ununterbrochenes Symbolisieren, worauf die erste Bildung der Sprache sich gründet, soll ja in der Wiederschöpfung der Sprache, der Poesie, hergestellt werden" (A.W. Schlegel, *Kants Kritik der ästhetischen Urteilskraft*, 83).

14 "Wie kann nun das Unendliche auf die Oberfläche, zur Erscheinung gebracht werden? Nur symbolisch, in Bildern und Zeichen. Die unpoetische Ansicht der Dinge ist die, welche mit den Wahrnehmungen der Sinne und den Bestimmungen des Verstandes alles an ihnen für abgetan hält; die poetische, welche sie immerfort deutet und eine figürliche Unerschöpflichkeit in ihnen sieht. ... Dadurch wird erst alles für uns lebendig. Dichten (im weitesten Sinne für das Poetische allen Künsten zum Grunde liegende genommen) ist nichts anderes als ein ewiges Symbolisieren: wir suchen entweder für etwas Geistiges eine äußere Hülle oder wir beziehen ein Äußeres auf ein unsichtbares Inneres" (A.W. Schlegel, *Kants Kritik der ästhetischen Urteilskraft*, 81–82).

15 See Ewton, *The Literary Theories*, 60–71.

CHAPTER EIGHT

THE TECHNIQUE OF THE SUBLIME

1 See Suzanne Guerlac, "The Sublime in Theory," *Modern Language Notes* 106, no. 3 (1991), 895–909, and Jean-Luc Nancy, "L'Offrande sublime," in *Du sublime*, ed. Jean-François Courtine, Michel Deguy, Jean-François Lyotard and Jean-Luc Nancy (Paris, 1988), 37–75. In this chapter, I have benefitted greatly not only from the critical comments of Susan Brantly and Scott Mellor, but also from their help with improving the English.

2 Words and poetry are the central issue in the small fifth part of Edmund Burke's *A Philosophical Enquiry into the Origin of our Ideas of the Sublime and Beautiful*, ed. James T. Boulton (Oxford, 1990), 170–175.

3 Peter de Bolla, *The Discourse of the Sublime: Readings in History, Aesthetics and the Subject* (Oxford, 1989). In speaking of "aesthetics," I primarily mean that discipline which defined itself by that name: obviously, ideas that could be called "aesthetic" are to be found much earlier. In speaking of an evolution, I certainly see no teleological project leading up to Kant or anyone else. See the discussion of aesthetics and teleology in Andrew Ashfield and Peter de Bolla, "Introduction," in *The Sublime: A Reader in British Eighteenth-Century Aesthetic Theory*, ed. Andrew Ashfield and Peter de Bolla (Cambridge, 1996), 1–16, 1–3.

4 See Charles P. Segal, "Hupsos and the Problem of Cultural Decline in the De Sublimitate," *Harvard Studies in Classical Philology* 64 (1959), 121–146.

5 John Dennis, quoted in *Longinus "On the Sublime."* Introduction and commentary by D.A. Russell (Oxford, 1964), xlvi–xlvii.

6 Samuel H. Monk, *The Sublime: A Study of Critical Theories in XVIII-Century England* (Ann Arbor, 1960 [1935]).

7 R.S. Crane, Rev. of Samuel H. Monk, *The Sublime: A Study of Critical Theories in XVIII-Century England*, in *Philological Quarterly* 15 (1936), 165–167.

8 Thomas Weiskel, *The Romantic Sublime: Studies in the Structure and Psychology of Transcendence* (Baltimore and London, 1976), 13.

9 Theodore E.B. Wood, *The Word "Sublime"*

and its Contexts 1650–1760 (The Hague and Paris, 1972), esp. 21, 205–210.

10 See Suzanne Guerlac, "Longinus and the Subject of the Sublime," *New Literary History* 16, no. 2 (1985), 275–289; Neil Hertz, *The End of the Line: Essays on Psychoanalysis and the Sublime* (New York, 1985), 1–20; and George B. Walsh, "Sublime Method: Longinus on Language and Imitation," *Classical Antiquity* 7 (1988), 252–269.

11 Paul H. Fry, *The Reach of Criticism: Method and Perception in Literary Theory* (New Haven and London, 1983), 47–48.

12 William K. Wimsatt Jr. and Cleanth Brooks, *Literary Criticism: A Short History* (New York, 1957), 103.

13 Weiskel, *The Romantic Sublime*, 17.

14 Fry, *The Reach of Criticism*, 49.

15 Walsh, "Sublime Method," 264–265.

16 "Ἐπεὶ δὲ πέντε, ὡς ἂν εἴποι τις, πηγαί τινές εἰσιν αἱ τῆς ὑψηγορίας γονιμώταται, προϋποκειμένης ὥσπερ ἐδάφους τινὸς κοινοῦ ταῖς πέντε ταύταις ἰδέαις τῆς ἐν τῷ λέγειν δυνάμεως, ἧς ὅλως χωρὶς οὐδέν, πρῶτον μὲν καὶ κράτιστον τὸ περὶ τὰς νοήσεις ἁδρεπήβολον, ὡς κἀν τοῖς περὶ Ξενοφῶντος ὡρισάμεθα· δεύτερον δὲ τὸ σφοδρὸν καὶ ἐνθουσιαστικὸν πάθος· ἀλλ’ αἱ μὲν δύο αὗται τοῦ ὕψους κατὰ τὸ πλέον αὐθιγενεῖς συστάσεις, αἱ λοιπαὶ δ’ἤδη καὶ διὰ τέχνης, ἥ τε ποιὰ τῶν σχημάτων πλάσις – δισσὰ δέ που ταῦτα, τὰ μὲν νοήσεως, θάτερα δὲ λέξεως – ἐπὶ δὲ τούτοις ἡ γενναία φράσις, ἧς μέρη πάλιν ὀνομάτων τε ἐκλογὴ καὶ ἡ τροπικὴ καὶ πεποιημένη λέξις· πέμπτη δὲ μεγέθους αἰτία καὶ συγκλείουσα τὰ πρὸ αὐτῆς ἅπαντα, ἡ ἐν ἀξιώματι καὶ διάρσει σύνθεσις" (*Longinus "On the Sublime,"* ed. and trans. W. H. Fyfe. Revised by Donald Russell, Loeb Classical Library 191 (Cambridge, MA, and London, 1999), 8.1. I render *tropikê* ... *lexis* as "tropical ... diction" instead of "metaphor").

17 *Peri hupsous* 44.12. See Russell, *Longinus "On the Sublime,"* xii–xiii.

18 Cf. Walsh, "Sublime Method," 264–269.

19 Fry, *The Reach of Criticism*, 75–76.

20 "Ὄγκου καὶ μεγαληγορίας καὶ ἀγῶνος ἐπὶ τούτοις, ὦ νεανία, καὶ αἱ φαντασίαι παρασκευαστικώταται· οὕτω γοῦν <ἡμεῖς> εἰδωλοποιΐας <δ’> αὐτὰς ἔνιοι λέγουσι· καλεῖται μὲν γὰρ κοινῶς φαντασία πᾶν τὸ ὁπωσοῦν ἐννόημα γεννητικὸν λόγου παριστάμενον, ἤδη δ’ ἐπὶ τούτων κεκράτηκεν τοὔνομα, ὅταν ἃ λέγεις ὑπ’ ἐνθουσιασμοῦ καὶ πάθους βλέπειν δοκῇς καὶ ὑπ’ ὄψιν τιθῇς τοῖς ἀκούουσιν. ὡς δ’ ἕτερόν τι ἡ ῥητορικὴ φαντασία βούλεται καὶ ἕτερον ἡ παρὰ ποιηταῖς, οὐκ ἂν λάθοι σε, οὐδ’ ὅτι τῆς μὲν ἐν ποιήσει τέλος ἐστὶν ἔκπληξις, τῆς δ’ ἐν λόγοις ἐνάργεια, ἀμφότεραι δ’ ὅμως τό τε <παθητικὸν> ἐπιζητοῦσι καὶ τὸ συγκεκινημένον" (*Peri hupsous* 15.1).

21 "Quas φαντασίας Graeci vocant (nos sane uisiones appellemus), per quas imagines rerum absentium ita repraesentantur animo ut eas cernere oculis ac praesentes habere videamur, has quisquis bene ceperit is erit in adfectibus potentissimus" (Quintilian, *Institutio oratoria* 6.2.29). See Russell, *Longinus "On the Sublime,"* 121.

22 "Insequetur ἐνάργεια, quae a Cicerone inlustratio et evidentia nominatur, quae non tam dicere videtur quam ostendere, et adfectus non aliter quam si rebus ipsis intersimus sequentur" (Quintilian, *Institutio oratoria* 6.2.32).

23 *On the Soul* III.iii; and *Rhetoric* I.xi.6 (1370a6): "And if pleasure consists in the sensation of a certain emotion, and imagination (*phantasia*) is a weakened sensation, then both the man who remembers and the man who hopes will be attended by an imagination of what he remembers or hopes" (Ἐπεὶ δ’ ἐστὶ τὸ ἥδεσθαι ἐν τῷ αἰσθάνεσθαί τινος πάθους, ἡ δὲ φαντασία ἐστὶν αἴσθησίς τις ἀσθενής, κἂν τῷ μεμνημένῳ καὶ τῷ ἐλπίζοντι ἀκολουθοῖ ἂν φαντασία τις οὗ μέμνηται ἢ ἐλπίζει).

24 Jeffrey Barnouw comments that the *phantasia* of Longinus seems derived from the Stoics, who had adapted Aristotle's notion, "The Morality of the Sublime: To John Dennis," *Comparative Literature* 35 (1983), 36.

25 See Lausberg, *Handbuch der literarischen Rhetorik*, § 810–19; and Russell's commentary, *Longinus "On the Sublime,"* 142–146.

26 Cf. Lausberg, *Handbuch der literarischen Rhetorik*, § 603.

27 Wimsatt and Brooks, *Literary Criticism*, 103–104.

28 Russell, *Longinus "On the Sublime,"* xlvi.

29 "ὅσσον δ’ ἠεροειδὲς ἀνὴρ ἴδεν ὀφθαλμοῖσιν, ἥμενος ἐν σκοπιῇ, λεύσσων ἐπὶ οἴνοπα πόντον, τόσσον ἐπιθρώσκουσι θεῶν ὑψηχέες ἵπποι.

τὴν ὁρμὴν αὐτῶν κοσμικῷ διαστήματι καταμετρεῖ. τίς οὖν οὐκ ἂν εἰκότως διὰ τὴν ὑπερβολὴν τοῦ μεγέθους ἐπιφθέγξαιτο, ὅτι ἂν δὶς ἑξῆς ὁφορμήσωσιν οἱ τῶν θεῶν ἵπποι, οὐκέθ' ὀύρήσουσιν ἐν κόσμῳ τόπον; ὑπερφυᾶ καὶ τὰ ἐπὶ τῆς θεομαχίας φαντάσματα" (*Peri hupsous* 9.5).

30 "ἔνθα μὲν Αἴας κεῖται ἀρήϊος, ἔνθα δ' Ἀχιλλεύς,
ἔνθα δὲ Πάτροκλος, θεόφιν μήστωρ ἀτάλαντος,
ἔνθα δ' ἐμὸς φίλος υἱός" (*Peri hupsous* 9.12).

31 *Peri hupsous* 9.5, fn.

32 "'Ζεῦ πάτερ,' φησίν, 'ἀλλὰ σὺ ῥῦσαι ὑπ' ἠέρος
υἷας Ἀχαιῶν,
ποίησον δ' αἴθρην, δὸς δ' ὀφθαλμοῖσιν ἰδέσθαι·
ἐν δὲ φάει καὶ ὄλεσσον'" (*Peri hupsous* 9.10).

33 "ἐν δ' ἔπεσ', ὡς ὅτε κῦμα θοῇ ἐν νηῒ πέσῃσι
λάβρον ὑπαὶ νεφέων ἀνεμοτρεφές, ἡ δέ τε πᾶσα
ἄχνῃ ὑπεκρύφθη, ἀνέμοιο δὲ δεινὸς ἀήτης
ἱστίῳ ἐμβρέμεται, τρομέουσι δέ τε φρένα ναῦται
δειδιότες· τυτθὸν γὰρ ὑπὲκ θανάτοιο φέρονται"
(*Peri hupsous* 10.5).

34 "φαίνεταί μοι κῆνος ἴσος θέοισιν
ἔμμεν' ὤνηρ, ὄττις ἐνάντιός τοι
ἰζάνει καὶ πλάσιον ἆδυ φωνεί-
σας ὐπακούει
καὶ γελαίσας ἰμερόεν, τό μ' ἦ μὰν
καρδίαν ἐν στήθεσιν ἐπτόαισεν.
ὣς γὰρ <ἐς> σ' ἴδω βρόχε' ὤς με φώνας
οὐδὲν ἔτ' εἴκει·
ἀλλὰ κὰμ μὲν γλῶσσα ἔαγε· λέπτον δ'
αὔτικα χρῷ πῦρ ὐποδεδρόμακεν
ὀππάτεσσι δ' οὐδὲν ὄρημμ', ἐπιρόμ-
βεισι δ' ἄκουαι·
ἀ δέ μ' ἴδρως κακχέεται, τρόμος δὲ
παῖσαν ἄγρει, χλωροτέρα δὲ ποίας
ἔμμι· τεθνάκην δ' ὀλίγω 'πιδεύης
φαίνομ' <ἐμαυτᾷ>·
ἀλλὰ πὰν τόλματον, ἐπεὶ †καὶ πένητα†
οὐ θαυμάζεις, ὡς, ὑπ<ὸ τὸ> αὐτὸ τὴν ψυχὴν τὸ σῶμα τὰς ἀκοὰς τὴν γλῶσσαν τὰς ὄψεις τὴν χρόαν, πάνθ' ὡς ἀλλότρια διοιχόμενα ἐπιζητεῖ καὶ καθ' ὑπεναντιώσεις ἅμα ψύχεται κᾴεται, ἀλογιστεῖ φρονεῖ [ἢ γὰρ φοβεῖται ἢ παρ' ὀλίγον τέθνηκεν] ἵνα μὴ ἕν τι περὶ αὐτὴν πάθος φαίνηται, παθῶν δὲ σύνοδος. πάντα μὲν τοιαῦτα γίνεται περὶ τοὺς ἐρῶντας, ἡ λῆψις δ' ὡς ἔφην τῶν ἄκρων καὶ ἡ εἰς ταὐτο συναίρεσις ἀπειργάσατο τὴν ἐξοχήν" (*Peri hupsous* 10.2–3).

35 Fry, *The Reach of Criticism*, 56–60.

36 See esp. Fry, *The Reach of Criticism*, 49, 66, 71. I also think that this verifies Fry's considerations on the relationship of the sublime to "grace" (83–84).

37 Walsh, "Sublime Method," esp. 259–264.

38 See, e.g., Malcolm Schofield, "Aristotle on the Imagination," in *Articles on Aristotle 4. Psychology and Aesthetics*, ed. Jonathan Barnes, Malcolm Schofield and Richard Sorabji (London, 1979), 103–132.

39 *The Spectator*, edited and with an introduction and notes by Donald F. Bond, III (Oxford, 1965), nos. 411–413, quotation 536.

40 For an extensive treatment of the notions of imagination, see Eva T. H. Brann, *The World of the Imagination: Sum and Substance* (Lanham, 1991).

41 Mats Malm, "On the Technique of the Sublime," *Comparative Literature: Journal of the American Comparative Literature Association* 52, no. 1 (2000), 1–10; Karl Axelsson, *The Sublime: Precursors and British Eighteenth-Century Conceptions* (Oxford, 2007). Axelsson, who curiously reads a discussion of the mental faculty where Longinus discusses the rhetorical figure *phantasia*, provides enlightening points concerning the reception of *Peri hupsous*.

42 On the early transmission of the text, see Bernard Weinberg, "Translations and Commentaries of Longinus, 'On the Sublime', to 1600: A Bibliography," *Modern Philology* 47, no. 3 (1950), 14–151, and "Une Traduction Française du 'Sublime' de Longin Vers 1645," *Modern Philology* 59, no. 3 (1962), 159–201.

43 Jules Brody, *Boileau and Longinus* (Geneva, 1958), 9–11, 18–20.

44 Nicolas Boileau-Despréaux, *Dissertation sur la Joconde, Arrest Burlesque, Traité du Sublime.* Texte établi et présenté par Charles-H. Boudhors. Œvres complètes de Boileau III (Paris, 1942), 59. Brody, *Boileau and Longinus*, 54.

45 "Ces *Images*, que d'autres appellent *Peintures*, ou *Fictions*, sont aussi d'un grand artifice pour donner du poids, de la magnificence, et de la force au discours. Ce mot d'*Image* se prend en general pour toute pensée propre à produire une expression, et qui fait une peinture à l'esprit de quelque maniere que ce soit. Mais il se prend encore dans un sens plus particulier et plus resserré, pour ces discours que l'on fait, "*lorsque par un* *enthousiasme et un mouvement extraordinaire de l'ame, il semble que nous voyons les choses dont nous parlons, et quand nous les mettons devant les yeux de ceux qui écoutent"* (*Traité du Sublime*, 76).

46 See Brody, *Boileau and Longinus*, 13–14: Longinus was translated into English by John Hall in 1652 and John Pulteney in 1680, but discussion here will be restricted to the 18th-century reception.

47 Leonard Welsted, *The works of Dionysius Longinus, on the sublime: or, a treatise concerning the sovereign perfection of writing. Translated from the Greek. With some remarks on the English poets* (London, 1712), 20 and 52.

48 William Smith, *Dionysius Longinus on the sublime. Translated from the Greek, with notes and observations, and some account of the life, writings and* character *of the author* (London, 1739), 16, 39–40.

49 The confusion of Longinus and his interpreters appears as late as in 2007, when Karl Axelsson commences a chapter on the imagination in Longinus by stating that "[a]n image is an idea, while the imagination is 'warm'd and affected' when presenting this idea, according to Longinus" (Axelsson, *The Sublime*, 108).

50 *A treatise of Dionysius Longinus upon the sublime. Translated from the Greek, with explanatory notes, by the late Rev. Charles Carthy, M.A.* (Dublin, 1762), 36 and 74.

51 Cf. Russell, *Longinus "On the Sublime,"* 120. On the continuous tradition of "imagination" in philosophy, see e.g. Brann, *The World of the Imagination*, 31–54. Longinus's use of the term is here described as a "poetic talent" (496), but should rather be defined as a "poetic technique."

52 Cf. Crane, Rev. of Samuel H. Monk, *The Sublime*, 166–167.

53 Cf., e.g., Ella Birmelin, "Die kunsttheoretischen Gedanken in Philostrats Apollonios," *Philologus. Zeitschrift für das klassische Altertum* 88 (1973), 149–180, 392–414, 395–402.

CHAPTER NINE

THE SYMBOL AND THE CATEGORIES OF RHETORIC

1 For a comprehensive study of the symbol, I refer to Tzvetan Todorov, *Theories of the Symbol* (1982 [1977]), from where some of my examples are taken. Todorov's subject is figurative referentiality in a broader sense than I discuss here and he does not make the concretion or actuality of the sign a base of discussion, although he treats the symbol theory of romanticism (147–221).

2 So, in the common example, Jerusalem is historically/literally a city, allegorically/typologically the Church. Tropologically/morally it is the believer's soul and anagogically/mystically it is the divine city of God. See Friedrich Ohly, "Vom geistigen Sinn des Wortes im Mittelalter," *Zeitschrift für deutsches Altertum* 89 (1958/59), 1–23, 10–11.

3 Allegory and metaphor may be the tropes that most unequivocally comply with the definition that the "right" word is substituted with the "wrong" word. One objection to the substitutivity of the trope system might be that a synecdoche such as "keel" for "ship" is not an adequate substitution since the keel is there regardless of whether it is the ship that is meant. But also here, the idea is that the *word* "keel" must be removed and replaced by "ship." The concepts of "substitutive" and "analogous" are inspired by J.A.Mazzeo, *Varieties of Interpretation* (London, 1978) and "Allegorical Interpretation and History," *Comparative Literature* xxx, no. 1 (1978), 1–21.

4 Augustine, *De trinitate libri XV*, XV.ix.15.

5 Beda Venerabilis, *De Schematibus et Tropis*, Corpus Christianorum Series Latina CXXIII A. Bedae Opera. Pars VI, 1, Turnholti MCMLXXV, 142–171, esp. 164–169; see Armand Strubel, "'Allegoria in factis' et 'Allegoria in verbis'," *Poétique* VI (1975), 342–357.

6 See the works treated in Barbara Kiefer Lewalski, *Protestant Poetics and the Seventeenth-Century Religious Lyric* (Princeton, 1979).

7 "Die auf diese Weise dargestellten Gegenstände scheinen bloß für sich zu stehen und sind doch wieder im tiefsten bedeutend und das wegen des Idealen das immer eine Allgemeinheit mit sich führt. Wenn das symbolische außer der Darstellung noch etwas bezeugt so wird es immer auf indirekte Weise geschehen. ... Nun gibt es auch Kunstwerke die durch Verstand, Witz, Galanterie brillieren wohin wir auch alle allegorischen rechnen; von diesen läßt sich am wenigsten Gutes erwarten weil sie gleichfalls das Interesse an der Darstellung selbst zerstören und den Geist gleichsam in sich selbst zurücktreiben und seinen Augen das was wirklich dargestellt ist entziehen; das Allegorische unterscheidet sich vom Symbolischen daß dieses indirekt, jenes direkt bezeichnet" (Johann Wolfgang Goethe, *Sämtliche Werke nach Epochen seines Schaffens. Münchner Ausgabe Band 4.2. Wirkungen der Französischen Revolution 1791–1797, 2*, ed. Klaus H. Kiefer, Hans J. Becker, Gerhard H. Müller, John Neubauer and Peter Schmidt (Munich, 1986), 123–124).

8 On ambiguity, see Päivi Methonen, *Obscure Language, Unclear Literature: Theory and Practice from Quintilian to the Enlightenment*, trans. Robert MacGillon (Helsinki, 2003).

9 "The allegory transforms the phenomenon into a concept, the concept into an image, but in such a manner that the concept is always kept, limited and full, within the image, and is expressed through it. The symbolism transforms the phenomenon into an idea, the idea into an image, in such a manner that the idea always remains infinitely active and unreachable, and, even if pronounced in all languages, yet ineffable" (Die Allegorie verwandelt die Erscheinung in einen Begriff, den Begriff in ein Bild, doch so dass der Begriff im Bilde immer noch begrenzt und vollständig zu halten und zu haben und an demselben auszusprechen sei. Die Symbolik verwandelt die Erscheinung in Idee, die Idee in ein Bild, und so dass die Idee im Bild immer unendlich wirksam und unerreichbar bleibt, und selbst in allen Sprachen ausgesprochen doch unaussprechlich bleibe) (Johann Wolfgang Goethe, *Sämtliche Werke nach Epochen seines Schaffens. Münchner Ausgabe Band 17. Wilhelm Meisters Wanderjahre. Maximen und Reflexionen*, ed. Gonthier-Louis Fink, Gerhard Baumann and Johannes John (Munich, 1991), 749).

10 With Quintilian: "A Trope is a shift of a word or phrase from its proper meaning to another, in a way that has positive value" (Tropos est verbi vel sermonis a propria significatione in aliam cum virtute mutatio), *Institutio oratoria* 8.6.1.

11 See note 31 below.

12 "Durch tiefes Gefühl das wenn es rein und natürlich ist mit den besten und höchsten Gegenständen koinzidieren und sie allenfalls symbolisch machen wird," Goethe, *Sämtliche Werke 1*, 767.

13 With Quintilian's words quoted above, the allegory is a *tropus sermonis*, not a *tropus verbi* (cf. Heinrich Lausberg, *Handbuch der literarischen Rhetorik*, § 894).

14 While Quintilian describes "pure" allegory as a series of metaphors (*continuatis translationibus*) in *Institutio oratoria* 8.6.44, Goethe contrasts the symbol to "discursive expansiveness" as Todorov puts it (Todorov, *Theories of the Symbol*, 204).

15 "Consideracio uero non est nisi ostensio dubiorum et hoc non per raciones aut persuasiones (quoniam hoc non spectat ad poetam) sed per representaciones tam certe et veraciter factas, ut non credatur res ficta esse. Et hoc contingit, quando res nichil vel modicum pertinentes ad propositum interseruntur tanquam intersignia rei facte. Vnde tale est illud Iohannis de miraculo quinque panum: 'Erat autem fenum multum in loco' et cetera" (*Poetria*, § 66–67).

16 "we translate *sêmeion* as *signum* – though some have used *indicium* ('indication') or *vestigium* ('trace') instead. It is that from which something else is inferred, for example murder from blood" (Signum vocatur, ut dixi, σημεῖον, (quamquam id quidam indicium, quidam vestigium nominaverunt): per quod alia res intelligitur, ut per sanguinem caedes) (*Institutio oratoria* 5.9.9).

17 Immanuel Kant, *Kritik der ästetischen Urteilskraft* (1790), *Werke in sechs Bänden*, Band V, ed. Wilhelm Weischeidel (Wiesbaden, 1957), § 59. See chapter 7.

18 "So bedeutet die heil. Magdalena nicht nur die Reue, sondern ist die lebendige Reue selbst. So ist das Bild der heil. Cäcilia, der Schutzheiligen der Musik, nicht ein allegorisches, sondern ein symbolisches Bild, da es eine von der Bedeutung unabhängige Existenz hat, ohne die Bedeutung zu verlieren. So das Bild

Christi, weil es die ganz einzige Identität der göttlichen und menschlichen Natur anschaulich darstellt," *Friedrich Wilhelm Joseph von Schellings Sämmtliche Werke* I.v (Stuttgart and Augsburg, 1859), 555. Cf. the discussion in Todorov, *Theories of the Symbol*, 201, 209.

19 "According to our explanation, the historical in itself is but a kind of the symbolic" (Nach unsrer Erklärung ist das Historische selbst nur eine Art des Symbolischen), *Schellings Sämmtliche Werke* I.v, 555; cf. Todorov, *Theories of the Symbol*, 211.

20 Yet another use of *signum* within rhetoric occurs in the art of memory, which does not concern composition but the preparations for presentation. The usual method is to create places, e.g. a house which one may wander through, finding images which function as reminders of what is to be said, and the rooms dictating the order of things. In Quintilian such an image is a *signum*, which can become a more or less analogous sign: "Let us suppose a symbol of navigation, such as an anchor, or of warfare, such as a weapon. Then this is how they arrange it. They place the first idea as it were in the vestibule, the second, let us say, in the atrium, and then they go round the open areas, assigning ideas systematically" (Sit autem signum navigationis ut ancora, militiae ut aliquid ex armis. Haec ita digerunt: primum sensum vestibulo quasi adsignant, secundum (puta) atrio, tum … per ordinem committunt) (*Institutio oratoria* 11.2.19–20).

21 See Todorov, *Theories of the Symbol*, 199.

22 Henry George Liddell and Robert Scott, *A Greek–English Lexicon*. Revised and augmented throughout by Sir Henry Stuart Jones, with the assistance of Roderick McKenzie (Oxford, 1940), s.v.

23 Todorov, *Theories of the Symbol*, 16.

24 *Dissertatio de Symbolis*, pres. Clas Arrhenius, resp. Simon Isogæus (Upsaliae, MDCLXXII). Cf. Allan Ellenius, *De Arte Pingendi. Latin Art Literature in Seventeenth-Century Sweden and its International Background*, Lychnos-bibliotek 19 (Uppsala and Stockholm, 1960), 272–277.

25 "signum quoddam symbolicè innuens aliquid & figurans" (*Dissertatio de Symbolis* chapter I § IV).

26 "*animalium figuris pro literis utebantur*" (*Dissertatio de Symbolis* chapter II § II). The reference is to Olaus Magnus, *Historia de gentibus septentrionalibus*, book I chapter 36.

27 When in chapter II § III "parabolis, symbolis & allegoricis figuris" are discussed, parable implies a verbal discourse while "allegorical figures" seem to specify "symbol" as a natural and analogous sign.

28 "Quod ut faustum esse queàt, faxis Tu quæso, qui sub columbæ Symbolo DEus hominibus apparere es dignatus!"

29 Tesauro, *Il Cannocchiale Aristotelico*, 305 and 611, cf. 731.

30 See Ernest B. Gilman, *Iconoclasm and Poetry in the English Reformation* (Chicago and London, 1986), 87.

31 "Es ist ein großer Unterschied, ob der Dichter zum Allgemeinen das Besondere sucht, oder im Besondern das Allgemeine schaut. Aus jener Art entsteht Allegorie, wo das Besondere nur als Beispiel, als Exempel des Allgemeinen gilt; die letztere aber ist eigentlich die Natur der Poesie: sie spricht ein Besonderes aus, ohne ans Allgemeine zu denken, oder darauf hinzuweisen. Wer nun dieses Besondere lebendig faßt, erhält zugleich das Allgemeine mit, ohne es gewahr zu werden, oder erst spät" (Johann Wolfgang Goethe, *Sämtliche Werke 1*, 767).

32 See the treatment of obscurity in Päivi Mehtonen, *Obscure Language, Unclear Literature: Theory and Practice from Quintilian to the Enlightenment*.

CHAPTER TEN

EMOTIONS AND THE SYSTEM OF GENRES

1 See, e.g., Hathaway, *The Age of Criticism*, 205–224; Richard Sorabji, *Emotion and Peace of Mind: From Stoic Agitation to Christian Temptation* (Oxford, 2000), esp. 17–28, 194–201; Susan James, *Passion and Action: The Emotions in Seventeenth-Century Philosophy* (Oxford, 1997), esp. 1–25; Thomas Dixon, *From Passions to Emotions: The Creation of a Secular Psychological Category* (Cambridge, 2003).

2 "καὶ γὰρ οὗτοι διὰ τῶν σχηματιζομένων

ῥυθμῶν μιμοῦνται καὶ ἤθη καὶ πάθη καὶ πράξεις" (*Poetics* 1447a).

3 "πάθος δέ ἐστι πρᾶξις φθαρτικὴ ἢ ὀδυνηρά, οἷον οἵ τε ἐν τῷ φανερῷ θάνατοι καὶ αἱ περιωδυνίαι καὶ τρώσεις καὶ ὅσα τοιαῦτα" (*Poetics* 1452b10, see the commentary to 1447a).

4 See primarily *Poetics* 1452b10–11, 1453b18–19, 1454a13 and 1453b39, 1459b9, 1459b14, 1455b34. *Pathos* is used in the sense of "stylistic anomality" in 1460b12.

5 "ἔστιν οὖν τραγῳδία μίμησις πράξεως σπουδαίας καὶ τελείας μέγεθος ἐχούσης, ἡδυσμένῳ λόγῳ χωρὶς ἑκάστῳ τῶν εἰδῶν ἐν τοῖς μορίοις, δρώντων καὶ οὐ δι' ἀπαγγελίας, δι' ἐλέου καὶ φόβου περαίνουσα τὴν τῶν τοιούτων παθημάτων κάθαρσιν" (*Poetics* 1449b24–28).

6 Stephen Halliwell, "Introduction," in *Aristotle. Poetics*, edited and translated by Stephen Halliwell, Loeb Classical Library XXIII (Cambridge, MA, 1999), 3–26, 15–16.

7 See Halliwell, "Introduction," in *Aristotle. Poetics*, 18–19; Halliwell, *Aristotle's Poetics*, 168–201; Plato, *The Republic* I–II. With an English translation by Paul Shorey (London and Cambridge, MA, 1930–35), 10.603c–6d.

8 See W. W. Fortenbaugh, *Aristotle on Emotion: A Contribution to Philosophical Psychology, Rhetoric, Poetics, Politics and Ethics*, 2nd edition (London, 2008), 9–22; Simo Knuutilla, *Emotions in Ancient and Medieval Philosophy* (Oxford, 2005), 24–47.

9 Halliwell, "Introduction," in *Aristotle. Poetics*, 18; see Halliwell, *The Aesthetics of Mimesis*, 177–206, 73–74.

10 *Gorgias* 465–507. See Jacqueline Lichtenstein, *The Eloquence of Color: Rhetoric and Painting in the French Classical Age* (Berkeley, Los Angeles and Oxford, 1993), 37–71.

11 *Republic* 10, 601B.

12 "Καὶ περὶ ἀφροδισίων δὴ καὶ θυμοῦ καὶ περὶ πάντων τῶν ἐπιθυμητικῶν τε καὶ λυπηρῶν καὶ ἡδέων ἐν τῇ ψυχῇ, ἃ δή φαμεν πάσῃ πράξει ἡμῖν ἕπεσθαι, ὅτι τοιαῦτα ἡμᾶς ἡ ποιητικὴ μίμησις ἐργάζεται; τρέφει γὰρ ταῦτα ἄρδουσα, δέον αὐχμεῖν, καὶ ἄρχοντα ἡμῖν καθίστησι, δέον ἄρχεσθαι αὐτὰ" (Plato, *Republic* 10.606D).

13 Most apparently so perhaps in Quintilian, who renders Plato's *hêdonê* with *adulatio*, accentuating falsehood and feigning even more (Quintilian, *Institutio oratoria* 2.15.24–26); Lichtenstein, *The Eloquence of Color*; Mats Malm, *Voluptuous Language and Poetic Ambivalence: The Example of Swedish Baroque* (Frankfurt am Main, 2011).

14 *Poetics* 1462a16.

15 Plato, *Cratylus* 431c–434a. See Lichteinstein, *The Eloquence of Color*, esp. 53–54.

16 "μανθάνειν οὐ μόνον τοῖς φιλοσόφοις ἥδιστον ἀλλὰ καὶ τοῖς ἄλλοις ὁμοίως" (*Poetics* 1448b13–14).

17 Robortello, *In Librum Aristotelis de Arte Poetica Explicationes* 12, Castelvetro, *Poetica D'Aristotile vulgarizzata* 9.

18 "Che cosa è la Poesia? M. Imitatione di uarie maniere di persone, in diuersi modi, ò con parole, ò con harmonia, ò con tempi; separatamente, ò con tutte queste cose insieme, ò con parte di loro. ... Tre cose in ogni imitatione considerarci conuiene. Prima quel, che ad imitar prendiamo; poi con che imitiamo; al fine in qual modo. Le cose, che ad imitar prendiamo, sono i costumi, gli affetti, & i fatti delle persone; le quali sono di tre qualità" (Minturno, *L'arte Poetica*, 2). With the three qualities, Minturno refers to Aristotle's words that poetry portrays people who are better, worse or the same as ourselves.

19 Minturno, *L'arte Poetica*, 14.

20 Minturno, *L'arte Poetica*, 177–178.

21 According to Irene Behrens, Minturno is not entirely alone in this view (Behrens, *Die Lehre von der Einteilung der Dichtkunst vornemlich vom 16. bis 19. Jahrhundert. Studien zur Geschichte der poetischen Gattungen* (Halle/Saale, 1940), 208–209). See also Scherpe, *Gattungspoetik im 18. Jahrhundert*, 61–63.

22 Minturno, *L'arte Poetica*, 167.

23 See Lichtenstein, *The Eloquence of Color*, 65.

24 "ubi vero animis iudicum vis adferenda est et ab ipsa veri contemplatione abducenda mens, ibi proprium oratoris opus est. ... Probationes enim efficiant sane ut causam nostram meliorem esse iudices putent, adfectus praestant ut etiam velint; sed id quod volunt credunt quoque. Nam cum irasci favere odisse misereri coeperunt, agi iam rem suam existimant, et, sicut amantes de forma iudicare non possunt quia sensum oculorum praecipit animus, ita omnem veritatis inquirendae rationem iudex omittit occupatus

adfectibus: aestu fertur et velut rapido flumini obsequitur" (*Institutio oratoria* 6.2.5–6).

25 See Michael Baxandall, *Giotto and the Orators: Humanist Observers of Painting in Italy and the Discovery of Pictorial Composition 1350–1450* (Oxford, 1971); Brian Vickers, *In Defence of Rhetoric* (Oxford, 1988), 340–374; Götz Pochat, "Rhetorik und bildende Kunst in der Renaissance," in *Renaissance-Rhetorik. Renaissance Rhetoric*, ed. Heinrich F. Plett (Berlin and New York, 1993), 266–284; Ellenius, *De Arte Pingendi*, esp. 71–96, and Plett, *Rhetoric and Renaissance Culture*, 295–334. On music, see the overview by Klaus Wolfgang Niemöller, "Die musikalische Rhetorik und ihre Genese in Musik und Musikanschauung de Renaissance," in *Renaissance-Rhetorik. Renaissance Rhetoric*, ed. Heinrich F. Plett (Berlin and New York, 1993), 285–311, and Plett, *Rhetoric and Renaissance Culture*, 365–412 and references there.

26 See Lichtenstein, *The Eloquence of Color*, esp. 171–173; Vickers, *In Defence of Rhetoric*, 358.

27 D. R. Edward Wright, who demonstrates the pedagogical structure and scope inherited from Quintilian by Alberti, stresses that Alberti's *compositio* was not adopted from rhetoric's category with corresponding name: instead, Wright draws the line from other tripartite distinctions than rhetoric's *inventio*, *dispositio* and *elocutio* (D. R. Edward Wright, "Alberti's *De Pictura*: Its Literary Structure and Purpose," *Journal of the Warburg and Courtauld Institute* 47 (1984), 52–71). However, when modelling his work on Quintilian's, Alberti was of course forced to handle both correspondences and divergences between rhetoric's categories and his own. See Vickers, *In Defence of Rhetoric*, 343–344.

28 *De Pictura* II 35–36. See Vickers, *In Defence of Rhetoric*, 342–353 with references; cf. Franciscus Junius's view on the matters (Ellenius, *De Arte Pingendi*, 74).

29 "Picturam in tres partes dividimus, quam quidem divisionem ab ipsa natura compertam habemus. Nam cum pictura studeat res visas repraesentare, notemus quemadmodum res ipsae sub aspectu veniant. Principio quidem cum quid aspicimus, id videmus esse aliquid quod locum occupet. Pictor vero huius loci spatium circumscribet, eamque rationem ducendae fimbriae apto vocabulo circumscriptionem appellabit. Proxime intuentes dignoscimus ut plurimae prospecti corporis superficies inter se conveniant; hasque superficierum coniunctiones artifex suis locis designans recte compositionem nominabit. Postremo aspicientes distinctius superficierum colores discernimus, cuius rei repraesentatio in pictura, quod omnes differentias a luminibus recipiat, percommode apud nos receptio luminum dicetur" (Leon Battista Alberti, *On Painting and On Sculpture. The Latin Texts of "De Pictura* and *De Statua,"* II, edited with translations, introductions and notes by Cecil Grayson (London, 1972), 30. I have inserted original terms instead of the translations).

30 Cf. *De Pictura* II 46.

31 *De Pictura* II 31.

32 *De Pictura* II 35.

33 "Animos deinde spectantium movebit historia, cum qui aderunt picti homines suum animi motum maxime prae se ferent. Fit namque natura, qua nihil sui similium rapacius inveniri potest, ut lugentibus conlugeamus, ridentibus adrideamus, dolentibus condoleamus. Sed hi motus animi ex motibus corporis cognoscuntur. Nam videmus ut tristes, quod curis astricti et aegritudine obsessi sint, totis sensibus ac viribus torpeant, interque pallentia et admodum labantia membra sese lenti detineant. Est quidem maerentibus pressa frons, cervix languida, denique omnia veluti defessa et neglecta procidunt. Iratis vero, quod animi ira incendantur, et vultus et oculi intumescunt ac rubent, membrorum que omnium motus pro furore iracundiae in eisdem acerrimi et iactabundi sunt. Laeti autem et hilares cum sumus, tum solutos et quibusdam flexionibus gratos motus habemus" (*De Pictura* II 41). The words on Nature's rapaciousness should be understood in the light of Cicero's *De amicitia* 50. I thank Hans Helander for kindly bringing this to my attention.

34 Vickers, *In Defence of Rhetoric*, 345–348; Lichtenstein, *The Eloquence of Color*, 199–207, both quoting the above passage. Lichtenstein emphasizes Alberti's will to identify painting's goal and means with rhetoric's – in order to enforce painting's superiority over poetry. See also Lichtenstein, *The Eloquence of Color*, 208–219 on *actio* in painting.

35 Plett, *Rhetoric and Renaissance Culture*, 315–328, esp. 324–328. Plett also offers an illustrating example of a rhetorical analysis of Poussin's *The Judgement of Solomon*, focusing on "*actio*, i.e. the symbolic grammar of gestures" (333–334).

36 Cf. Batteux, *Les beaux arts*, 258–259.

37 *Thomas Thorild. Att följa ögonblicken. Texter i urval*, ed. and intro. Horace Engdahl (Stockholm, 2000), 328–340, 328–329.

38 *The Poetical Works of William Wordsworth* 2, edited from the manuscripts with textual and critical notes by E. de Selincourt (Oxford, 1944), 400.

39 *The Poetical Works of William Wordsworth* 2, 394–395. "Correspondingly, the poet is endued with more lively sensibility, more enthusiasm and tenderness, who has a greater knowledge of human nature, and a more comprehensive soul, than are supposed to be common among mankind; a man pleased with his own passions and volitions, and who rejoices more than other men in the spirit of life that is in him; delighting to contemplate similar volitions and passions as manifested in the goings-on of the Universe, and habitually impelled to create them where he does not find them. To these qualities he has added a disposition to be affected more than other men by absent things as if they were present; an ability of conjuring up in himself passions ... whence, and from practice, he has acquired a greater readiness and power in expressing what he thinks and feels, and especially those thoughts and feelings which, by his own choice, or from the structure of his own mind, arise in him without immediate external excitement" (*The Poetical Works of Wordsworth*, 751).

Bibliography

ABRAMS, M. H., *The Mirror and the Lamp: Romantic Theory and the Critical Tradition* (New York, 1953).

ADDISON, Joseph, *The Spectator*, edited and with an introduction and notes by Donald F. Bond, III (Oxford, 1965).

AILI, Hans, "St. Birgitta and the Text of the *Revelationes*: A Survey of Some Influences Traceable to Translators and Editors," in *The Editing of Theological and Philosophical Texts from the Middle Ages*, edited by Monika Asztalos (Stockholm, 1986), 75–91.

ALBERTI, Leon Battista, *On Painting and On Sculpture. The Latin Texts of "De Pictura* and *De Statua,"* edited with translations, introductions and notes by Cecil Grayson (London, 1972).

AQUINAS, Thomas, *Summa theologiæ*, edited by Thomas Gilby (New York, 1964–81).

ARISTOTLE, *Poetics*, edited and translated by Stephen Halliwell, Loeb Classical Library XXIII (Cambridge, MA, 1999).

ARISTOTLE, *Aristoteles Latinus XXXI 1–2. Rhetorica. Translatio Anonyma sive Vetus et Translatio Guillelmi de Moerbeka*, edited by Bernhardus Schneider (Leiden, 1978).

ARISTOTLE, *Aristoteles Latinus XXXIII. Editio altera. De arte poetica. Translatio Guillelmi de Moerbeka...,* edited by L. Minio-Paluello, *Accedunt Expositio media Averrois sive "Poetria" Hermanno Alemanno interprete et Specimina Translationis Petri Leonii* (Brussels and Paris, 1968).

ARISTOTLE, *Poetics*. Introduction, commentary and appendices by D.W. Lucas (Oxford, 1968).

ARISTOTLE, *Rhetoric*. English translation by John Henry Freese (London and New York, 1926).

ARRHENIUS, Clas (pres.), *Isogæus*, Simon (resp.), *Dissertatio de Symbolis* (Upsaliae, MDCLXXII).

ASHFIELD, Andrew and Peter de Bolla, "Introduction," in *The Sublime: A Reader in British Eighteenth-Century Aesthetic Theory*, edited by Andrew Ashfield and Peter de Bolla (Cambridge, 1996), 1–16.

AUERBACH, Erich, *Mimesis. Dargestellte Wirklichkeit in der abendländischen Literatur* (Berne, 1946).

AUGUSTINE, *Sancti Aurelii Augustini de Trinitate Libri XV [Libri XIII–XV]*, Cura et Studio W.J. Mountain, Corpus Christianorum L, A (Turnholti, 1968).

AUGUSTINE, *Writings of Saint Augustine 18. The Trinity*, translated by Stephen McKenna (Washington, 1963).

AXELSSON, Karl, *The Sublime: Precursors and British Eighteenth-Century Conceptions* (Oxford, 2007).

BARNOUW, Jeffrey, "The Morality of the Sublime: To John Dennis," *Comparative Literature* 35 (1983).

BATTEUX, Charles, *Les quatre poëtiques: d'Aristote, d'Horace, de Vida, de Despréaux*, Avec les Traductions & des Remarques, Par M. l'Abbé Batteux.... I–II (Paris, 1771).

BATTEUX, Charles, *Herrn Abt Batteux, königlichen Professors, Mitglieds der französischen Akademie, auch der Akademie der J[n]schriften und schönen Wissenschaften, Einschränkung der schönen Künste auf einen einzigen Grundsatz; aus dem Französischen übersetzt, und mit verschiednen eignen damit verwandten Abhandlungen begleitet von Johann Adolf Schlegeln*, I–II (Leipzig, 1770).

BATTEUX, Charles, *Principes de la litterature. Nouvelle édition* (Paris, 1764).

BATTEUX, Charles, *Einschränkung der schönen Künste auf einen einzigen Grundsatz. Aus dem Französischen übersetzt, und mit einem Anhange einiger eignen Abhandlungen versehen*, translated by J. A. Schlegel (Leipzig, 1759).

BATTEUX, Charles, *Einleitung in die Schönen Wissenschaften; nach d. Französischen, mit Zusätzen vermehret von C.W. Ramler* (Leipzig, 1756–58).

BATTEUX, Charles, *Les beaux arts réduits à un même principe par l'abbé C. Batteux* (Paris, 1746).

BAXANDALL, Michael, *Giotto and the Orators: Humanist Observers of Painting in Italy and the Discovery of Pictorial Composition 1350–1450* (Oxford, 1971).

BEDA Venerabilis, *De Schematibus et Tropis*, edited by B.C. Kendall, Corpus Christianorum Series Latina CXXIII, A. Bedae Opera. Pars VI, 1 (Turnholti, 1975).

BEHLER, Ernst, *German Romantic Literary Theory* (Cambridge, 1993).

BEHRENS, Irene, *Die Lehre von der Einteilung der Dichtkunst vornemlich vom 16. bis 19. Jahrhundert. Studien zur Geschichte der poetischen Gattungen* (Halle/Saale, 1940).

BERGH, Birger, "Birgittas djävulsskildringar," *Credo* 54 (1973), 108–115.

BERGH, Birger, "Introduction," in *Magister Mathias Lincopensis. Testa Nucis and Poetria*, edited and translated by Birger Bergh, Samlingar utgivna av Svenska fornskriftsällskapet 2:IX:2 (Stockholm, 1996), 7–13.

BERGH, Birger, "Matts Övidsson, 'Nötskalet' och den heliga Birgitta," in *Vetenskap och retorik. En gammal konst i modern belysning*, edited by Kurt Johannesson (Stockholm, 2001), 88–95.

BIEBER, Hugo, *Johann Adolf Schlegels poetische Theorie* (Berlin, 1912).

BIRGITTA, *Sancta Birgitta. Revelaciones* IV, edited by Birger Bergh, Samlingar utgivna av Svenska fornskriftsällskapet 2:VII:6 (Stockholm, 1991).

BIRGITTA, *Sancta Birgitta. Revelaciones* VI, edited by B. Bergh, Samlingar utgivna av Svenska fornskriftsällskapet 2:VII:6 (Stockholm, 1991).

BIRGITTA, *Acta et processus canonizacionis beate Birgitte*, edited by Isak Collijn, Samlingar utgivna av Svenska fornskriftsällskapet 2:1 (Uppsala, 1924–31).

BIRMELIN, Ella, "Die kunsttheoretischen Gedanken in Philostrats Apollonios," *Philologus. Zeitschrift für das klassische Altertum* 88 (1973), 149–180.

BLACK, Deborah, *Logic and Aristotle's "Rhetoric" and "Poetics" in Medieval Arabic Philosophy* (Leiden, New York, Copenhagen and Cologne, 1990).

BOILEAU-DESPRÉAUX, Nicolas, *Dissertation sur la Joconde, Arrest Burlesque, Traité du Sublime.* Texte établi et présenté par Charles-H. Boudhors. Œvres complètes de Boileau III (Paris, 1942).

BOLLA, Peter de, *The Discourse of the Sublime: Readings in History, Aesthetics and the Subject* (Oxford, 1989).

BRANN, Eva T. H., *The World of the Imagination: Sum and Substance* (Lanham, 1991).

BRANN, Eva T.H., *The World of the Imagination: Sum and Substance* (Lanham, 1991).Brody, Jules, *Boileau and Longinus* (Geneva, 1958).

BUCK, August, "Einleitung," in Julius Caesar Scaliger, *Poetices libri septem.* Faksimile-Neudruck der Ausgabe Leipzig von Lyon 1561 mit einer Einleitung von August Buck (Stuttgart–Bad Cannstatt, 1987).

BUCK, August, "Einleitung," in Emanuele Tesauro, *Il Cannocchiale Aristotelico,* herausgegeben und eingeleitet von August Buck, Bad Homburg v.d.H. (Berlin and Zurich, 1968).

BURKE, Edmund, *A Philosophical Enquiry into the Origin of our Ideas of the Sublime and Beautiful,* edited by James T. Boulton (Oxford, 1990).

CASTELVETRO, Lodovico, *Poetica D'Aristotile vulgarizzata, et sposta (1570),* Poetiken des Cinquecento 1 (Munich, 1967).

CAVE, Terence, "The Afterlife of the *Poetics,*" in *Making Sense of Aristotle: Essays in Poetics,* edited by Øivind Andersen and Jon Haarberg (London, 2001), 197–214.

CHAPELAIN, Jean, *Opuscules critiques,* introduction by Alfred C. Hunter (Paris, 1936).

COOPER, Lane and Alfred Gudeman, *A Bibliography of the Poetics of Aristotle,* Cornell Studies in English XI (New Haven and London, 1928).

CORNEILLE, Pierre, *Œuvres complètes* III. Textes établis, présentés et annotés par George Couton (Paris, 1987).

CRANE, R. S., Rev. of Samuel H. Monk, *The Sublime: A Study of Critical Theories in XVII Century England, Philological Quarterly* 15 (1936), 165–167.

CULLHED, Anna, *The Language of Passion: The Order of Poetics and the Construction of a Lyric Genre 1746–1806* (Uppsala, 2002).

DAHIYAT, Ismail M., *Avicenna's Commentary on the "Poetics" of Aristotle: A Critical Study with an Annotated Translation of the Text* (Leiden, 1974).

DIXON, Thomas, *From Passions to Emotions: The Creation of a Secular Psychological Category* (Cambridge, 2003).

DONATO, Eugenio, "Tesauro's Poetics: Through the Looking Glass," *Modern Language Notes* 78 (1963), 15–30.

EDEN, Kathy, *Poetic and Legal Fiction in the Aristotelian Tradition* (Princeton and Guildford, 1986).

ELLENIUS, Allan, *De Arte Pingendi. Latin Art Literature in Seventeenth-Century Sweden and its International Background,* Lychnos-bibliotek 19 (Uppsala and Stockholm, 1960).

ELSE, Gerald F., *Plato and Aristotle on Poetry,* edited with an introduction by Peter Burian (Chapel Hill, 1986).

EWTON Jr, Ralph W., *The Literary Theories of August Wilhelm Schlegel* (The Hague and Paris, 1972).

FORTENBAUGH, W.W., *Aristotle on Emotion: A Contribution to Philosophical Psychology, Rhetoric, Poetics, Politics and Ethics,* 2nd edition (London, 2008).

FREDE, Dorothea, "Necessity, Chance, and 'What Happens for the Most Part' in Aristotle's *Poetics,*" in *Essays on Aristotle's "Poetics,"* edited by Amélie Oksenberg Rorty (Princeton and London, 1992), 197–219.

FRIEDRICH, Hugo, *Epochen der italienischen Lyrik* (Frankfurt am Main, 1964).

FRIIS-JENSEN, Karsten, "Horace and the Early Writers of Arts of Poetry," in *Sprachtheorien in Spätantike und Mittelalter,* edited by Sten Ebbesen (Tübingen, 1993), 360–401.

FRY, Paul H., *The Reach of Criticism: Method and Perception in Literary Theory* (New Haven and London, 1983).

GILMAN, Ernest B., *Iconoclasm and Poetry in the English Reformation* (Chicago and London, 1986).

GILMAN, Ernest B., *The Curious Perspective: Literary and Pictorial Wit in the Seventeenth Century* (New Haven and London, 1978).

GOETHE, Johann Wolfgang, *Sämtliche Werke nach Epochen seines Schaffens. Münchner Ausgabe Band 17. Wilhelm Meisters Wanderjahre. Maximen und Reflexionen*, edited by Gonthier-Louis Fink, Gerhard Baumann and Johannes John (Munich, 1991).

GOETHE, Johann Wolfgang, *Sämtliche Werke nach Epochen seines Schaffens. Münchner Ausgabe Band 4.2. Wirkungen der Französischen Revolution 1791–1797, 2*, edited by Klaus H. Kiefer, Hans J. Becker, Gerhard H. Müller, John Neubauer and Peter Schmidt (Munich, 1986).

GOTTSCHED, Johann Christoph, *Versuch einer Critischen Dichtkunst vor die Deutschen* (Leipzig, 1730).

GREEN, Lawrence D., "Aristotelian Lexis and Renaissance Elocutio," in *Rereading Aristotle's Rhetoric*, edited by Alan G. Gross and Arthur E. Walzer (Carbondale and Edwardsville, 2000), 149–165.

GREEN, Lawrence D., "The Reception of Aristotle's *Rhetoric* in the Renaissance," in *Peripatetic Rhetoric after Aristotle*, edited by William W. Fortenbaugh and David C. Mirhady (New Brunswick, NJ, 1994), 320–348.

GRIFOLO, Jacopo, *Horatii Flacci liber De arte poetica Iacobi Grifoli Lucinianensis interpretatione explicatus (1550)*, Poetiken des Cinquecento 3 (Munich, 1967).

GUERLAC, Suzanne, "The Sublime in Theory," *Modern Language Notes* 106, no. 3 (1991), 895–909.

GUERLAC, Suzanne, "Longinus and the Subject of the Sublime," *New Literary History* 16, no. 2 (1985), 275–289.

GUSTAFSSON, Lars, *Le poëte masqué et démasqué. Étude sur la mise en valeur du poète sincère dans la poétique du classicisme et du préromantisme* (Uppsala, 1968).

GUSTAFSSON, Lars, "'Imitation' och 'äkthet'. En linje i 1700-talets diskussion om mimesisprincipen," *Samlaren. Tidskrift för svensk litteraturvetenskaplig forskning* (1959), 39–59.

HALLIWELL, Stephen, *The Aesthetics of Mimesis: Ancient Texts and Modern Problems* (Princeton and Oxford, 2002).

HALLIWELL, Stephen, "Introduction," in *Aristotle. Poetics*, edited and translated by Stephen Halliwell, Loeb Classical Library XXIII (Cambridge, MA, 1999), 3–26.

HALLIWELL, Stephen, *Aristotle's Poetics* (London, 1986).

HARDISON, O. B., "The Place of Averroës' Commentary on the *Poetics* in the History of Medieval Criticism," in *Medieval and Renaissance Studies* (Durham, NC, 1970), 57–81.

HARDISON, O. B., *The Enduring Monument: A Study of the Idea of Praise in Renaissance Literary Theory and Practice* (Chapel Hill, 1962).

HATHAWAY, Baxter, *The Age of Criticism: The Late Renaissance in Italy* (Ithaca, NY, 1962).

HEINRICHS, Wolfhart, *Arabische Dichtung und griechische Poetik. Hazim al-Qartagannis Grundlegung der Poetik mit Hilfe aristotelischer Begriffe* (Beirut, 1969).

HERTZ, Neil, *The End of the Line: Essays on Psychoanalysis and the Sublime* (New York, 1985).

HOOK, J.W. van, "'Concupiscence of Wit': The Metaphysical Conceit in Baroque Poetics," *Modern Philology* 84, no. 1 (1986), 24–38.

JAMES, Susan, *Passion and Action: The Emotions in Seventeenth-Century Philosophy* (Oxford, 1997).

JAVITCH, Daniel, "The Assimilation of Aristotle's *Poetics* in Sixteenth-Century Italy," in *The Cambridge History of Literary Criticism* III, edited by Glyn P. Norton (Cambridge, 1999), 53–66.

KANT, Immanuel, *Kritik der ästetischen Urteilskraft* (1790), *Werke in sechs Bänden,* Band V, edited by Wilhelm Weischeidel (Wiesbaden, 1957).

KARDAUN, Maria, *Der Mimesisbegriff in der griechischen Antike. Neubetrachtung eines umstrittenen Begriffes als Ansats zu einer neuen Interpretation der platonischen Kunstauffassung* (Amsterdam, New York, Oxford and Toronto, 1993).

KELLY, H. A., "Aristotle-Averroës-Alemannus on Tragedy," *Viator: Medieval and Renaissance Studies* 10 (1979), 161–210.

KEMAL, Salim, *The Philosophical Poetics of Alfarabi, Avicenna and Averroës: The Aristotelian Reception* (London and New York, 2003).

KLOCKARS, Birgit, *Birgitta och böckerna* (Stockholm, 1973).

KNUUTILLA, Simo, *Emotions in Ancient and Medieval Philosophy* (Oxford, 2005).

KOLLER, Hermann, *Die Mimesis in der Antike. Nachahmung, Darstellung, Ausdruck* (Berne, 1954).

LAUSBERG, Heinrich, *Handbuch der literarischen Rhetorik. Eine Grundlegung der Literaturwissenschaft.* 3.e Auflage (Stuttgart, 1990).

LEWALSKI, Barbara Kiefer, *Protestant Poetics and the Seventeenth-Century Religious Lyric* (Princeton, 1979).

LICHTENSTEIN, Jacqueline, *The Eloquence of Color: Rhetoric and Painting in the French Classical Age* (Berkeley, Los Angeles and Oxford, 1993).

LIDDELL, Henry George and Robert Scott, *A Greek–English Lexicon.* Revised and augmented throughout by Sir Henry Stuart Jones, with the assistance of Roderick McKenzie (Oxford, 1940).

LIEDGREN, Jan, "Magister Matthias' svenska kungörelse om Birgittas första stora uppenbarelse. Ett förbisett dokument i riksarkivet," in *Meddelanden från svenska riksarkivet för år 1958* (Stockholm, 1961), 101–116.

LINDGREN, Mereth, "Birgitta och bilderna," in *Heliga Birgitta – budskapet och förebilden,* edited by Alf Härdelin and Mereth Lindgren (Stockholm, 1993), 231–251.

LONGINUS, *Longinus "On the Sublime,"* edited and translated by W. H. Fyfe. Revised by Donald Russell, Loeb Classical Library 191 (Cambridge, MA, and London, 1999).

LONGINUS, *On the Sublime,* introduction and commentary by D. A. Russell (Oxford, 1964).

LONGINUS, *A treatise of Dionysius Longinus upon the sublime. Translated from the Greek, with explanatory notes, by the late Rev. Charles Carthy, M.A.* (Dublin, 1762).

LONGINUS, *Dionysius Longinus on the sublime. Translated from the Greek, with notes and observations, and some account of the life, writings and* character *of the author,* translated by William Smith (London, 1739).

LONGINUS, *The works of Dionysius Longinus, on the sublime: or, a treatise concerning the sovereign perfection of writing. Translated from the Greek. With some remarks on the English poets,* translated by Leonard Welsted (London, 1712).

LÜHE, Irmela von der, *Natur und Nachahmung. Untersuchungen zur Batteux-Rezeption in Deutschland* (Bonn, 1979).

MALM, Mats, *Voluptuous Language and Poetic Ambivalence: The Example of Swedish Baroque* (Frankfurt am Main, 2011).

MALM, Mats, "On the Technique of the Sublime," *Comparative Literature* 52, no. 1 (2000), 1–10.

MAZZEO, Joseph Anthony, "Allegorical Interpretation and History," *Comparative Literature* 30, no. 1 (1978), 1–21.

MAZZEO, Joseph Anthony, *Varieties of Interpretation* (London, 1978).

MAZZEO, Joseph Anthony, "Metaphysical Poetry and the Poetic of Correspondence," *Journal of the History of Ideas* 14 (1953), 221–234.

MCKEON, Richard, "Aristotle's Conception of Language and the Arts of Language," in *Critics and Criticism: Ancient and Modern*, edited by R.S. Crane (Chicago, 1952), 176–231.

MCKEON, Richard, "Literary Criticism and the Concept of Imitation in Antiquity," in *Critics and Criticism: Ancient and Modern*, edited by R.S. Crane (Chicago, 1952), 147–175.

MEHTONEN, Päivi, "Essential Art: Matthew of Linköping's Fourtheenth-Century Poetics," *Rhetorica* XXV (2007), 125–139.

MEHTONEN, Päivi, "A Medieval and Modern Battle of Arts," in *The Rhetoric of Cicero in its Medieval and Early Renaissance Commentary Tradition*, edited by Virginia Cox and John O. Ward (Leiden and Boston, 2006), 289–312.

METHONEN, Päivi, *Obscure Language, Unclear Literature: Theory and Practice from Quintilian to the Enlightenment*, translated by Robert MacGillon (Helsinki, 2003).

MELBERG, Arne, *Theories of Mimesis* (Cambridge, 1995).

MINNIS, A.J. and A.B. Scott, *Medieval Literary Theory and Criticism c. 1100–c. 1375: The Commentary-Tradition* (Oxford, 1988).

MINTURNO, Antonio Sebastiano, *L'arte poetica (1564)*, Poetiken des Cinquecento 6 (Munich, 1976).

MONK, Samuel H., *The Sublime: A Study of Critical Theories in XVIII-Century England* (Ann Arbor, 1960 [1935]).

NANCY, Jean-Luc, "L'Offrande sublime," in *Du sublime*, edited by Jean-François Courtine, Michel Deguy, Jean-François Lyotard and Jean-Luc Nancy (Paris, 1988), 37–75.

NIEMÖLLER, Klaus Wolfgang, "Die musikalische Rhetorik und ihre Genese in Musik und Musikanschauung de Renaissance," in *Renaissance-Rhetorik. Renaissance Rhetoric*, edited by Heinrich F. Plett (Berlin and New York, 1993), 285–311.

NORÉN, Kjerstin, "The Soul Is Far Better by Nature than the Body," in *The History of Nordic Women's Literature* (http://nordicwomensliterature.net/article/soul-far-better-nature-body) (Själen är av långt bättre natur än kroppen. Om Birgitta av Vadstena," in *Nordisk kvinnolitteraturhistoria* I, edited by Elisabeth Møller Jensen, Eva Hættner Aurelius and Anne-Marie Mai (Höganäs, 1993), 120–134).

ODELMAN, Eva, "Lärd och folklig retorik hos Birgitta," in *Vetenskap och retorik. En gammal konst i modern belysning*, edited by Kurt Johannesson (Stockholm, 2001), 96–105.

ODELMAN, Eva, "Uppenbarelsernas retorik," in *Heliga Birgitta – budskapet och förebilden*, edited by Alf Härdelin and Mereth Lindgren (Stockholm, 1993), 15–21.

OHLY, Friedrich, "Vom geistigen Sinn des Wortes im Mittelalter," *Zeitschrift für deutsches Altertum* 89 (1958/59), 1–23.

OLAUS Magnus, *Historia de gentibus septentrionalibus* (Rome, 1555).

OLIN, Martin, *Views on Portraiture from Vasari to Jonathan Richardson*, Studies in Italian, French and English Art Theory (Lund, 1996).

PALLAVICINO, Sforza, *Da "Del Bene", Trattatisti e narratori del Seicento*, a cura di Ezio Raimondi (Naples, 1960), 218–262.

PILTZ, Anders, "Inspiration, vision, profetia. Birgitta och teorierna om uppenbarelsen," in *Heliga Birgitta – budskapet och förebilden*, edited by Alf Härdelin and Mereth Lindgren (Stockholm, 1993), 67–88.

PILTZ, Anders, "Uppenbarelserna och uppenbarelsen. Birgittas förhållande till bibeln," in *Birgitta. Hendes værk og hendes klostre i Norden*, edited by Tore Nyberg (Odense, 1991), 447–469.

PIRHOLT, Mattias, *Metamimesis: Ideology and Representation in the Novels of Early German Romanticism* (forthc.).

PLATO, *Cratylus, Parmenides, Greater Hippias, Lesser Hippias*, with an English translation by H.N. Fowler (London and Cambridge, MA, 1953).

PLATO, *The Republic* I–II, with an English translation by Paul Shorey (London and Cambridge, MA, 1930–35).

POCHAT, Götz, "Rhetorik und bildende Kunst in der Renaissance," in *Renaissance-Rhetorik. Renaissance Rhetoric*, edited by Heinrich F. Plett (Berlin and New York, 1993), 266–284.

PREMINGER, Alex, O.B. Hardison Jr. and Kevin Kerrane, eds. *Classical and Medieval Literary Criticism: Translations and Interpretations* (New York, 1974).

PROCTOR, Robert E., "Emanuele Tesauro: A Theory of the Conceit," *Modern Language Notes* 88, no. 1 (1973), 68–94.

RACINE, Jean, *Principes de la Tragédie en Marge de la Poétique d'Aristote*, Texte établi et commenté par Eugène Vinaver (Paris, 1951).

RICOEUR, Paul, *Time and Narrative* I (Chicago, 1984).

ROBORTELLO, Francesco, *In Librum Aristotelis de Arte Poetica Explicationes. Paraphrasis in Librum Horatii, Qui Vulgo de Arte Poetica ad Pisones Inscribitur (1548)*, Poetiken des Cinquecento 8 (Munich, 1968).

RUTLEDGE, Joyce S., *Johann Adolph Schlegel* (Berne and Frankfurt am Main, 1974).

SCALIGER, Julius Caesar, *Poetices libri septem*. Faksimile-Neudruck der Ausgabe Leipzig von Lyon 1561 mit einer Einleitung von August Buck (Stuttgart, 1987).

SCHELLING, Friedrich, *Friedrich Wilhelm Joseph von Schellings Sämmtliche Werke* I.v (Stuttgart and Augsburg, 1859).

SCHENKER, Manfred, *Charles Batteux und seine Nachahmungstheorie in Deutschland* (Leipzig, 1909).

SCHENKEVELD, Dirk M., "*Ta asteia* in Aristotle's *Rhetoric*: The Disappearance of a Category," in *Peripatetic Rhetoric after Aristotle*, edited by William W. Fortenbaugh and David C. Mirhady (New Brunswick, NJ, 1994), 1–14.

SCHERPE, Klaus R., "Analogon Actionis und lyrisches System. Aspecte normativer Lyriktheorie in der deutschen Poetik des 18. Jahrhunderts," *Poetica. Zeitschrift für Sprach- und Literaturwissenschaft* 4 (1971), 32–59.

SCHERPE, Klaus R., *Gattungspoetik im 18. Jahrhundert. Historische Entwicklung von Gottsched bis Herder*. Studien zur allgemeinen und vergleichenden Literaturwissenschaft (Stuttgart, 1968).

SCHLEGEL, A. W., *Vorlesungen über Ästhetik I [1798–1803]*, edited by Ernst Behler, *Kritische Ausgabe seiner Vorlesungen* I, Kritische Ausgabe der Vorlesungen I, edited by Ernst Behler and Frank Jolles (Paderborn, Munich, Vienna and Zurich, 1989).

SCHLEGEL, A. W., *Geschichte der klassischen Literatur, Kritische Schriften und Briefe* III, edited by Edgar Lohner (Stuttgart, 1964).

SCHLEGEL, A. W., *Kants Kritik der ästhetischen Urteilskraft, Die Kunstlehre. Kritische Schriften und Briefe* II, edited by Edgar Lohner (Stuttgart, 1963).

SCHLEGEL, A. W., *Briefe über Poesie, Silbenmaß und Sprache, Sämmtliche Werke*, edited by Eduard Böcking (Leipzig, 1846).

SCHLÜTER, Renate, *Zeuxis und Prometheus. Die Überwindung des Nachahmungskonzeptes in der Ästhetik der Frühromantik*, Bonner romanische Arbeiten (Frankfurt am Main, 1995).

SCHOFIELD, Malcolm, "Aristotle on the Imagination," in *Articles on Aristotle 4. Psychology and Aesthetics*, edited by Jonathan Barnes, Malcolm Schofield and Richard Sorabji (London, 1979), 103–132.

SEGAL, Charles P., "Hupsos and the Problem of Cultural Decline in the De Sublimitate," *Harvard Studies in Classical Philology* 64 (1959), 121–146.

SELLARS, Wilfrid, "Substance and Form in Aristotle," in *Aristotle: Substance, Form and Matter*, edited with introductions by Terence Irwin (London, 1995), 140–151.

SORABJI, Richard, *Emotion and Peace of Mind: From Stoic Agitation to Christian Temptation* (Oxford, 2000).

SÖRBOM, Göran, "The Theory of Imitation is Not a Theory of Art: Some Stages in a Conceptual Tradition," in *Understanding the Arts: Contemporary Scandinavian Aesthetics*, edited by Jeanette Emt and Göran Hermerén, Studies in Aesthetics 3 (Lund, 1992).

SÖRBOM, Göran, *Mimesis and Art: Studies in the Origin and Early Development of an Aesthetic Vocabulary* (Uppsala, 1966).

STRÖMBERG, Bengt, *Magister Mathias och fransk mendikantpredikan* (Stockholm, 1944).

STRUBEL, Armand, "'Allegoria in factis' et 'Allegoria in verbis'," *Poétique* VI (1975), 342–357.

SUNDÉN, Hjalmar, *Den heliga Birgitta. Ormungens moder som blev Kristi brud* (Stockholm, 1973).

TAVERNIER, Ludwig, "L'imitation de la belle nature. Zum Verständnis des Künstlers in der Nachahmungstheorie von Charles Batteux," in *Empfindung und Reflexion. Ein Problem des 18. Jahrhunderts*, edited by Hans Körner, Constanze Peres, Reinhard Steiner and Ludwig Tavernier (Hildesheim, Zurich and New York, 1986), 49–98.

TESAURO, Emanuele, *Il Cannocchiale Aristotelico*, herausgegeben und eingeleitet von August Buck, Bad Homburg v.d.H. (Berlin and Zurich, 1968).

The New English Bible. New Testament (Oxford, 1961).

THORILD, Thomas, *Thomas Thorild. Att följa ögonblicken. Texter i urval*, edited and introduced by Horace Engdahl (Stockholm, 2000).

TIGERSTEDT, E.N., "Observations on the Reception of the Aristotelian *Poetics* in the Latin West," *Studies in the Renaissance* 15 (1968), 7–24.

TODOROV, Tzvetan, *Theories of the Symbol*, translated by Catherine Porter (Oxford, 1982 [1977]).

UNDHAGEN, Carl Gustaf, "General Introduction," in *Sancta Birgitta. Revelaciones* I, edited by Carl-Gustaf Undhagen, Samlingar utgivna av Svenska fornskriftsällskapet 2:VII:1 (Uppsala, 1978), 1–37.

UNDHAGEN, Carl-Gustaf, "Special Introduction," in *Sancta Birgitta. Revelaciones* I, edited by Carl-Gustaf Undhagen, Samlingar utgivna av Svenska fornskriftsällskapet 2:VII:1 (Uppsala, 1978), 38–226.

VETTORI, Pietro, *Commentarii in primum librum Aristotelis de arte poetarum (1560)*, Poetiken des Cinquecento 9 (Munich, 1967).

VICKERS, Brian, *In Defence of Rhetoric* (Oxford, 1988).

WALSH, George B., "Sublime Method: Longinus on Language and Imitation," *Classical Antiquity* 7 (1988), 252–269.

WALTON, Kendall, *Mimesis as Make-Believe: On the Foundations of the Representational Arts* (Cambridge, MA, 1990).

WALZER, Richard, *Greek into Arabic: Essays on Islamic Philosophy* (Oxford, 1962).

WEINBERG, Bernard, *Aristotle's "Poetics" and English Literature: A Collection of Critical Essays*, edited and with an introduction by Elder Olson (Chicago and London, 1965).

WEINBERG, Bernard, "From Aristotle to Pseudo-Aristotle," in *Aristotle's "Poetics" and English Literature: A Collection of Critical Essays*, edited and with an introduction by Elder Olson (Chicago and London, 1965), 192–200.

WEINBERG, Bernard, "Une Traduction Française du 'Sublime' de Longin Vers 1645," *Modern Philology* 59, no. 3 (1962), 159–201.

WEINBERG, Bernard, *A History of Literary Criticism in the Italian Renaissance* I–II (Chicago, 1961).

WEINBERG, Bernard, "Castelvetro's Theory of Poetics," in *Critics and Criticism: Ancient and Modern* (Chicago, 1952), 349–371.

WEINBERG, Bernard, "Robortello on the *Poetics*," in *Critics and Criticism: Ancient and Modern* (Chicago, 1952), 319–348.

WEINBERG, Bernard, "Translations and Commentaries of Longinus, 'On the Sublime', to 1600: A Bibliography," *Modern Philology* 47, no. 3 (1950), 14–151.

WEISKEL, Thomas, *The Romantic Sublime: Studies in the Structure and Psychology of Transcendence* (Baltimore and London, 1976).

WESTMAN, Knut B., *Birgitta-studier* (Uppsala, 1911).

WIMSATT Jr., William K. and Cleanth Brooks, *Literary Criticism: A Short History* (New York, 1957).

WOOD, Theodore E. B., *The Word "Sublime" and its Contexts 1650–1760* (The Hague and Paris, 1972).

WORDSWORTH, William, *The Poetical Works of William Wordsworth* 2, edited from the manuscripts with textual and critical notes by E. de Selincourt (Oxford, 1944).

WRIGHT, D. R. Edward, "Alberti's *De Pictura*: Its Literary Structure and Purpose," *Journal of the Warburg and Courtauld Institute* 47 (1984), 52–71.

ZANARDI, Mario, "La metafora e la sua dinamica di significazione nel 'Cannocchiale Aristotelico' di Emanuele Tesauro," in *Giornale storico della letteratura italiana* CLVII (Turin, 1980), 321–368.

ZEUCH, Ulrike, "Aporien in der Literaturtheorie der Frühen Neuzeit. Francesco Robortellos *In Librum Aristotelis De arte poetica explicationes* und die Folgen," in *Mimesis – Repräsentation – Imagination. Literaturtheoretische Positionen von Aristoteles bis zum Ende des 18. Jahrhunderts*, edited by Jörg Schönert and Ulrike Zeuch (Berlin and New York, 2004), 181–214.

Index